The Exceptional Child
through Literature

The Exceptional Child through Literature

edited by

Elliott D. Landau
University of Utah

Sherrie L. Epstein
*Psychological Services, Millbrae School District
Millbrae, California*

Ann P. Stone
*San Mateo Union High School District
San Mateo, California*

Prentice-Hall, Inc., Englewood Cliffs, New Jersey 07632

Library of Congress Cataloging in Publication Data
Main entry under title:

The Exceptional Child through literature

    Bibliography: p.
    Includes index.
    1. Exceptional children—Fiction. 2. Short stories,
American. I. Landau, Elliott D. II. Epstein,
Sherrie Landau. III. Stone, Ann Plaat.
PZ1.E93 [PS648.E95]   813′.009352   77-16317
ISBN 0–13–293860–X

© 1978 by Prentice-Hall, Inc.
Englewood Cliffs, New Jersey 07632

10   9   8   7   6   5   4   3   2   1

Printed in the United States of America

PRENTICE-HALL INTERNATIONAL, INC., *London*
PRENTICE-HALL OF AUSTRALIA PTY. LIMITED, *Sydney*
PRENTICE-HALL OF CANADA, LTD., *Toronto*
PRENTICE-HALL OF INDIA PRIVATE LIMITED, *New Delhi*
PRENTICE-HALL OF JAPAN, INC., *Tokyo*
PRENTICE-HALL OF SOUTHEAST ASIA PTE. LTD., *Singapore*
WHITEHALL BOOKS LIMITED, *Wellington, New Zealand*

For Carolyn

Contents

Introduction   xi

To the Instructor   xv

CHAPTER ONE   1 √

Who Is Exceptional?
"Hunting Season" *by Joanne Greenberg*   *6*

CHAPTER TWO   14

The Mentally Retarded
"The Boy Who Laughed" *by Ivy Litvinov*   *26*

CHAPTER THREE   37

The Gifted
"Clancy Wants an Orangoutang" *by Sara*   *47*

CHAPTER FOUR   61

The Learning Disabled and Neurological Dysfunction
Gideon: A Boy Who Hates Learning
    by Gladys Natchez   69

CHAPTER FIVE   82

The Speech and Language Impaired
A Walker in the City by Alfred Kazin   90

CHAPTER SIX   98

The Orthopedically Handicapped
    and the Multiply Handicapped
"Little Baseball World" by Robert Lowry   108
Cannery Row by John Steinbeck   125

CHAPTER SEVEN   130

The Hearing Impaired
"And Sarah Laughed" by Joanne Greenberg   142

CHAPTER EIGHT   156

The Blind and the Partially Sighted
The Fourth World by Daphne Athas   166

CHAPTER NINE   176

The Behaviorally Disordered
    and the Emotionally Disturbed
"The Life You Save" by William Melvin Kelley   185
"Something Missing" by John L'Heureux   196

CHAPTER TEN   209

The Severely Emotionally Disturbed and the Autistic

"Wednesday's Child" *by Joyce Carol Oates*   *218*

CHAPTER ELEVEN   233

The Exceptional Child in the Family

"The Scarlet Ibis" *by James Hurst*   *239*

CHAPTER TWELVE   252

The Exceptional Child in the Community

"Clothe the Naked" *by Dorothy Parker*   *257*

SUGGESTED READINGS   266

Adult Fiction, Biography and Autobiography

Children's Literature About the Disabled

Index   273

Introduction

This volume, which is for everyone interested in working with exceptional children, uses literature to complement the usual research-oriented approach to the field of child development and education. Whether you are a mental health worker, are preparing to teach children with disabilities, or are a teacher participating in mainstreaming in the regular classroom, working well with the exceptional person requires particular sensitivity to one's own feeling about the disabled. Literature is capable of evoking emotional responses and can therefore be especially helpful to explore those feelings. Most students have some preconceived ideas about how well they will relate to people with disabilities. In some cases students are overly confident and may need to learn to expect some frustrations. Through the short stories and excerpts in this book, the reader can identify with an exceptional person and with the person's parents, teachers, or siblings while maintaining enough distance from the story to evaluate characters as well as his or her own reactions and feelings.

The ability to feel comfortable with a severely disabled person takes time, exposure to carefully planned educational experience, and some examination of the stereotypes, myths, and early experiences that have helped shape attitudes and feelings about particular handicaps.[1]

[1]An innovative program and materials are being used and developed by Barbara Schneiderman's group, You, Me, and Us, Inc. (P.O. Box 7009, Menlo Park, California 94025) to prepare the way for the acceptance of the exceptional child by "normal" peers and their teachers and parents.

Despite students' preparation to deal with people with pronounced differences in physical appearance or behavior, students' initial reactions may nevertheless include intense feelings of pain, pity, and rejection. Many successful teachers and contributors to the field of special education have not forgotten their ambivalent feelings when they first visited a state institution for the mentally ill and retarded or a class for the severely emotionally disturbed.[2] They had not been as detached and objective as they had envisioned.

A text providing an overview of the major disabilities in special education cannot, of course, prepare all students to deal successfully with all handicapped children. There are no magic formulas for teaching all blind children as there are none for teaching all sighted children. Handicapped children are, first, children with individual moods, likes and dislikes, abilities and dreams; second, they are disabled. A wise teacher once observed that handicapped children are just like other children, only more so. How others respond to exceptional children has a lot to do with how the children see and value themselves. Recent developments in the fields of psychotherapy and behavior suggest that professionals should pay particular attention to what they do and say in relation to what they feel and think when working with handicapped children. Given an opportunity to observe exceptional children in school and home situations, students should pay close attention to what parents *do*, what children *do*, and what teachers *do* as they interact with one another. Such observations afford insight into the ways in which individuals in the child's environment shape his or her behavior.

Those who become involved in the lives of handicapped children find that the emotional effects of being disabled are often more debilitating than the disability. Frequently it is not enough to remediate problems in academic learning, speech, or mobility when a young person's emotional growth is hampered by feelings of alienation or rejection, and often the disparity between what the handicapped child wants and what is possible for him or her to achieve may seem extremely great. Patience and skill are required to encourage the child to be persistent and courageous. No one who works with the exceptional child should expect instant, positive results. Progress for most of the disabled is only attainable in steps, with long periods on one level before making a little progress up to the next. In the field of special education, the professional must be willing to try, to accept failure, and then to try again.

The emotionally moving stories in this text may help students to

---

[2]See C. Milton Blue, "An Open Letter to A Prospective Teacher of Handicapped Children," *Focus on Exceptional Children* (Denver, Colo.: Love Publishing Co., September 1975), pp. 8–10.

decide whether or not they have the personal attributes that are necessary to work effectively with the handicapped. If students are drawn to the field of special education primarily by pity or a desire to serve the less fortunate, they may be fulfilling their own needs rather than those of the disabled. Reading about, observing, and participating with exceptional children may, however, turn initial feelings of pity into empathy and compassion. Feelings of shock may in time be replaced by optimism and acceptance of the challenge.

Acknowledgments

We would like to make special mention of the assistance, advice, and counsel we have received from the following persons in the Department of Special Education of the University of Utah: Dean Robert Erdman of the Graduate School of Education and past chairman of the Department of Special Education; Cliff Drew, assistant dean and professor of Special Education; Grant Bitter; Winn Egan; Cy Freston; Michael Hardman; Jeanette Misaka; and Joan Wolf. Invaluable help in understanding the child with special needs has been provided by Polly Amrein, Vera Foster, Adele Lackey, and Henry Richanbach. We are indebted to Bea Landau for help in typing the manuscript. Special editorial work was done by Dennis R. Dobbs and Janet Lloyd. Thanks also go to Dan Stone for his support throughout this project.

To the Instructor

The best use of this text is made by assigning the appropriate section to accompany the instructor's discussion of an area of exceptionality. The essays in this book are designed to be provocative rather than substantive. They point toward major ideas but are not to be construed as definitive surveys. Many instructors use the "springboards" as regular assignments because they too lead the student into intriguing personal explorations in each area of exceptionality. Students who regularly use the springboards build up a file of responses to the stories that chronicle their journey through the affective world of exceptionality. Making full use of the text so that there is maximum involvement of students may be achieved using the following four well-tested college classroom techniques:

1. *Panel discussion.* Four to six students form a panel for each chapter. They survey the related literature for that particular topic, criticize the essay, and discuss the story or stories. A moderator starts the discussion by referring to any part of the chapter (essay, story, discussion, or springboards) and letting students amplify or criticize the facet that gains their interest.
2. *6-6-6.* Six-six-six refers to six groups of six students for six minutes, with either the springboards or the students' personal responses as the basis for discussion.
3. *Role play.* Using the critical incidents theory, students stop at

any point in the story that is critical (because of what is said or unsaid or what is done or not done) and change the story (for example, changing what is said to what may have been said), giving it a whole new twist. The students participating in this exercise either role play an alternative response or suggest another direction for the story. If it is possible for the students to prepare in advance, a brief dialogue may be developed that could be played out before the rest of the class.

4. *Small group-guided discussion.* Assuming that the students have all read a chapter or two of the book, key questions, comments, and activities designed by the instructor may be geared for each chapter. In the typical college class of twenty-five to thirty students, five or six different groups discuss one or two chapters. By appointing a spokesperson for each group, the class shares opinions and attitudes in an open, yet structured, discussion.

The Exceptional Child
through Literature

CHAPTER ONE

Who Is Exceptional?

It is tempting to respond to the question, Who is exceptional? with the equally challenging, Who isn't exceptional? The flippancy of the latter query begs the question and diverts our attention from the gravity of one of America's most desperate and pressing educational issues. As Edward B. Fiske has written, "Societies . . . can be judged by the way in which they treat those who are different. By this standard, American education has never distinguished itself."[1]

In a volume dedicated to using an affective approach to alert the student of special education to the "quiet revolution" now taking place in the education of exceptional children, it would be dereliction of duty not to respond to the question without at least partial reference to *Christmas in Purgatory*, the distinguished volume of pictures of people languishing in institutions for the retarded.[2] In his preface to this photographic essay, the printed forerunner to *Titicut Follies*,[3] Seymour Sara-

---

[1]Edward B. Fiske, "Special Education is Now a Matter of Civil Rights," *New York Times,* April 25, 1976, p. 1.

[2]Burton Blatt and Fred Kaplan, with an introduction by Seymour Sarason, *Christmas in Purgatory* (Boston, Mass.: Allyn & Bacon, Inc., 1966).

[3]This is Frederick Wiseman's film (Grove Press Film Division) about an institution in Massachusetts. It earned for its producer-director virtual banishment from that state's "schools" for the retarded because he portrayed on film the modern horrors of incarceration in a public institution. The film won first prize at the Mannheim Film Festival, 1968.

son[4] writes, "it became increasingly clear to me that the conditions I saw—and which are documented in the present book—were not due to evil or incompetent or cruel people but rather to a conception of human potential and an attitude toward innovation, which when applied to the mentally defective, result in a self-fulfilling prophecy . . . if one thinks that defective children are beyond help, one acts towards them in ways which then confirm one's assumptions."[5] This visual saga of life in five state institutions in four eastern states, which left the authors of *Christmas in Purgatory* in "the depths of despair" and with the realization that "man's inhumanity to man makes countless thousands mourn,"[6] seems to make an attempt to define exceptionality as merely an academic exercise. Nevertheless, the sobriety of formal definitions of exceptionality are needed to balance the emotional upheaval the reader may expect while reading the fiction of this volume.

    Robert M. Smith and John T. Neisworth, objecting to standard definitions of exceptionality that have "focused on attributes, deficiencies, or defects of the child,"[7] propose a definition that shifts the emphasis from characteristics of the child to manipulation of educational variables for intervention. Thus they define special education rather than exceptional children: "special education is that profession concerned with the arrangement of educational variables leading to the prevention, reduction or elimination of those conditions that produce significant defects in the academic, communicative, locomotor or adjustive functioning of children."[8] We commend this approach and cite three more child-oriented definitions of exceptionality. Samuel A. Kirk defines an exceptional child as "a child who deviates from the average or normal child (1) in mental characteristics, (2) in sensory abilities, (3) in neuromuscular or physical characteristics, (4) in social or emotional behavior, (5) in communication abilities, or (6) in multiple handicaps to such an extent that he requires a modification of school practices, or special educational services, in order to develop to his maximum capacity."[9] Bill R. Gearheart states, "The exceptional child shall be consid-

---

[4]Blatt and Kaplan, *Christmas in Purgatory*, p. iv.
[5]Compare the Sarason quote with Thomas S. Szasz's statement, "If one wishes to understand the term HOLY WATER, one should not study the properties of water, but rather the assumptions and beliefs of the people who use it. That is, holy water derives its meaning from those who attribute a special essence to it (Thomas S. Szasz, *Ceremonial Chemistry: The Ritual Persecution of Drugs, Addicts, and Pushers* [Garden City, N.Y.: Doubleday & Company, Inc., 1974])."
[6]Robert Burns in *Familiar Quotations*, 13th ed., ed. John Bartlett (Boston, Mass.: Little, Brown and Company, 1955).
[7]Robert M. Smith and John T. Neisworth, *The Exceptional Child: A Functional Approach* (New York: McGraw-Hill Book Company, 1975), p. 12.
[8]Ibid., p. 13.
[9]Samuel A. Kirk, *Educating Exceptional Children*, 2nd ed. (Boston, Mass.: Houghton Mifflin Company, 1972), p. 4.

ered to be one whose educational requirements are so different from the average or normal child, that he cannot be effectively educated without the provision of special educational programs, services, facilities, or materials."[10] Lloyd M. Dunn writes, "An exceptional pupil is so labeled only for that segment of his school career (1) when his deviating physical or behavioral characteristics are of such a nature as to manifest a significant learning asset or disability for special education purposes; and, therefore, (2) when, through trial provisions, it has been determined that he can make greater all-around adjustment and scholastic progress with direct or indirect special education services than he could with only a typical regular school program."[11]

In November 1975, the Congress of the United States passed the Education for All Handicapped Children Act (P.I.. 94–142) that requires states to locate and provide free, appropriate education by 1978 for all handicapped children.[12] Federal funds up to at least 1 billion dollars a year are expected to flow into special education efforts. The United States Office of Education estimates that there are 7.8 million handicapped in the country (1 million in Canada) between the ages of three and twenty-one, 1 million of whom are not receiving any education and only half of whom are in adequate programs. The most recent statistics breaking this figure down into specific disability categories comes from the 1968–69 summary from the Bureau of Education for the Handicapped. Of the nearly 8 million exceptional children, there are "2.5 million with speech problems, 1.4 million with emotional problems,·1.7 million with some degree of mental retardation, 700,000 with learning disabilities, 400,000 with hearing problems, 350,000 with crippling conditions and 70,000 with visual impairments."[13]

Aside from the question of the validity of the figures just quoted, we must examine the rationale for the classification of exceptional children. In the first of a two-volume comprehensive study, *Issues in the Classification of Children,* Prudence M. Rains and her collaborators state the following:

> What is an "exceptional child" and who says so? . . . What makes this category of child exceptional to those who define it as such, and why this child and not others? The answer to this question is likely to be considered

---

[10]Bill R. Gearheart, ed., *Education of Exceptional Children* (Scranton, Pa.: International Textbook, 1972), p. 2.

[11]Lloyd M. Dunn, ed., *Exceptional Children in the Schools,* 2nd ed. (New York: Holt, Rinehart and Winston, Inc., 1973), p. 7.

[12]It is interesting to note that the Congress used the term "handicapped" whereas the professionals cited so far in this book rarely or never do.

[13]Jerry W. Willis, Jeane Crowder, and Joan Willis, *Guiding the Psychological and Educational Growth of Children* (Springfield, Ill.: Charles C. Thomas, Publisher, 1976), p. 183.

obvious, but some cases are more obvious than others. Surely, the blind are more "exceptional" than the left-handed, and the mentally retarded are more exceptional than the child with a speech impediment. But is the bilingual child more exceptional than the black child, or are the children of migrants more exceptional than those from the upper-middle class? It is just as sensible to ask why blind, mentally retarded, or culturally deprived children should be considered exceptional as to ask about left-handed, upper-middle class, or gifted children. Clearly, the children considered "exceptional" are the children who create "social problems" for institutions responsible for their welfare. Thus, categories of exceptional children are expressions of values that may vary with time and place. This conception of social problems—a conception that contains assertions about the existence of certain "social conditions" considered undesirable, harmful, or otherwise detrimental to the individuals in question and to the welfare of society—provides the basis, then, for identifying populations of children as exceptional.[14]

The editors of this volume ask the question, Who is exceptional? not merely to identify those with whom the book is concerned but also to raise a more fundamental question. It should be somewhat disturbing to the student of special education to learn that the classification of a person as exceptional is not based on the degree of incapacity but on the application of socially generated rules. Rains and her collaborators state, "Just as it has been said that law is the formal cause of crime, so it can be said that classification is the formal cause of mental retardation, speech impediments, and school phobias."[15] Howard S. Becker writes, "Social groups create deviance by making the rules whose infraction constitutes deviance and by applying those rules to particular people and labeling them as outsiders."[16] In other words, socially generated rules define the exceptional child and produce a specific category. Of necessity the categories of exceptionality are made very broad so that despite the immense heterogeneity of people included in any particular category, all children with deviance from the norms accepted by society are differentiated as members of the same population.

Once classified in a particular category of exceptionality for the convenience of professionals, the effects upon those classified (and those who have made the classification) are readily apparent. Once stereotyped, a person is apt to think differently of himself and to be

[14]Prudence M. Rains et al., "The Labeling Approach to Deviance," in *Issues in the Classification of Children*, ed. Nicholas Hobbs (San Francisco, Calif.: Jossey-Bass, Inc., Publishers, 1975), pp. 88–100.

[15]Ibid., p. 92.

[16]Howard S. Becker, *Outsider: Studies in the Sociology of Deviance* (New York: The Free Press, 1963), p. 9.

thought of differently by others, including specialists in any particular category. Although the stereotype may reflect either positive or negative behavior and beliefs, "it generally reflects a negative attitude about a population as a whole."[17] Rains and her collaborators ask, "When an agency designates a person as *deviant*, then, is the agency thereby producing deviants rather than simply identifying them?"[18] Social scientists have used the term *self-fulfilling prophecy* to indicate what happens when a person feels the effects of labeling.[19]

Our thesis is that society creates labels, therefore it creates distinct categories that encompass wide differences, and those differences are lumped together. An article by Robert Bogdan and Steven Taylor documents vividly all of the assertions we have promulgated.[20] Erving Goffman[21], David L. Rosenhan[22], Burton Blatt[23], and Dorothea and Benjamin Braginsky[24] have all shown that persons in institutions designated for a special purpose have their conduct interpreted by others as if all of them were identical. Further, these persons soon view themselves with a lowered self-image. The beautiful interview in Bogdan and Taylor's article highlights this idea. Ed Murphy, a twenty-six-year-old man labeled mentally retarded and institutionalized since he was fifteen, states, "You have an image of yourself deep down. You try to sort it all out. You know what you are deep inside but those around you give you a negative picture of yourself. It's that umbrella over you."[25]

Who is exceptional? Whoever we say is exceptional. Bogdan and Taylor state, "We have told the world that there are two kinds of human beings. . . . It is through intimacy that we learn how the subject views himself or herself and what he or she has in common with all of us becomes clear. Difference takes on less importance . . . and categories of all kinds become less relevant."[26]

---

[17]Bill R. Gearheart and Mel W. Weishahn, *the Handicapped Child in the Regular Classroom* (St. Louis, Mo.: The C. V. Mosby Co., 1976).

[18]Rains et al., "The Labeling Approach to Deviance," p. 97.

[19]The effect of labels in the political arena is deftly described by Stuart Chase in "Label and Libel," *ETC: A Review of General Semantics*, vol. XIX, no. 3 (October 1962), 262–68.

[20]Robert Bogdan and Steven Taylor, "The Judged, Not the Judges," *American Psychologist*, vol. 31, no. 1 (January 1976), 47–52. Also see Robert Bogdan and Douglas Biklen, "Handicapism," *Social Policy*, vol. 7, no. 5, (April 1977), 14–19.

[21]Erving Goffman, *Asylums* (New York: Anchor Books, 1961).

[22]David L. Rosenhan, "On Being Sane in Insane Places," *Science*, 179 (January 1973), 1–9.

[23]Burton Blatt, *Exodus from Pandemonium* (Boston, Mass.: Allyn & Bacon, Inc., 1970).

[24]Dorothea Braginsky and Benjamin Braginsky, *Hansels and Gretels: Studies of Children in Institutions for the Mentally Retarded* (New York: Holt, Rinehart and Winston, Inc., 1971).

[25]Bogdan and Taylor, "The Judged, Not the Judges," p. 51.

[26]Ibid., p. 52.

Hunting Season

by Joanne Greenberg

"Maybe I'll go down to the creek bank and see if some deers were there last night," he said. The top of his head was level with the counter top where she was working. He put his head all the way back to look up at her, as if she were a sky above him. "Can I, Mommy?"

"Just a minute, will you?" She was measuring flour, and when she had finished and was ready to pay attention to him, his head was still tilted all the way back, because he knew he had to wait and wait for her to get finished with the complicated things she did, and then repeat everything, and even then, half the time it was *no*, anyway. "Now, what was that?" she said.

He asked again.

"All right, you can go, but wear your heavy jacket, because it's getting cold outside."

His heavy jacket wasn't for the cold alone, and they both knew it. It had been made in fear of the Cruel Season. In these bright cold-yellow days, town men put on their talisman clothes, gulped their whiskey, and went up into the hills to hunt and kill. Sometimes they killed one another, and although no hill children had been hurt in many years, it was hard to send them out to play in the sound of the guns.

The little boy was lonely, with all the others in school now. She couldn't keep him indoors, the way some of the other women tried to do—not with everything leading away from their house, trails and tracks and the woods all calling to be explored. So she had made him a little turquoise jacket, unmistakable and in the most unnatural color she could think of.

"Button it up," she said. "I told you it was cold." He began to work the buttons clumsily. Next year he would be going to school; all the kids could walk together down the Notch to the county road. *"To* the creek, not *in* the creek," she told him. "And please, no more smooth stones— we have a whole basketful already. And if you see any of the hunters on the trail————"

He bore her fussing with stoic patience; his face had the removed look of someone who had already started off, and finally she told him to have a good time, and then he knew he could go. He said good-bye and, yes, he would be back before lunchtime, and he went out into the shivering gold-yellow of the hillside.

She went back into the kitchen, crumbled two cakes of yeast into the potato water she had saved, and started to get the dishes ready to wash. I keep nagging him, she thought. I have such a good eye to peer out and see what he has done wrong once and might do wrong again. . . . She thought about it occasionally, what a shame it was that the boys would never know her as she had been—someone who laughed easily at silly things; who played and didn't care how much it messed up the room; someone

who had once liked to stamp windowpanes out of frozen puddles; who had prized laughter, wind, and freedom. Her mind went to the ways she had changed in the years of being a mother. Some of the ways made her a little ashamed.

There was one time when Joseph was trying to tell her about his best friend, Tim. Tim was moving away, and Joseph was shaken with a foretaste of loneliness. There would be nobody to play with on this side of the Notch. She had found herself looking into his ear as he talked, and then going for the small glob of wax with the edge of her apron; then noticing the little crust of sleep at the corner of his eye, and getting that; then straightening his hair—and all the while he was trying to show her his pain, hoping that she could share, from her height, his tragedy—a child's tragedy, written in miniature, told in a small, high voice.

She fussed and fussed and missed the important things. In defense of herself, she knew this was one of the penalties of being a "good" wife and mother. Her life was a mass of details, endless and entangled, all together, all unsorted: trivial things and important things wound into and against one another, all warring for her attention. Changing the goldfish water wasn't vital, but it couldn't wait; teaching the children their Bible was vital, but it could wait. Listening to them, growing with them, that was vital; but the bills had to be paid now, the dinner was burning right now. . . .

She finished with the dishes and went back to the bread, beating the foamed yeast into the well she had made in the flour. Three palmfuls of sugar, one of salt, two eggs. Here it was Friday already, and . . .

Friday! How could she have let him go out today? She put down the bread paddle at the edge of the bowl, where it fell over into the dough and sank. Friday. Had the week gone so fast? He had been on his new medicine since last Friday. His last seizure had been on Friday. They had gone down-mountain to the doctor, and the doctor had changed the medicine again.

"Don't worry about your little boy," he had said. "We'll get control of the seizures; it will take time, that's all." He had given her medication for two weeks. "And if he has no trouble with it, you can just call the office, and I'll have it made up for him, the way we did it before."

She had had to tell him humbly that she didn't like to use the phone to call him because of the party line.

"Maybe it's a good idea not to, then," he had said gently. "It wouldn't do to put a stigma on him. We're going to get him under control before he starts to school, and then nobody need

know. Until we find the right combination of medicine—something that gives control without getting him too groggy—well, there are going to be problems." Then the doctor had got up, his way of ending their conversation. "The difficulty will be for you, not for him. You can be grateful that epilepsy is most merciful to the people who have it—he's not conscious of his seizures, doesn't know he has them. The loss of all the time he's out—that might puzzle him; that, and your attitude, perhaps. But—you just let me worry. In every other way, he's a fine, healthy boy."

One week and no seizure, though she had waited, half wanting it to come and be over, fearful of a vain hope that his medicine might be right at last. Every evening when Cal came home, his eyes asking, "Did it happen?" and her eyes answering, "Not today" went before all other greetings, questions, news, kiss at the door.

Now it was Friday again, and he had never gone longer than a week without a seizure. Now he was walking up over Pickax Hill, past the old mine and then down the steep gully, all rock. Guns would be going off over his head and frightened animals bursting the thickets to outrun their panic. Death would be all around him. He was sure to stop at the creek, enchanted with the round stones, bending down to play with them and watch the water go over; he would be bending over the shocking chill water. . . .

She couldn't stop seeing her Mother-Pictures—how a seizure could catch him at the top of the hill, no warning. He could fall, thrashing, unable to breathe, his face going gray for lack of air, and then down the rocky gully, falling, and there was the water. He would be in the water while the paroxysms slowed and the unconsciousness began. How could he begin to breathe again, with his head in the water? (Always the first infinitesimal breath after a seizure had been a miracle to her. It was a promise that the next breath would come, and the next, each one a little longer, until Breath itself had been given back to him, and slowly, slowly, his life.) It was an awful picture, the water holding him so that his breath could never again promise. . . .

She shook herself free of the picture, but it didn't leave her. It stayed, brimming the edges of her mind, ready to flow back when she relaxed her vigil against it. "He had his medicine this morning," she said to the empty house. "He looked fine when he went out."

Of course he looked fine. Didn't the seizures catch him in the middle of a word, a step, a thought across his mind? He might be in the midst of running: leg up, arm out, his face eager with success. Motion would be frozen, and then a cry squandering all his breath. Then he would fall into the rhythmic spasms that conquered everything, and an eternity without breathing. It took only a second for the happy, healthy boy to disappear. Now he was going up Pickax Hill, up near the old mine, the sudden hunters, the gully, the rocks, the water.

"I can't stay here any more!" she said to the house. She pulled her old work jacket off the hook and ran out the door.

For a single eye-struck moment she forgot what had brought her outside. She stood still, gasping with the beauty of the sunlight that was still slanting from the east, catching itself in the hillside's trees, its golden light pouring through a million translucent screens of veined paper. The colors trembled and vibrated with the light, but the leaf sound was brittle in the wind, like a scattering applause of old people, dry and hesitant. Above the feverish trees there was a sky cut clean by the sharp edge of a harder wind.

She followed the little path and crossed the Notch. After that, there were only deer trails up the near side of Pickax Hill. The mines and roads were over the summit. How she hated and feared those old mine shafts! These hills were full of raped land the takers had plundered and left unhealed. Mines and quarries still poured yellow tailings from their wounds. She heard a gun, then another. Now the hunters too. A world of rape and murder, a whole world. Her head ached with the horror of all the possibilities. She had to find him and stop the pictures in her head.

The shimmering golden forest moved in upon the trail. Where was the little turquoise jacket? Ahead of her, the way wound and sought upward, hidden by trees and brush. Where was he? Could he have gone so far? She nosed the wind like an animal. Was that he, calling? Was that his cry? She began to run, listening, smelling the air for danger. And then she saw, on the trail ahead of her, the turquoise jacket going up and down with his steps as he marched along. She cut over and off into the woods, keeping behind him, tracking. I mustn't let him see me, she thought. He doesn't know what he has, what takes him and transforms him. She could see his face as he said, "Everybody else goes up the hill and down to the creek. You don't think I'm big enough! You think I'm a *baby!*" Oh, that worst of all insults!

She kept uphill of him and behind the beacon jacket, tracking him warily, stopping when she got too close, not daring to let her breath sob out on a wind that

might carry the sound to him. It was hard not to pant for breath. She thought: When did I get so old and fat—a middle-aged huntress in a ratty apron, puffing uphill with the grace of a runaway tractor?

He put his head up, reading the air for something, and she crouched lower.

For a while, he dawdled over a fork in the trail, and she watched from her cover, seething against him. (Why do you tell me you are going to go someplace and then turn right around and go someplace else instead! What if I had to look for you one day, when you'd told me, oh, the creek, and it wasn't the creek you had gone to, but the canyon? Don't you know that you could be lost or finished in a moment? Don't you know that you are a miracle, and irreplaceable—you stupid, stupid boy!) Below her, he made up his mind idly and turned uptrail again, and she followed him, tracking.

They skirted the summit, leveled, and started over toward the south. The scattered heaps of tailings from the mines began. They lay spewed from the openings of shafts or drill holes, and the water that they leached turned acid and killed the plants it touched.

Over to the north, she heard the guns of the hunters. The boy crossed again and started down toward the sound of the guns, cutting obliquely down the north side to where the creek ran. She backtracked and came up again at his left, being careful not to stumble, not to make noise in the leaves that lay blown in heaps for the afternoon schoolboys to play in. When she came up again, she didn't see him. The panic and pictures flooded back. She went to the brow of the hill, tracking.

She kept away from the top, where they had been, and looked out toward the north and east. The downward slope was more gentle there; there were fewer rocks, and the creek flowed almost level and had laid banks of soft, alluvial sand for itself on either side.

He was standing close to the bank, immediately below her, looking across the creek and picking his nose intently. In the midst of her relief, her hand came up in the gesture that had become automatic to her—and her mouth opened to say, "Don't do that." She thought suddenly: I'm not saving him, I'm saving myself. I'm not even looking out for him—I'm *spying*. What am I doing here, invading his pitiful little private time?

He stood very small and straight against all the land and sky that reached around her. His back was to her, and his ears stuck out so bravely, and his neck was set bravely on his thin shoul-ders. What if it wasn't a seizure now, but a wasp stinging him—wouldn't she run down to the bank to comfort him? When the creek bed froze, he would want to skate with the other boys on the pond downstream, to go sled riding, howling down the hillsides in his joyfear. What if he should be thrown over in the snow, hit a tree, hit a rock? Could she follow him everywhere to pick him up? Weren't there tunnels in the mine?

Over north, the shooting started up again.

He was standing on the bank, sifting sand through his fingers, and he began to talk in his high, clear voice—his own thoughts, which she was not meant to hear. "Listen, you rocks over there—you better shape up! You're not so tough, you big, damn rocks! My brothers go to school. When I go to school, I'm going to learn all about *you*, but you will never know about *me*, and you will be in my power." Then he shouted at them, *"Do you hear me?"* It was her intonation exactly, all the querulous anger of her impatience and all the long-suffering in her tone, captured with unconscious, searing honesty.

It was his world of rape and murder, too—he had to make it his.

"Yes, I hear you," she whispered, and turned and walked back down the hill.

DISCUSSION

There are some handicaps, such as epilepsy, that are invisible to the outsider. No one looking at the little boy in this story could detect that he is subject to seizures. His parents, however, are constantly concerned about the boy's neurological defect. Each night the mother and father exchange glances of relief that the little boy has not had a seizure; this wordless exchange takes precedence over actual words of greeting. The doctor is the only person with whom the parents share their fear and pain. The doctor, however, encourages the silence over the boy's epilepsy by using the term "stigma" to emphasize the socially damaging aspects of this disorder. The doctor hopes to get the boy's seizures under control through medication before he enters school, thereby implying that if the boy's condition is kept out of school records, no one in the community need ever know that he is subject to seizures.

Fortunately this doctor's attitude is less prevalent today. Parents are encouraged to be open about a child's medical hsitory in filling out forms for the school. School authorities do not use this information to restrict a child's activities. The schools are an important force in changing old-fashioned ideas concerning disorders such as epilepsy. Teachers are usually alerted by the school nurse to any children in the class who may be on medication. In the case of epilepsy, the child would not be excluded from a regular school placement. Instead the teacher would be given instructions regarding first aid for a seizure. National organizations such as the Epilepsy Foundation of America (1828 L. Street, N.W., Washington, D.C. 20036) have been formed to disseminate accurate information to the public and to encourage healthier attitudes. Thus, individuals with certain handicapping conditions are spared the additional emotional trauma associated with false fears or restrictions.

The little boy in the story is not aware that his parents have restricted his activities for a medical reason. He views their attitudes as minimizing his abilities and attempting to keep him "a baby." He rejects their protectiveness, but at a subconscious level he may be anxious about his adequacy. Joanne Greenberg has effectively portrayed the mother as a woman who has made her role as wife and mother her sole concern, thereby neglecting her own needs as a person. Guilt and fear for her child are overriding aspects of her life. She never permits herself the freedom to laugh unburdened or the freedom to nurture her own child state—the child that is within every adult.

The end of the story can be interpreted in a number of ways. One interpretation may be that the boy is reacting to the mother's controlling ways. He mimics her tone and her varied emotions as she mothers. He lets the unanswering rocks know that overcontrol saps strength and power. His mother keeps control over him by making sure she knows about every aspect of his life. Nevertheless, the ending hints that the boy has learned the secret of control and power and that he will take over his own life.

SPRINGBOARDS FOR INQUIRY

1. If you were the parent in this story, would you share with your child knowledge of his handicap? Explain how you would communicate this information or why you would withhold information.
2. Do you think that epilepsy still holds a social stigma? How can an individual with a handicap work toward educating the public about false stereotypes concerning his or her disorder?
3. In view of the child's handicap, what do you think of the way the doctor handled the parents? How could he have advised these parents differently?
4. Discuss the mother's reactions to her boy's handicap. Was she overprotective or realistic?
5. How would you feel about having an epileptic child in your class? What measures would you take to handle the situation?
6. List five national organizations and five professional journals devoted to disseminating information about particular disabilities.

CHAPTER TWO

The Mentally Retarded

> When I first saw her, she lay nude in a small, dirty, solitary confinement cell. She wouldn't talk to anyone—wouldn't even hold out her hand. Tests couldn't register her low IQ. We got her out of that seclusion cell. We placed her in a program with one staff member for her, three shifts a day.
>
> In four months I went back to visit her. She was dressing herself. She played a record for me and showed me the paintings she had done. She talked to me. Now, she is no longer considered to be severely retarded.[1]

Bruce Ennis, a lawyer, wrote that nearly a decade ago. In contrast to the description above is the following nearly verbatim account of an NBC radio broadcast in June 1976:

> In Menomonie, Wisconsin, a conference on the mentally retarded was completely planned by a committee of mentally retarded persons. They planned the program, invited speakers, outlined fifteen seminars and chose seminar leaders and planned the meals. The only help they received was from a committee of students of special education and their professor.

In between these extremes—the incarceration of the mentally retarded and their liberation—lies a plethora of problems still needing solutions. In October 1961, President John F. Kennedy appointed the President's Committee on Mental Retardation and charged them with

---

[1]President's Committee on Mental Retardation, *Silent Minority* (Washington, D.C.: United States Government Printing Office, 1970), p. 9.

the study of all aspects of mental retardation and the preparation of a comprehensive and long-range plan for dealing with the crucial problems. Their report was published in October 1962. A second report was published in March 1976. The committee presented the following statistics, which still have some validity:

1. There were approximately 5.5 million mentally retarded in the United States. By 1970, there would be approximately 1 million more (3 percent of the population).
2. Only 400,000 of the mentally retarded required constant care and supervision.
3. There were 15–20 million people living in families with a retarded child. 96 percent of all retarded persons lived in private homes.
4. Over 200,000 mentally retarded were cared for in public institutions at a cost of over $300 million per year.
5. Over $250 million were spent in special education by state and local groups. The federal government spent an additional $164 million.[2]
6. During World War II, 4 percent of all persons examined for induction into the armed forces were mentally retarded.
7. One in four beds in mental institutions was occupied by a mentally retarded patient.
8. Mental retardation disabled twice as many perons as blindness, polio, cerebral palsy, and heart disease combined; ten times as many as diabetes; and twenty times as many as muscular dystrophy.[3]

The definition of mental retardation still accepted by most professionals is the one published by the American Association on Mental Deficiency (AAMD): "Mental Retardation refers to significantly subaverage general, intellectual functioning existing concurrently with deficits in adaptive behavior, and manifested during the developmental period."[4] Nancy M. Robinson and Halbert B. Robinson, who quote di-

[2]According to the "Spring Survey of Education," *New York Times,* April 25, 1976, the United States Office of Education reports that since 1972 the local and state expenditures for all handicapped were approximately $4 billion. After 1978, because of the Education for All Handicapped Children Act, $1 billion a year will be spent for the handicapped. What share of this will go specifically for the mentally retarded is, of course, still unknown.
[3]President's Committee on Mental Retardation, *Mental Retardation: Century of Decision* (Washington, D.C.: United States Government Printing Office, 1976).
[4]Herbert J. Grossman, ed., *Manual on Terminology and Classification in Mental Retardation* (Washington, D.C.: AAMD, 1973), p. 11.

rectly from the AAMD manual, provide further clarification of the terminology used in the definition. They refer to six key terms, four of which are reproduced here:

> *Mental retardation* denotes a level of behavioral performance without reference to etiology. Mental retardation is descriptive of current behavior and does not imply prognosis.
>
> *Intellectual functioning* may be assessed by one or more of the standardized tests developed for that purpose. (It is emphasized that despite current practice, a finding of low IQ is never by itself sufficient to make the diagnosis of mental retardation.)
>
> *Developmental period* is the period from birth to eighteen years old and is considered the time during which there is or may be intellectual growth (development). After eighteen, either progress or retardation is negligible.
>
> *Adaptive behavior* is defined as the effectiveness or degree with which the individual meets the standards of personal independence and social responsibility expected of his age and cultural group.[5]

A concise review of the history and background of definition and classification in mental retardation may be found in the volume by Phillip C. Chinn and his colleagues[6] and in a recent work by Nicholas Hobbs.[7] Generally, some of the controversy over a usable definition for mental retardation has been around the inclusion of terms such as "constitutional origin" and "essentially incurable." Although most lay people think of the mentally retarded exclusively in terms of the visibly observable characteristics associated with Down's syndrome (mongolism), microcephaly (an abnormally small head and marked mental deficiency), or hydrocephaly (marked enlargement of the head and an underdeveloped brain), 75–85 percent of the total population of retarded persons in this country fall into the category of cultural familial retardation that is not associated with biomedical factors or with visible, abnormal physiological features but totally with environmental factors.

---

[5]Nancy M. Robinson and Halbert B. Robinson, *The Mentally Retarded Child*, 2nd ed. (New York: McGraw-Hill Book Company, 1976), pp. 30–32.

[6]Phillip C. Chinn, Clifford J. Drew, and Don R. Logan, *Mental Retardation: A Life Cycle Approach* (St. Louis, Mo.: The C. V. Mosby Co., 1975), pp. 7–23.

[7]Nicholas Hobbs, *Issues in the Classification of Children*, vols. I and II (San Francisco, Calif.: Jossey-Bass, Inc., Publishers, 1975). See especially chapter 8, "Mental Retardation," written by John W. Filler, Jr., et al. Other issues concerning mental retardation in vol. II are in chapter 17, "Mental Retardation System," by Robert B. Edgerton, Richard K. Eymen, and Arthur B. Silverstein.

Therefore a definition that includes "constitutional origin" is erroneous in the majority of cases. A definition suggesting that mental retardation is incurable is also misleading because the majority of the mentally retarded are not identified until school age and lose the label when they leave the school system and enter the general population. Jane Mercer uses the term "six-hour retardate" to emphasize that many individuals in her study considered "normal" by neighbors and family were labeled "retarded" for school purposes; the label was relevant only for the six hours that the individual was in the school setting.[8]

There has been much confusion and contradiction in the development of classification schemes. Medicine and education, the two disciplines most interested in the retarded, have not been able to agree upon the same limits for classification. Educators employed a classification based upon expected educational achievement and employed the descriptive terms "educable-trainable" and "custodial" to distinguish among the groups. This kind of classification served administrative purposes well. Students were more easily counted when assigned to a particular educational grouping, and funds were distributed according to the count in each category. Grouping also aided the legal system to arrive at decisions regarding responsibility for action or guardianship.

With the Education for All Handicapped Children Act, 1975 (PL. 94–142), there is now mandated a more individualized approach to the educational goals and objectives for each handicapped child. Since the law requires that the child be educated in the least restrictive educational placement, many mildly retarded children will go from classes specifically designated for the educable mentally retarded into the mainstream of education, with provisions for special tutorial services. The learning abilities and disabilities of each child will be evaluated using instruments that are not racially or culturally discriminatory, and an individualized educational program will be written for each handicapped child. The act safeguards the due process rights of the children and their parents; it is now incumbent upon the schools to include the parent as one of the members of the educational team that approves the educational program and decides on educational placement.

At the present time, classification of mentally retarded as recommended by the AAMD guidelines stresses the degree to which the retarded person is able to cope with his or her everyday environment, that is, adaptive behavior,[9] and his or her score on an IQ test. Terminol-

---

[8]Jane R. Mercer, *Labeling the Mentally Retarded* (Berkeley, Calif.: University of California Press, 1973), p. 94.

[9]Adaptive behavior refers primarily to three types of coping behavior. These are (1) the level of independent functioning, (2) the ability of the retarded person to accept personal responsibility, and (3) the social responsibility of the retarded person. Nancy and Halbert Robinson, *The Mentally Retarded Child* (New York: McGraw-Hill Book Company, 1976), p. 356.

ogy such as "idiot," "imbecile," and "moron" (IQ's of 0–30, 30–50, 50–70 respectively), which was used for the subgroupings within the trainable category, have been dropped. Table 2–1 summarizes both the intellectual functioning data and the adaptive behavior characteristics.

The literature on mental retardation is vast. A content analysis of every article that appeared in the journal *Mental Retardation* revealed that during 1976 the literature was most often concerned with institutionalization/normalization issues. There is a body of nonfiction literature that is equally, if not more, effective in helping lay people and professionals to gain insight into the problems of the retarded. The reports of Dorothea D. and Benjamin M. Braginsky and Burton Blatt are eloquent testimonials to the unacceptable warehousing of too many of the retarded in America.[10] The Braginsky studies, dedicated to the "surplus" children, have triggered considerable thought about how and why certain children are classified as retarded and then housed in state institutions.[11] Theodore R. Sarbin writes:

> They offer experiment and argument to demonstrate that so-called retardates are in fact undifferentiated from their unlabeled peers, committing themselves well on psychological dimensions relevant for adaptation in an imperfect and changing world. The "retardates," not unlike their extramural peers, display power strategies, adaptive styles, and the ability to take into account the roles of others in their own behavioral choices. In short, they are not psychologically different from other specimens of humanity.[12]

---

[10]Dorothea D. Braginsky and Benjamin M. Braginsky, *Hansels and Gretels: Studies of Children in Institutions for the Mentally Retarded* (New York: Holt, Rinehart and Winston, Inc., 1971); Burton Blatt, *Exodus from Pandemonium* (Boston, Mass.: Allyn & Bacon, Inc., 1970), and *Souls in Extremis* (Boston, Mass.: Allyn & Bacon, Inc., 1973).

[11]Braginsky and Braginsky, *Hansels and Gretels*. This work is also cited in Robert Bogdan and Steven Taylor, "The Judged, Not the Judges," *American Psychologist*, vol. 31, no. 1 (January 1976) 47–52. Bogdan and Taylor rely heavily upon the verbatim account of a person placed in an institution for the retarded at the age of fifteen. The following statement by this person should give pause to the student of exceptionality who has a predetermined opinion about the thinking ability of the retarded: "My mother protected me. It wasn't wrong that she protected me, but there comes a time when someone has to come in and break them away. I can remember trying to be like the other kids and having my mother right there pulling me away. She was always worried about me. You can't force yourself to say to your mother, 'stop, I can do it myself.' Sometimes I think the pain of being handicapped is that people give you so much love that it becomes a weight on you and a weight on them. There is no way that you can break from it without hurting them—without bad feelings—guilt. It is like a trap because of the fact that you are restricted to your inner thoughts. After a while you resign yourself to it. The trap is that you can't tell them, 'Let me go.' You have to live with it and suffer. It has to do with pity. Looking back on it I can't say it was wrong. She loved me. You do need special attention, but the right amount."

[12]Braginsky and Braginsky, *Hansels and Gretels*, p. iv.

Table 2–1
IQ Scores and Expected Level of Adaptive Behavior for Levels of Retardation

Level	Obtained intelligence quotient (Stanford Binet)	(Wechsler Scales)	Expected level of adaptive behavior
Mild	68–52	69–55	Capable of maintaining themselves in a job; need help with social and financial affairs
Moderate	51–36	54–40	Able to care for themselves adequately within the context of a family; able to do simple jobs in industry and around the house
Severe	35–20	39–25 (extrapolated)	Need special help in even the simplest everyday behavior; exhibit little independent behavior
Profound	19 and below	24 and below (extrapolated)	Total supervision required; little learning is evident

Source: The IQ Score index is from Nadine M. Lambert, Margaret R. Wilcox, and W. Preston Gleason, *The Educationally Retarded Child* (New York: Grune & Stratton, Inc., 1974), p. 8. The "expected level of adaptive behavior" material has been added by the editors of this volume.

Along with the vast numbers of institutionalized individuals and the shocking conditions in many of the large hospitals where they are confined, the Braginskys also draw attention to the disproportionately high number of minority group children enrolled in special classes for the mentally retarded. Jane Mercer's study of children who were referred to pupil-personnel services in the city of Riverside, California, found that the 1,234 referred children were similar in ethnic distribution and socioeconomic status to the total population of the school district. *"As soon as the intelligence test was used, the higher failure rate of children from lower socioeconomic background and from minority homes produced the disproportions characteristic of classes for THE mentally retarded."* [13] A bias became evident at the juncture in the referral process when a standardized intelligence measure was used for diagnosis. In their study conducted in Pima County, Arizona, Daniel Reschly and Frederick J. Jipson found that when they used the Perfor-

[13] Mercer, *Labeling the Mentally Retarded*, p. 101.

mance IQ (the IQ obtained in subtests requiring visual motor skills and manual problems solving) rather than using the Verbal IQ and the Full Scale IQ on the Wechsler Intelligence Scale for Children, Revised (WISC-R), overrepresentation was eliminated for Mexican-Americans and greatly reduced for Black and Papago Indian children.[14]

Because a bias is evident in many of the most frequently used standardized tests, psychologists, sociologists, and others interested in mental retardation are working toward developing instruments that are more useful in identifying the retarded. More accurate assessment procedures are becoming increasingly available. Nadine M. Lambert and her colleagues recommend assessment procedures in eleven essential evaluation areas. They also recommend a complete reevaluation at least every three years of all educationally retarded children. "In addition the psychologist should consider a complete reevaluation at any time the parent . . . a special class teacher, or other staff members . . . feel that this process is indicated because of a change in behavioral patterns."[15]

Jane Mercer has authored a System of Multicultural Pluralistic Assessment (SOMPA).[16] The assessment procedure was standardized in California with a white, Hispanic surname and a Black sample of children from five to eleven years of age. The WISC-R, one of the most frequently used tests of intellectual functioning, is retained, but SOMPA includes an interview with the parent to determine sociocultural family characteristics, an adaptive behavior rating, and a health history. Graphs are drawn showing the distribution of scores for subsets of students homogeneous for racial, cultural, socioeconomic, and other characteristics. A student's individual score is then compared to the norm for his unique subset group. Better designed tests and more inclusive criteria, as well as a heightened sensitivity to cultural difference rather than cultural disadvantage, should help to eliminate mislabeling in the schools.

The education of retarded children should be concentrated in the following four curricular areas:

1. Self-help, basic readiness, and independent living skills
2. Communication, oral language, and cognitive development skills

---

[14]Daniel Reschly and Frederick J. Jipson, "Ethnicity, Geographic Locale, Age, Sex, and Urban-Rural Residence As Variables in the Prevalence of Mild Retardation," *American Journal of Mental Deficiency*, vol. 8, no. 2 (September 1976), 154–61.

[15]Nadine M. Lambert, Margaret R. Wilcox, and W. Preston Gleason, *The Educationally Retarded Child* (New York: Grune & Stratton, Inc., 1974), pp. 91–92.

[16]Jane Mercer and June F. Lewis, *Manual for System of Multicultural Pluralistic Assessment* (New York: The Psychological Corporation, 1977).

3. Socialization and personality development skills
4. Vocational, recreational, and leisure skills

Retarded children can learn—they can learn to read, to write, to socialize, and to work. There are specific methodologies that stimulate the retarded to learn. The institutional picture of warehousing retarded persons is giving way to the application of learning and teaching techniques that work. Martin A. Kozloff's book is an example of the many behaviorally oriented texts that can help teachers to do something specific to teach the retarded to cope with life by developing each of the curricular areas.[17] His text covers techniques of teaching such skills as looking and listening, motor and verbal imitation, functional speech, and self-help chores and skills.

What is known of the cognitive development of the retarded should dictate the type of instruction attempted. For example, knowing that a slowly emerging cognitive development characterizes the intellectual growth of the mildly retarded, the aware teacher must carefully monitor the rate at which both verbal and nonverbal materials are presented to the child. Under these circumstances, such concepts as the engineered classroom[18] and precision teaching[19] may be important. Klaus Wedell states that "it is evident from even the most cursory scrutiny of the available literature that retarded children constitute the largest and most important group of subjects for behaviour modification programmes."[20] This educational technology is not concerned with etiology. What does matter is the evidence of specific problems, such as not being able to tie his or her shoes, use the toilet, or add two one-digit numbers, and the manipulation of the learning environment and learner so that these problems may be approached. The reasons why a child cannot feed himself or learn to zip his zipper are inconsequential. The core of any program for changing a child's behavior is what is known as the functional analysis of the problem. A standard six step procedure is followed:

1. Identification of the behaviors to be controlled or instituted. The more precise these descriptions are the more exact the methodology may be.

---

[17]Martin A. Kozloff, *Educating Children with Learning and Behavior Problems* (New York: John Wiley & Sons, Inc., 1974).

[18]Frank Hewett, *Education of Exceptional Learners* (Boston, Mass.: Allyn & Bacon, Inc., 1974).

[19]Ogden Lindzley, "Direct Measurement and Prosthesis of Retarded Children," *Journal of Education*, 147 (1964), 62–81.

[20]Klaus Wedell, *Orientations in Special Education* (London: John Wiley & Sons, Inc., 1975), p. 81.

2. Observing target behaviors in terms of frequency (f) and intensity of emission. The second step is called the collection of baseline data.

3. Identification of methods by which behavior may be modified or elicited. Both antecedent events (curriculum, teacher behavior, organization of the classroom) and setting stimuli (the educational setting itself, for example, a teacher with a negative attitude or parents who cannot follow a discussion of their children) need consideration in deciding on methodology.

4. Implementation. In order to have a planned change or initiation of behavior, all concerned need to agree with the aims of the program, to be trained, and to realize that an effective operant approach allows for variations and alternatives in the basic strategies.

5. Monitoring. This refers to the continuance of adequate observation of specific behaviors.

6. Evaluation. Behavior modification programs are judged solely by whether the target behaviors have been taught or brought under control. Included in evaluation is the relative efficiency of the program in terms of the length of time it took to change, extinguish, or develop new behavior, of the number of trials required, and of the level of reinforcement required to maintain desirable behavior.[21]

Cecil D. Mercer and Martha E. Snell assure teachers that mildly retarded individuals often experience so much failure by the middle and secondary school levels that externally supplied reinforcement and programming for the achievement of success in school are essential teaching strategies.[22] While it is true that B. F. Skinner's psychology has encouraged behavior modification techniques that hasten the appearance of behavior that would otherwise be acquired slowly or not at all, Donald L. Macmillan and Steven R. Forness express concern that behavior modification will be seen as the way to "treat" mental retardation.[23] They acknowledge its effectiveness but caution against misuse of the strategy. They contend that possibly too much responsibility is put in

[21]Ibid., p. 74.

[22]Cecil D. Mercer and Martha E. Snell, Learning Theory Research in Mental Retardation (Columbus, Ohio: Charles E. Merrill Publishing Co., 1977).

[23]Donald L. Macmillan and Steven R. Forness, "Behavior Modification: Savior or Savant?" in Sociobehavioral Studies in Mental Retardation, ed. C. Edward Meyers (Los Angeles, Calif.: American Association of Mental Deficiency, 1973), p. 207.

Table 2–2

Components of the Learning Process and Respective Theories and
       Implications

Learning components	Proponents	Major implication
Expectancy ↓	Social Learning Theory	Provide continuous success
Selective Attention ↓	Zeaman and House Fisher and Zeaman Denny (Incidental)	Make cues of task stimuli distinctive
Organizing Input for Storage ↓	Spitz	Organize or group input Pair material with meaningful event or object
Memory and Recall ↓	Ellis	Use verbal rehearsal
Transfer ↓		Train in a variety of settings Use modeling
Performance ↓	Dependent measure of all the research Skinner	Develop appropriate tasks
Feedback	Skinner	Provide systematic consequation

Source: Cecil D. Mercer and Martha E. Snell, *Learning Theory Research in Mental Retardation* (Columbus, Ohio: Charles E. Merrill Publishing Co., 1977), p. 321. Reprinted by permission of publisher.

the hands of the modifier (teacher) who may select behavior goals that are in the best interest of the teacher rather than the student. Also, behavior modification programs may be directed to group outcomes rather than individualized goals. The authors point out that behavior technology has been more successful in producing results when the goals involved defined response sequences and less successful in producing changes when the goals involved complex behaviors, such as adjustment and socialization processes.

    It is urgent that professionals be cognizant of other learning paradigms and the implication(s) of each for teaching the retarded. Table 2–2 presents a concise summarization of the learning components essential to theory, the persons identified with that component, and the major implications for teaching the retarded based upon the learning components. A brief description of each learning theory follows, including the major piece of research responsible for the theory:

1. Ellis's multiprocess memory model. Retarded individuals tend to have a deficiency in short-term memory. This deficiency springs from failure to use rehearsal strategies or from using inadequate rehearsal strategies. (N. R. Ellis, "Memory Processes in Retardates and Normals," in *International Review of Research in Mental Retardation*, vol. 4, ed. N. R. Ellis [New York: Academic Press, Inc., 1973].)

2. Spitz's input organization theory. Mentally retarded individuals have difficulty in organizing input and thus retrieval processes are impaired. (H. H. Spitz, "Consolidating Facts into the Schematized Learning and Memory System of Educable Retardates," in *International Review of Research in Mental Retardation*, vol. 6, ed. N. R. Ellis [New York: Academic Press, Inc., 1973].)

3. Zeaman and House's attention theory and the attention-retention theory of Fisher and Zeaman. In discrimination-learning tasks, retarded individuals have difficulty selecting and attending to the relevant dimensions. Fisher and Zeaman's work added the retention factor. (D. Zeaman and B. J. House, "The Role of Attention in Retardate Discrimination Learning," in *Handbook of Mental Deficiency*, ed. N. R. Ellis [New York: McGraw-Hill Book Company, 1963].)

4. Denny's elicitation theory and incidental learning. Learning depends on consistent elicitation of the to-be-learned response in close temporal contiguity with a particular stimulus situation. Also, retarded persons are poorer incidental learners than normals. All of these are related to a deficient attention behavior. (M. R. Denny, "A Theoretical Analysis and its Application to Training the Mentally Retarded," in *International Review of Research in Mental Retardation*, vol. 2, ed. N. R. Ellis [New York: Academic Press, Inc., 1966].)

5. Social Learning Theory (SLT)–Rotter's 1975 Formula–Behavior Potential = f (Expectancy and Reinforcement Value). The implications of this theory are retarded children need (1) realistic success, (2) specific goals, (3) realistic goals, (4) specific feedback, and (5) intense social reinforcement. (E. Zigler, "Research on Personality Structure in the Retardate," in *International Review of Research on Mental Retardation*, vol. 1, ed. N. R. Ellis [New York: Academic Press, Inc., 1966].)

6. Observational learning theory. Retarded individuals at all levels learn through observation. (J. L. Gewirtz, "The Role of

Stimulation in Modes for Child Development," in *Early Child Care,* ed. L. L. Dittman [New York: Atherton, 1968].)[24]

With these theoretical models in mind, specific teaching procedures in content areas[25] of the curriculum should be based as much as possible on a certain degree of eclecticism. Putting theory into practice is the challenge.

[24]Mercer and Snell, *Learning Theory Research in Mental Retardation.*

[25]Numerous volumes are available. Among the better ones are Oliver P. Kolstoe, *Teaching Educable Mentally Retarded Children,* 2nd ed. (New York: Holt, Rinehart and Winston, Inc., 1976); and Kathryn A. Blake, *Teaching the Retarded* (Englewood Cliffs, N.J.: Prentice-Hall, Inc., 1974).

The Boy
Who Laughed

by Ivy Litvinov

I

The specialists consulted by Slava's anxious parents all agreed that Slava was retarded. None would commit themselves further. All had known, or at least heard of, otherwise normal children who did not speak till they were five, six, indeed seven years old. By the time he was eight everyone could see that Slava, while patently a human being, would never be a full member of society; the slack underlip, the straight, spaced fingers, the curious angle at which he habitually carried his head, were more articulate than poor Slava's unmanageable tongue. Many people advised Yuri Vladimirovich and Valentina Matveyevna to send their child to a Home. Yuri Vladimirovich might have agreed, but he never dared propose it to his wife or mother. And many who knew Slava in his home thought it would be a tragedy to send him away. One doctor went so far as to say that to deprive Slava of the only things he understood—his mother's affection and the passionate devotion of his grandmother—would cause a trauma from which Slava would never recover. "And it would kill Babushka," Valentina Matveyevna said. Yuri Vladimirovich knew it was true—his mother lived for Slava, without him her life would have no meaning.

The move from Odessa, where Slava was born, to Moscow—occasioned by Yuri Vladimirovich's astounding success in nuclear physics—had a most unfortunate effect on Slava.

In Odessa the family had inhabited the ground floor of a dilapidated two-story house, in a weed-grown yard where Slava spent hours on end picking grass stalks which he afterward placed one by one on the stone path in subtle, never-repeating patterns. Upstairs lived two old ladies who had known Slava all his life and were used to him. In Moscow the family had two rooms in an old-fashioned communal apartment on the ninth floor. The yard was a thoroughfare for motor traffic and Slava had to make his patterns from spent matches on the top of a trunk in the tiny room he shared with Babushka. He soon came down with a severe case of flu. Thanks to Babushka's fanatical conscientiousness in carrying out the doctor's orders, still more perhaps to the purity and intensity of her love, Slava recovered, but he was a different boy in his relations with the outside world forever after.

Before his illness he had taken no notice when the other tenants spoke to him; now he responded to the kindliest greetings with maniacal chuckles. He was quiet with his gentle mother and grandmother, but on Sundays and in the evenings when his father came home, harsh laughter was heard in the other room every time a door was opened. Housewives at work in the communal kitchen set down a rolling pin on a floured board or upended an iron to shut out the horrid sound with a hand at each ear. And one day Yuri Vladimirovich packed up his bag and went away never to return. And no wonder, the other tenants said. It was all the fault of his mother and wife for not sending Slava to a Home; how could one of the most promising young physicists in the Soviet Union be expected to live at close quarters with a hopeless imbecile, even if it *was* his own child? Where was he to write, to receive his friends and colleagues after work hours? There were even people who said Slava should have been "allowed to die" of the flu. They asked: what would become of Slava when his grandmother died or (more delicately) if anything happened to his mother? They said such children live for ever. Valentina Matveyevna and her mother-in-law shrugged their shoulders helplessly. What was meant by "allowing Slava to die"? Were they to withhold succor from a sentient being who gazed trustfully at them from fringed eyes, and accepted their ministrations with the wavering smile only seen on the lips of infants and dying persons? Did Slava need love and security less than other children? Or, he being defective, didn't his needs matter? For the first four years of Slava's life had she not been as proud and happy as any mother? Was his mother to give him up because he was unfortunate?

Two attempts were made to

put Slava in a day school for retarded children, once when he was six years old and once after his father left them. Each had ended in catastrophe; the doctor said Slava could only be dealt with in a Home, but held out no hopes of a "cure"—the trauma might be too strong for treatment to be of any use. And gradually, under Babushka's gentle, unrelaxing pressure, Slava became amenable to certain social disciplines: he learned to stand aside to let a neighbor pass him in the hall, to wait till everyone else was in the lift before stepping in himself, to wipe his boots on the mat. He still snarled quietly at play, but the horrid outbreaks of harsh laughter grew less frequent, only occurring under stress of novelty or fear.

Slava loved to draw. He drew by the hour during the day, and in the night Babushka was sometimes awakened by a low continuous growling from the window and knew it was Slava standing behind the window curtains, drawing by the light from the neon lamps in the street. Friends encouraged Valentina Matveyevna to believe Slava had artistic talent (weren't Van Gogh and Utrillo both mad?). But the obsession subsided; the albums and crayons lay untouched in the top drawer of the bureau. And yet the indefatigable Babushka managed to graft certain skills on what the doctors said were the empty cells of Slava's brain. She taught him to read. He would read aloud in a low murmur by the hour from any book put into his hands, without any apparent preferences; Russian folk tales, *Robinson Crusoe*, and *Tales for Tiny Tots* seemed to give him equal pleasure, and once his mother had had trouble in tearing him away from a street guide to Leningrad which had been given to him in mistake for a copy of the *Arabian Nights*. Apparently the only thing Slava couldn't do was to make sense out of his senses.

Babushka's supreme achievement was teaching Slava to play the piano. Her method was crude to the point of subtlety: she placed his great paws over the backs of her own delicately arched hands and played a few bars of music over and over again, then slipped her hands from beneath Slava's hollowed palms, leaving the tips of his fingers poised on the keys; Slava's excellent ear and sense of rhythm did the rest, and soon he had a repertoire of six songs, ranging from the "Song of the Volga Boatmen" to "Silent Night," all of which he played "with the left hand too," as Babushka never failed to point out, by which she meant she had somehow taught him to shift from the tonic to the dominant and back again. Hopes of musical talent were now indulged in. As a little girl Valentina Matveyevna had been taken to hear Pachmann play Chopin at the Petersburg Conservatory. All she could remember of it was that Pachmann's antics on the piano stool had made the audience laugh. Poor Pachmann was mad. But that had not prevented him from being a great pianist, had it? A teacher said to have had much experience with "maladjusted" children was found. Slava played his six pieces for her and waited for the outburst of admiration to which he was accustomed. When the teacher said nothing but took up his forearm to demonstrate the proper position of the hand before striking the note, Slava tossed her hand away with a powerful gesture and once again went through his repertoire, wagging his heavy head and laughing loudly and harshly all the time. When she tried to steady his exuberant but essentially rhythmic tempo by marking time with a pencil on the edge of the piano, Slava turned on her with bared teeth, snatched the pencil from her fingers, and broke it in half. After this even Babushka couldn't teach him any new pieces, though he still played the original six from time to time, and when his mother came home from work she was always greeted by the strains of "Birdie, birdie where've you been?" and knew that behind the door of her room two smiling faces waited for her kiss. It was sweet, it was bitter, she was used to it.

By the time Slava was fifteen he could be left alone in the yard with no danger that he would stray into the street. He even earned money shoveling snow for the yard woman and hammering nails into boards outside a carpenter's workshop in the basement. The foreman soon discovered that Slava was perfectly safe with saw or hatchet, and his strength and endurance made him a valuable worker during the building season, though he couldn't be employed indoors because his chuckling laugh got on the other men's nerves. And you couldn't count on him; as soon as he was paid he was apt to stray from work till by some mysterious urge to increase his hoard he went in search of another job. He never spent his earnings, of that his mother and grandmother were sure, but for a long time nobody had any idea where he kept them, till one day Babushka, intent on mending a rent in the pocket of Slava's wadded jacket, came upon a cache of paper rubles and small change in a corner of the lining. It was decided not to risk upsetting Slava by taking it out; seeing that the amount never lessened but rather increased, the women got into a lazy habit of slipping nickels and quarters, sometimes even a silver ruble, into the slit, with a vague idea of one day buying something special for Slava.

All in all you could scarcely have found a more tranquil home in the whole of Moscow than the two rooms in the communal apartment on the ninth floor where the women lived and cherished their helpless charge. Everything went smoothly till the fatal day when Babushka was summoned to Riga, to the bedside of her daughter Galina.

The women discussed trains and timetables in writing, like people who believe there is a concealed microphone in every room; there was no time to prepare Slava, and you never knew what he took in—he had a disconcerting habit of watching lips. They packed hastily when Slava was asleep and at midnight Babushka kissed his pure forehead and tiptoed out of the room. Valentina Matveyevna, who had arranged a week's leave from the office, thought Slava looked strangely at her when she sat down to breakfast with him. It's not Sunday, his look seemed to say. (Pulling yesterday from the calendar was Slava's duty and privilege, and he always knew when it was Sunday—Sundays were red.) The only other sign that he knew something was amiss was a rapid glance over his mother's shoulder every time she came into the room. But he said nothing about Babushka, and Valentina Matveyevna said nothing. Waiting for Slava's lead had become second nature.

After breakfast Slava without a word allowed himself to be dressed for going out, and fol-lowed his mother with his usual docility in and out of the milk-shop and the bread store, then into the vegetable store, but when she turned from the fruit counter Slava was nowhere to be seen. Nobody in the store had noticed him, but some little boys outside said they had seen him cross the road and get on a tram.

II

"Everywhere," Valentina Matveyevna said. "I've tried everywhere—the hospitals, the police station, the streetcar depots, the bus parks, the railway stations. Nobody has seen him."

"You didn't try Odessa," Babushka said. Her daughter had recovered and she had come back to Moscow as soon as she got Valentina Matveyevna's telegram. The neighbors had advised Valentina Matveyevna not to send for Babushka; it would only upset her, and what could Slava's grandmother do that his mother hadn't done? But Valentina Matveyevna had sent a telegram just the same—she knew it was what Babushka would have wanted her to do. And when she arrived Babushka had not asked a single question; all she had said was, "You didn't try Odessa."

Neighbors crowding into the hall folded their arms and shook their heads compassionately. The poor old thing!

"He's gone to look for me," Babushka said.

Nobody believed Slava capable of finding his way to the railway station and ordering a ticket to Odessa till Babushka brought out of the top drawer of the bureau an old candy box in which, neatly arranged, were used tickets and a pile of "rubles" and cardboard coins that had come with a shopping game. Playing at "going to the dacha" had been almost a daily occupation.

"And where did he get the money?"

Valentina Matveyevna flung herself on the quilted jacket hanging from a hook in the hall and thrust her hand deep into the pocket. Her fingers groped knowingly among the loose wads of cotton but brought out nothing but a soiled lump with a two-kopeck coin sticking to it. Slava must have planned his escapade in advance; the money had been in its hiding place the night before he disappeared, Valentina Matveyevna was sure of that— she had put a paper ruble and a quarter into the slit when clearing her pocketbook after Babushka had left.

The next day Valentina Matveyevna started for Odessa, afraid that if she didn't, Babushka would go. As soon as she arrived she went straight to the little street on the outskirts where Slava was born. The house wasn't there any more, the *street* wasn't there any more, all had been swallowed up by high tenements which enclosed the original yard, with no grasses and bushes waving in the breeze, nothing but asphalt and garbage cans. Not quite nothing. In a corner of the yard was a shed Valentina Matveyevna remembered, though when she knew it there had been no iron pipe projecting through the roof to speak of a stove within. She made for it instinctively and was immediately hot on Slava's tracks. For in the doorway stood an ancient crone peering across the yard, and when Valentina Matveyevna came closer she recognized the younger of the two old ladies from upstairs in the now-vanished house she had lived in for the first ten years of Slava's life. Old Rosa told her that she had refused to go out of the yard when the street of small houses was demolished to make room for the new buildings, and they had allowed her to move into the shed and even have a stove put in. Valentina was surprised to see how snug she had made it; the shiny samovar, the Bokhara rugs on the wall, and two nineteenth-century portraits in heavy gilt frames gave it quite a prosperous, not to say aristocratic look. And there, it appeared, Slava had found her; he had always loved to play in the shed, and like his mother had gone to it instinctively in the shadow of the new houses. He stayed with her two days, Rosa said; she fed him and washed his clothes, and oh how hungry and dirty the poor lad was, and on the third day he went away with a wayfaring tinker who had just finished three days mending saucepans in the yard. She thought they went on a steamer.

The militia in Odessa were sure they would find Slava if he was anywhere on the islands, but by the time they got in touch with local authorities the scent was cold. A boy who had worked some time for a tinker on the outskirts of a kolkhoz had suddenly left; people could only remember of him that he laughed at his work. After visiting the hospitals and railway stations—even the prisons—there was nothing for Valentina Matveyevna to do but go back to Moscow.

Old Rosa had wrapped a card with his mother's name and address on it in a handkerchief and put it into Slava's pocket while he slept, and from time to time over the years news came in illiterate scrawls of a "man" who had worked three months, six months in a remote village, and gone away. Babushka and Valentina Matveyevna followed Slava's itinerary on the map as best they could by the help of the postmarks. "He's working his way back," Babushka said. "He's coming back to us."

Once a snapshot of a tall figure grasping a rake in a cornfield came; it was pale and blurred, but they recognized Slava's deep mindless eyes in the mustached and bearded face, his small neat ear flattened against the closely cropped head—and wept. Soon after, Babushka died.

Galina Vladimirovna, who had after all not died that dreadful time in Riga, came to Moscow for her mother's funeral. The sisters-in-law scarcely knew one another, but each had an intimate knowledge of the other's sad life (Galina had her own tragedy, more common but no less painful than Valentina's). The day of the funeral they talked far into the night, fascinated by a relationship made up of intimacy and strangeness. Yes, they went to bed early after a cozy supper the day they followed Babushka to the grave, and left the door open between the two rooms. "I don't remember that I ever slept in a room all to myself," Galina said. "Do you think they'll leave you the two rooms, Valya?" Valentina told her the question wouldn't even be raised; Slava's name had never been officially removed from the register, and his room was so tiny and could only be reached through her own, so that nobody could be put into it. "Couldn't they offer you one room instead of two?" Valentina didn't let this worry her. The room was Slava's and one day Slava would come back and claim it. "Valya, darling, do you still really believe Slava will come back?" Valya was sure of it, he would come back to his own home, as he had gone back to the old home in Odessa. Shuddering, Galina envisaged a Neanderthal figure plodding over plains and hills, through towns and villages, toward his mother in far-off Moscow.

"Why don't you marry again, Valya?" Galina asked on a sudden impulse. Valya sighed impatiently. "I told you. I'm waiting for Slava to come back. I can't expect a man to live in the same apartment with Slava. His own father couldn't."

"Yuri told me he never loved you more than when you refused to send Slava to a Home. It was just that he couldn't stand living with the poor boy." "I know," said Valentina. "I never blamed him."

"I think it broke his heart when you chose to give your life to Slava and not to him."

"He married again within the year," Valentina said shortly.

"And why couldn't you— after all these years?"

"Why are *you* so eager for me to get married, Galya? Have you found marriage so satisfactory? I should have thought you would envy me my freedom." "I have been unfortunate," Galya said. "Everybody doesn't have such bad luck as I had." She pushed a tear out of the corner of each eye with a sidewise action of the heels of her palms; much as she liked talking about her woes, she did not mean to be led away from the subject of her sister-in-law's life by subtle evasions on Valya's part. So she said, "I can't see what use you make of your freedom." "I do my best," Valya said. "Only I won't let any man come here. I wouldn't while Babushka was alive, and I still won't as long as there's a possibility of Slava coming back." Galya turned and looked at her sister-in-law through the open door, eyes now perfectly dry and wide open, round. "Oh, so you *do* have somebody!" she exclaimed. "I had no idea." "For goodness' sake, Galya, I'm a woman, aren't I?"

Galya went back to her own particular tragedy in Riga, nothing more was heard of Slava, and Valentina Matveyevna went to work every morning and came back every evening as usual. Even Galya, who should have known better, made a halfhearted attack on her sister-in-law's freedom. She already had three children, and a few months after her return the poor foolish woman found herself again pregnant, she who was never tired of saying how she detested and despised her deplorable husband. "Oh, Valya," she wrote, "I can hardly bear to say it, but perhaps after all you could take Natasha to live with you! She's only two, and she's such an affectionate little thing you'd soon get used to each other—I mean I wouldn't ask you to take one of the others, they're too difficult already. But I'm sure it would be no trauma for Natashka. The new baby would be much more of a trauma." (Galya had written "shock" but was happy to cross it out and use the more fashionable terminology.) "Even if Slava came back it would be all right, I mean not like him finding a man beside you, *that* I can understand would be too hard, dear Valya. Oh, Valya, you can understand how desperate I must be before I could ask this . . . ." And a man who had been happy enough for years in a gentle and undemanding union with her, now felt that the occasional weekend in the country, the month in the south, were not enough; his whole happiness depended on living all the time with Valentina Matveyevna, now that this was made possible by her mother-in-law's death. He did not get his way, and as a result they drifted apart.

By now Valentina Matveyevna was beginning to think she wanted nothing more from any man. She settled down peacefully to wait for Slava.

DISCUSSION

The numerous decisions that must be made concerning the care, management, and education of a mentally retarded child are well illustrated in this story set in Russia. The concerns regarding Slava are not very different from what they would be in any culture, and they are equally compelling. Advice comes from all quarters; there seems to be the ever present "they" passing judgment about the decisions made in regard to Slava.

It is very difficult for doctors and psychologists to determine the eventual intellectual and social potential of the retarded child. Tests given in the early years have poor levels of validity and predictability. When a child is without language or has very little language, as is the case with Slava, it is even more difficult to test intellectual functioning adequately.

The issue of residential care for Slava becomes fraught with guilt for all involved. Even the doctors seem unable to sort out professional objectivity from human sentiment in contemplating separating the child from his parents. This issue is so painful that Yuri and Valentina cannot openly discuss it. The devotion of Yuri's mother to Slava adds an additional emotional strain. In the chapter "The Exceptional Child in the Family," the multifaceted strains a child with special needs places on the marital relationship is discussed. It is not surprising that Yuri, who needs time and quiet for his own work, finds his cramped and tense home life unbearable and chooses to leave.

Philosophy regarding residential placement for the retarded as opposed to home care and day school placement varies from country to country. For example, England has a network of residential schools where children live and attend school during the week and come home for weekends and holidays. In the United States the trend is away from residential placement with emphasis on community resources for the mentally handicapped. Unfortunately, in the United States there are still large institutions in outlying areas that are supposed to provide residential care and schooling for the retarded, but most do not meet even minimal standards for care and education because of their size and restricted funds.

This story emphasizes the central role the grandmother plays in caring for Slava. Because of the mother's initial grief at the birth of an imperfect child, the father or grandparents are sometimes needed to take a more active role in the child's care. In this story, caring for Slava gives Babushka a reason to live. Providing supervision for him while Valentina works makes her feel needed and useful. Babushka is able to teach Slava a surprising number of skills. Although Slava cannot use his ability to read, draw, or play the piano in terms of a vocation, it is important for all people to have some forms of recreation that are satisfying. Standardized testing would probably not have predicted his potential in these areas, but patient and loving teaching tapped resources that were evidently intact in Slava's otherwise damaged brain.

Babushka's exclusive care of Slava may have denied him the opportunity to learn better social skills that he might have learned had he been in school with other children. His bizarre laugh makes him particularly objectionable to others. It is important for exceptional children to receive guidance in social behavior and appearance. Most school programs give a great deal of attention to these important aspects of living. Well-run schools include parent education as an adjunct to their program.

The ending of this story attests to Slava's adaptability. He can do enough physical labor to earn a marginal existence. As an itinerant person he is fortunate to find in each community someone who affords him some small amount of protection. Slava has made the move from being wholly in protective custody of his mother and grandmother to being fairly self-sufficient. Slava's unpredictable self-sufficiency attests to the fact that it is impossible to know if the limits of any individual's potential have ever been fully explored. Slava is an excellent example of a mentally retarded child who finds at least some of his potential skills.

SPRINGBOARDS FOR INQUIRY

1. Do you think Valentina should have sought residential care for Slava in view of her husband's needs?

2. Read any of the texts suggested in this chapter and list tests used for identification of the retarded. Comment on their advantages and disadvantages.

3. What special considerations should be kept in mind when planning curriculum for the mildly mentally retarded? Plan a lesson in any subject area that interests you and indicate grade level for your plan.

4. If you know a mentally retarded person, discuss his or her unique behavioral chracteristics. In which ways is this person like other people in your acquaintance?

5. What facilities are available in your community for educating the retarded? Are there distinctions made between the mildly retarded, trainable retarded, and developmentally disabled? What are the recreational provisions in your area specifically for the mentally retarded?

6. Visit your regional center for the retarded and list the reading materials they offer. List the services they provide.

7. Use the children's library, and research several titles about the retarded, in addition to those that appear in the suggested readings, in both juvenile and young adult literature. Outline the plot and discuss the insights to be gleaned about the mentally retarded.

CHAPTER THREE

The Gifted

On April 11, 1962, Dr. Donald W. MacKinnon, giving the Walter Van Dyke Bingham Lecture at Yale University, repeated a story credited to Mark Twain. Twain's story is about a man who sought the greatest general who ever lived. At the Pearly Gates he informed Saint Peter of the purpose of his quest, whereupon Saint Peter pointed to a soul nearby. "But that," protested the inquirer, "isn't the greatest of all generals. I knew that person when he lived on earth, and he was only a cobbler." "I know that," replied Saint Peter, "but if he had been a general, he would have been the greatest of them all."[1]

A review of the vast literature on the identification of gifted children in America reads much like the story just recounted. For example, in the Marland study of 1972, 57.5 percent of elementary and secondary school principals reported in 1970 that they had no gifted students in their schools.[2] The same landmark study reports that the gifted and talented population by a conservative estimate ranges "between 1.5 and 2.5 million children out of a total elementary and secondary school population [1970 estimate] of 51.6 million."[3] Further, existing services to the

[1]As reported in Donald W. MacKinnon, "The Nature and Nurture of Creative Talent," in *Psychology and Education of the Gifted*, 2nd ed., ed. Walter B. Barbe and Joseph S. Renzulli (New York: Irvington Publishers, 1975), p. 151.
[2]Sidney Marland, *Education of the Gifted and Talented* (Washington, D.C.: United States Office of Education, 1971), p. iii–9.
[3]Ibid., p. xi.

gifted and talented do not serve even a fraction of that 1.5 to 2.5 million figure and certainly "do not reach large and significant sub-populations (e.g., minorities and disadvantaged)."[4] How many of today's "cobblers" are hiding "generals" is anyone's guess.

The following vignette illustrates further the possible losses to society because of the educational deprivation of a gifted but inadequately educated person:

> Dorothy J. is a middle-aged member of the Cahuilla Indian tribe. When she started school at age eight, she experienced immediate difficulties because of her lack of knowledge of English and her fear of teachers. Eventually she succeeded in learning English with no special help and she finally finished high school at 19.
>
> In school she and other Indian children encountered teachers who regarded Indians as "dumb" and incapable of learning. Many Indian children believed this, and of a dozen Indian children who entered school, Dorothy was the only one to finish. She maintained her interest in learning, but her only opportunity to apply for a college scholarship for Indians (when she was 42) was denied.
>
> Dorothy's favorite subject in school was history, but she found that the contributions of Indians were either denied or ignored, and their culture was denigrated by teachers. On the other hand, persons like Andrew Jackson, who was responsible for the slaughter of countless Indians, were presented as heroes.
>
> Dorothy, largely self-taught, has compensated well for her lack of opportunity. She is co-author, with university professors, of several books in linguistics, ethnobotany, and music and has served as a university lecturer both in the United States and abroad. Meanwhile, because she lacks formal higher education, she earns a living on an assembly line in a factory near her reservation home.[5]

The answer to the question, Who are the gifted? is not a simple one. Ruth A. Martinson defines them as children with "superior cognitive abilities. Their common element includes outstanding promise, or an unusual level of ability, whether in academic attainment, in creative performance, in talent, in ability to deal with advanced concepts and generalizations, or in the generation of ideas of uncommon merits."[6] James J. Gallagher's currently accepted definition reflects more recent concerns with a variety of dimensions of giftedness:

---

[4]Ibid.

[5]Ruth A. Martinson, "Children with Superior Cognitive Abilities," in *Exceptional Children in the Schools*, 2nd ed., ed. Lloyd M. Dunn (New York: Holt, Rinehart and Winston, Inc., 1973), p. 205.

[6]Ibid., p. 191.

Gifted and talented children are those identified by professionally qualified persons who by virtue of outstanding abilities are capable of high performance. These are children who require differentiated educational programs and services beyond those normally provided by the regular school program in order to realize their contribution to self and society.

Children capable of high performance include those with demonstrated achievement and/or potential ability in any of the following areas:

1. General intellectual ability
2. Specific academic aptitude
3. Creative or productive thinking
4. Leadership ability
5. Visual and performing arts
6. Psychomotor ability[7]

In an attempt to put an end to haggling over the complexity of a definition of the gifted, many people simply say that the gifted have uncommonly high IQ scores. Such a definition, however, is too simplistic. Mary Meeker contends that "no one who is entrenched in the problem of education of gifted children would for a moment seriously contend that the numerical definition of a 98 percentile score on an IQ test is sufficient to identify the gifted."[8] Jacob W. Getzels and Philip W. Jackson write, "Involved in this unidimensional definition of giftedness [that is, IQ test score] are several types of confusion, if not outright error."[9] They contend that using a single measurement blocks a generalized phenomenon and blinds us to other forms of excellence. They also discuss attitudes and value judgments that relate to creativity and giftedness. Although there is a definite relationship of IQ to measures of creativity, Getzels and Jackson contend that most people still look at creativity as related only to the arts and that the simple IQ definition is unrelated to the values placed upon giftedness by teachers, parents, and children. Getzels and Jackson compared twenty-nine high IQ, "low creativity" students with twenty-four high IQ, "high creativity" students and found the following:

1. Despite a difference of twenty-three points between the mean IQ's of the two groups, they were *equally* superior in school achievement.

[7]James J. Gallagher, *Teaching the Gifted Child* (Boston, Mass.: Allyn & Bacon, Inc., 1975), p. 10.

[8]Mary Meeker, "The Prophecy of Giftedness," *The Gifted Child Quarterly*, vol. xx, no. 1 (Spring 1976), 100.

[9]Jacob W. Getzels and Philip W. Jackson, "The Meaning of 'Giftedness'—An Examination of an Expanding Concept," in *Psychology and Education of the Gifted*, 2nd ed., Barbe and Renzulli, p. 56.

2. Teachers exhibited a clear-cut preference for the high IQ child.
3. The creative child rates high marks, IQ, pep, and energy *lower* than do members of the highly intelligent group; he or she rates wide range of interests, emotional stability, and sense of humor *higher* than members of the highly intelligent group.
4. The high IQ child desires to possess *now* that which he or she believes leads to success. The creative child does not seem to value success.
5. The high IQ child holds a self-ideal that he or she believes teachers most readily approve; the creative child shows a slight *negative* response to the teacher-approved model.[10]

Yet as late as the summer of 1975, Joy P. Guilford was still maintaining that if what we want is high grade-getters in the gifted children we educate, then the criterion of the IQ score alone is "very likely the best basis" for identifying the gifted.[11] Specifically, Guilford attempted to search for and identify aptitudes beyond those measured by traditional intelligence tests. If we are to educate gifted children, we need to know who they are. In other words, when the IQ score is used alone, gifted children may indeed be selected, but other gifted people whose abilities are not necessarily obvious may be omitted when the single criterion of an intelligence test score becomes the *sole* criterion. Guilford developed the SI (structure-of-intellect model) that identifies one hundred twenty different kinds of intellectual abilities.[12] According to Guilford, his SI model resulted in "the development of a unified theory of human intellect, which organizes the known, unique or primary intellectual abilities into a single system called the 'structure of intellect.'"[13] Guilford postulated three faces of intellect:

1. Operations.   The mind uses at least five processes, or operations, as it functions. These are cognition, memory, divergent thinking, convergent thinking, and evaluation. Guilford de-

[10]Jacob W. Getzels and Philip W. Jackson, "The Meaning of 'Giftedness'—An Examination of an Expanding Concept," *Phi Delta Kappan*, vol. xxxx, no. 2 (November 1958), 76–77.

[11]Joy P. Guilford, "Varieties of Creative Giftedness, Their Measurement and Development," *The Gifted Child Quarterly*, vol. xix, no. 2 (Summer 1975), 119.

[12]Joy P. Guilford, *The Nature of Human Intelligence* (New York: McGraw-Hill Book Company, 1967).

[13]Joy P. Guilford, "Three Faces of Intellect," *American Psychologist*, vol. 14, no. 8 (August 1959), 469.

fines them as follows: *cognition* means discovery; *memory* means retention; *divergent thinking* means that people think in different directions; *convergent thinking* means that the information leads to one best or conventional answer; and *evaluation* means that people reach a decision as to the goodness or correctness, suitability or adequacy of what is known.[14]

2. Contents.   The four kinds of contents are figural, symbolic, semantic, and behavioral. According to Guilford, however, the last category is purely theoretical and represents the general area called "social intelligence." In 1959, no behavioral traits were described but Guilford suggested that there were as many as thirty abilities.[15] *Figural* content is concrete material perceived through the senses. *Visual* material has properties such as size, form, color, location, or texture. *Symbolic* content is composed of letters, numbers, and other conventional signs. *Semantic* content is in the form of connotative meanings and ideas.

3. Products.   Guilford writes, "When a certain operation is applied to a certain kind of content, as many as six general kinds of products may be involved. There is enough evidence available to suggest that, regardless of the combination of operations and content, the same six kinds of products may be found associated. The six kinds of products are units, classes, relations, systems, transformations, and implications. So far as we have determined from factor analysis, these [are] the only fundamental kinds of products that we can know. As such, they may serve as basic classes into which one might fit all kinds of information psychologically."[16]

For those trying to identify the gifted using the IQ test as a sole criterion for giftedness, Guilford's SI model means that there are at least one hundred intellectual factors already known. The SI is a theoretical model that predicts as many as one hundred twenty distinct abilities if every cell of the model contains a factor. Guilford maintains that the major "implication for the assessment of intelligence is that to know an individual's intellectual resources thoroughly we shall need a surpris-

---

[14]Ibid., pp. 470–71.
[15]The abilities in the area of social intelligence will loom large in the 1970s and 1980s. Environmental, scientific, and social concerns are very significant today. The student might try to discover whether or not Guilford has amplified this since 1959.
[16]Guilford, "Three Faces of Intellect," p. 470.

ingly large number of scores."[17] The educational implications Guilford asserts are, however, provocative of "rank heresy."[18]

Both the group and the individual IQ test as sole measures of identifying the gifted have their shortcomings. Carl W. Pegnato studied the entire population of a junior high school.[19] "If a cutoff point of 125 on the Otis Group Test had been employed, over half of the gifted in his study would have failed to qualify, including nine whose actual scores on the Binet ranged from 146–61. Only thirty-five out of Pegnato's sample of eighty-four gifted pupils achieved scores on the group test of 125 or more."[20]

Individual tests of IQ, while more accurate than group tests, still leave much to be desired. Joy P. Guilford notes that the Stanford-Binet probably encompasses twenty-eight of the factors in his Structure of Intellect.[21] John C. Gowan and Catherine B. Burch quote Mary Meeker who maintains that the Stanford-Binet contains fifty-four of the one hundred twenty abilities hypothesized.[22] Clearly, no single test can either quantify or qualify any individual in all of his or her complexity. Thus, one needs to use multiple methods to identify the gifted. The school systems of Illinois, according to Sidney P. Marland, use six major procedures to identify the gifted.[23] These are summarized in Table 3–1. Ruth A. Martinson reports that Ohio uses pupil self-opinion and all the other criteria used by Illinois to identify gifted students.[24]

Joseph Renzulli of the University of Connecticut sums up rather neatly how to recognize the gifted amongst us:

> "You have to start with the assumption that if there was no such thing as gifted in the adult world, then we wouldn't go looking for it in children. . . . There is a cluster of three characteristics that make the eminent . . . gifted adult. . . . [1] above average, but not necessarily superior

[17]Ibid., p. 477.

[18]Ibid., p. 478. Three books by Dr. Darrell Allington, *Building an Igloo*, *About Those Thinking Skills*, and *For Those Concerned with Children* (Owl Enterprises, Box 15402, Salt Lake City, Utah 84115), all build upon J. P. Guilford's SI and then add the pioneer work of Dr. Calvin Taylor (University of Utah, Department of Psychology) and his materials in the field of creativity.

[19]Carl W. Pegnato, "An Evaluation of Various Initial Methods of Selecting Intellectually Gifted Children at the Junior High School Level" (Ed.D. dissertation, Pennsylvania State University, 1955).

[20]Ruth A. Martinson, *The Identification of the Gifted and Talented* (Ventura, Calif.: Ventura County Schools, 1974), p. 41.

[21]Joy P. Guilford et al., *The Structure of Intellect Text, Code Name CT* (Beverly Hills, Calif.: Sheridan Psychological Services, 1971).

[22]John C. Gowan and Catherine B. Burch, *The Academically Talented Student and Guidance* (New York: Houghton-Mifflin Company, 1971).

[23]Marland, *Education of the Gifted and Talented*, p. 261.

[24]Martinson, *The Identification of the Gifted and Talented*, p. 63.

intelligence. . . . [2] task commitment . . . the ability, the capacity, to hang in with a difficult problem over a long period of time. . . . And that's my criticism of what has happened in a lot of gifted programs. It's the quick game that's played for two hours in the morning and that's the end of it. . . . [3] And the third trait in this little cluster . . . yet we can't measure it . . . creativity.[25]

After the identification of the gifted, what? Under the auspices of National Public Radio and the Institute for Educational Leadership, a series of five radio programs, "Gifted Children in the Schools," was aired.[26] The first program concerned whether or not special education should be provided at all. After noting that there were 2 million children with superior intellect out of the 45 million school-aged children, Dr. Bruno Bettleheim was quoted, "I feel that the gifted child . . . is well able to take care of himself. If he isn't, then he isn't gifted. But I think that the deprived child or the child with handicaps is a child who is entitled to special help."[27] One criticism of singling out the gifted was that such

[25]Program 28, "Gifted Children in the Schools," National Public Radio, 1976, pp. 5–6.
[26]What follows are excerpts from transcripts of these five programs. We refer to programs 27–31, aired during 1976.
[27]Ibid., p. 1.

Table 3–1
Major Procedures Used and Recommended in the Identification of Gifted Students

Major identification procedures	Percent using (and rank order)	Percent recommending (and rank order)	Rank order difference
Teacher observation and nomination	93 (1)	75 (3)	−2
Group school achievement test scores	87 (2.5)	74 (4.5)	−2
Group intelligence test scores	87 (2.5)	65 (6)	−3.5
Previously demonstrated accomplishments (including school grades)	56 (4)	78 (2)	+2
Individual intelligence test scores	23 (5)	90 (1)	+4
Scores on tests of creativity	14 (6)	74 (4.5)	+1.5

Source: Sidney P. Marland, *Education of the Gifted and Talented* (Washington, D.C.: United States Office of Education, 1972). Column 1 data are drawn from this report on identification practices in the local school systems of Illinois and are reported as averages of elementary and secondary school practices. Column 2 data are from page 122 of the report and are based on what was considered important by 204 experts in the education of the gifted.

grouping would lead to elitism. Responding to this, Dr. Bruce Boston of Project Coordination of the ERIC Clearing House for Handicapped and Gifted Children in Reston, Virginia, argued, "If American society is going to develop the human resources that it has, then these resources have to be singled out. . . . It is no more elitist to identify and provide special programming for a gifted child than it is to identify and provide special programs for a handicapped child, or for a black child, or for a Spanish-speaking child, or for a woman."[28]

John Curry succinctly describes why, according to the Marland report of 1971, "gifted and talented children in average schools are, in fact, deprived and can suffer psychological damage and permanent impairment of their ability to function well."[29]

> We were driving by some tulip beds and there was a gardener out there cutting off some of the tulips, and we were wondering why he was doing that. And [the gardener] said [his employers] liked all the tulips to come up at one time, and that kind of reminded me of the way we are in education—we want everyone to be at the mean; you know, we have this terrible feeling, like everyone has to be the same on their basic skills test. And we don't want too many flowers coming up early and too many coming up late.[30]

There seems to be little question but that the gifted are "a population differing to a marked degree from their age peers, so that often traditional education is completely irrelevant for them."[31] The fundamental question concerns whether educators should create separate schools or the schools and their personnel should respond to the needs of these students through enrichment of the curriculum.[32] Sandra Kaplan, an advocate of differentiating the curriculum rather than isolating the gifted, states, "Curriculum for the gifted and talented can only be marked as such if it encompasses elements which distinguish it from being suitable for the education of all children."[33] Intellectually gifted children exhibit characteristics that distinguish them from others of their peers:

---

[28]Ibid., pp. 2–3.
[29]Marland, Education of the Gifted and Talented, p. viii–3.
[30]Ibid., p. 11.
[31]Martinson, "Children with Superior Cognitive Abilities," in Exceptional Children in the Schools, 2nd ed., Dunn, p. 236.
[32]In New York City, there are the Bronx High School of Science, the High School of Music and Art, and other schools that cater to gifted children interested in the school's particular focus.
[33]Sandra Kaplan, Providing Programs for the Gifted and Talented (Ventura, Calif.: Ventura City Superintendent of Schools, 1974), p. 111.

CHARACTERISTICS OF THE GIFTED PUPIL	SHOULD LEAD TO	IMPLICATIONS FOR CURRICULUM
Highly advanced achievement; advanced general language skills	→	Open access to content; grade-level materials often irrelevant at *any* age; need for freedom to learn apart from usual curriculum (special interests may enhance class learnings in a given curriculum field)
Multiple, specialized, unique interests	→	Specialization for indeterminate period, independent of age.
Intense, long-range concentration on topic of interest	→	Interest that may produce choice of topic ordinarily seen as irrelevant, but legitimate to pupil
Pleasure in learning	→	Interesting activities not seen as work
Curiosity, interest in the unusual	→	Interest that may produce choice of topic ordinarily seen as irrelevant, but legitimate to pupil; high interest in search for truth; incisive examination of issues
Independence in learning	→	Individual pursuits that may produce more satisfaction than a committee-based task; anticipated schedules that may need alteration for student needs; teacher as facilitator of access to needed learning opportunities; contacts spaced and used for communication and challenge rather than for direct supervision
Intense, long-range concentration on a given topic	→	Anticipated schedules that may need alteration for student needs; interest that may produce choice of topic ordinarily seen as irrelevant, but legitimate to pupil; need for freedom to learn apart from usual curriculum (special interests may enhance class learnings in a given curriculum field)
Interest in application of concepts	→	Use of learning in analysis and debate on societal problems and issues; key questions and issues as focus

| Ability to conceptualize, develop relationships | ⟶ | High interest in search for truth; incisive examination of issues |
| Independence | ⟶ | Individual pursuits that may produce more satisfaction than a committee-based task; need for freedom to learn apart from usual curriculum (special interests may enhance class learnings in a given curriculum field)[34] |

Reading the chart from left to right, it is evident that the theoretical constructs about the gifted pupil ("characteristics of the gifted pupil") should result in ("should lead to") a program of education ("implications for curriculum") that springs from those theoretical foundations. The burden upon teacher ingenuity is particularly heavy. Kaplan stresses that there are both cognitive and affective functions that the teacher must stress. For example, fluent and original thinking are cognitive tasks that need to be developed through teacher stress. Such affective attributes as curiosity, risk-taking, complexity, and imagination need to be understood by teachers who place premiums upon their development.

Though perhaps somewhat extreme in his point of view, Paul Plowman of the California State Department of Education summarizes the point of view of those who maintain that the mentally gifted need no longer go uneducated! "The future of our country, the very survival of our nation and of our way of life, depends upon the values, patterns of behavior, analytical and problem solving skills, and creativity fostered . . . in the upper 2 percent of general mental ability."[35]

[34]Adapted from Kaplan.
[35]GRC *(Gifted Resource Center) Newsletter* (San Mateo, Calif.: San Mateo County Superintendent of Schools, January–February 1975), p. 4.

Clancy Wants an Orangoutang

by Sara

Should she or should she not. It was like blowing at a dandelion in the fields back home. Whisking one way, then the other. Waiting for the last floating speck of fluff to rise gently with the wind, the decision made.

In staccato counterpoint, short and high, like the trailing tail end of a policeman's whistle, Clancy punctuated her indecision.

. . . Should she . . .

"'. . . Clancy's Program . . .'"

. . . or should she . . .

"'. . . Se-lek-shuns for the . . .'"

. . . not . . .

"'. . . geetar . . .'"

They sat at the Victorian dining table that was never used for eating, only for grading papers and piling Clancy's model air-planes. All three doors were shut tight, and the electric heater burned red hot midway between them. Still, the cold cut through with a bone-raw dampness that Hilda would forever associate with the city of San Francisco.

It was a ridiculous room, and a ridiculous apartment—the sort of impractical, furnished, railroad affair that only Flynn could have run into, and only a man like Flynn could possibly have been persuaded to rent. Flynn had vanished years ago, like the dandelion fluff blown to a greener hillside beyond. And the stem still trembling in his wake, should she or should she not, left rooted to the departed ground, but quavering and uncertain.

In the narrow mirror over the mantel, she caught a reflection of

"Clancy Wants an Orangoutang" from *A House Divided* by Sara is reprinted by the kind permission of the author.

Clancy's bent and clipped head. Whenever she considered her son, it was always with a sense of shock, shamefully repressed. Clancy was altogether too much.

He bore down with left-handed vigor now on the "program" he was carefully preparing for his "debut" tomorrow. At seven, Clancy didn't depend on dandelions or the wind. He had very simply requested Miss Agnews' permission to perform on the guitar for his second grade classmates. In a severely phrased note that began, "My Dear Miss Agnews. . . ."

Certainly, he looked like any other child. But that was all part of the deception. Old ladies on the cable car invariably smiled and patted him over the stub ends of his butch haircut; a chunky, green-eyed cherub with a pumpkin face and two black buttons where his nose belonged. Hilda sighed. Clancy was like no other child in the world. If she knew nothing else, she knew this. Clancy was Clancy.

His voice bounced around the room. Whenever he was deeply involved, he always spoke aloud, as if one-half of his implacable self pronounced the orders, the other half promptly and dutifully carrying them out. ". . . For his first se-lek-shun . . ." It took a while, however, to get the words printed down. ". . . Clancy will pre-sent . . . 'Shoo-Fly'. . . ."

She turned back to the application form that still lay neatly folded before her. In the kitchen, the dishes sat piled over the sink, breakfast as well as dinner, and four classes worth of papers yet to be graded. She absolutely had to make a decision, one way or the other. The awful thing was that it didn't really matter. Nothing really mattered. If you took the loan, you had to pay it off. Which, piled on top of Clancy's nephritis bills and her own bridge work, meant taking on another summer session, and more evening courses for an increment. And if you didn't, you had to work just about as hard anyhow, with the frantic uncertainty every morning that the old Chevy wouldn't get off the ground.

". . . For his third se-lek-shun . . ." Clancy nibbled at the eraser on the back end of his pencil. "Hilda . . ." It was the first time all evening that he had addressed her. "You know 'Old Smoky?'"

She looked vague and felt infinitely small.

Quickly, he piped, "'On top of old Smoky, all covered with snow, I met my true lover, a' courtin' to go. . . .' It's a bit adult, don't you think?"

"A love song?" she asked.

"Sort of. More a triangle, though. Two men and a woman."

She wiped her glasses on a Kleenex.

"Well, I can explain it, I suppose." And he bent again to his Program.

Music always embarrassed Hilda. Face to face with it and forced to a judgment, she would excuse herself, her gray eyes dimming, with, "I'm one of those people who just aren't musical, you know." The guitar was a legacy from Flynn.

As she recalled it, it seemed as though, quite absurdly, the guitar had walked in as the doctor walked out. Christmas Eve, a little more than a year ago . . .

"Nephritis," the young man from Permanente, who had given her all the sample drugs he had in his case, had said. She had never even heard of such a disease. Clancy lying motionless and yellow, the green eyes closed, and the mouth open only to breathe heavily and sucking.

At the front door, he had turned. "The next twenty-four hours will tell," he had said. And, as an afterthought, "Merry Christmas."

She had remained motionless on the steps, staring at the street, at a ring of holly on a door across the way, and a small white tree with golden lights in the window next to it. A messenger boy on a bike rode by, turned back, checked the address on his package.

She had managed very well, she thought, until then. No wringing of handkerchiefs, or of hands. But Flynn, who hadn't written or made any attempt to contact them since the day he'd left when Clancy was barely a year old, shipping on this particular Christmas Eve a package marked "FRAGILE . . . SPECIAL DELIVERY . . . GUITAR. . . ." That broke her. She stood,

looking at the messenger boy, dazed and unbelieving, and finally she laughed, head flung back, shouting at the sky, the salt of tears commingled with the spittle that ran from her throat.

Yet in the end, it was only the guitar that had made the four months in bed at all bearable for the boy. Blind as she was, even she could see that. . . .

Clancy was still working at his Program.

"Whatever do you expect to do with it?" she asked, suddenly, it only now having occurred to her that apparently he did intend to do something.

"Pin it up on the bulletin board." He spoke with an absolute certainty that ended any further discussion.

She had arranged to take the morning off tomorrow to be present at the recital, and more important, to make her appearance at the Credit Office. As if he read her mind, he asked, "You'll be there, won't you?" She nodded.

He thrust out his tongue. "Blast off. . ." he said. "It's finished!"

She frowned, squelched by his enthusiasm. She would never get the form filled out.

"Let's have a game of chess," said Clancy, the board already spreading before him.

"You always win," said Hilda, an automatic, unthinking reply. The forms were blurred.

Clancy shot a paper airplane through the air. "Zow . . ie. . . !"

She banged her fist on the table. "Dammit, Clancy, why can't you do something constructive?

He thought for a moment. "What's constructive, Hilda?"

She was silent, taken aback. Clancy rarely asked questions, he was one of those children who seemed somehow always *to know*. But when he did, as now, it had the effect only of sinking her deeper into that cesspool of uncertainty which drowned her days.

"I think I'd like an orangoutang . . ." he was off on another tack already, leafing through a booklet from the Junior Museum, ". . . for a pet, Hilda. Wouldn't that be keeno?"

"Yes," she said, "Just keeno."

He was still reading the pamphlet as he went through the door toward his bedroom.

Again she looked at the questions on the credit application. ". . . And do you solemnly swear to tell the truth, the whole truth, and nothing but the truth . . .?" Why should it remind her of the witness stand? She was only trying to borrow $300 to buy a used car that would be, she hoped, in better running condition than the used car she had now. But there it was. The brown room, the thin little lawyer shooting, shooting question after question, the high box that caged her and the judge above smiling. She was little older than Clancy at the time. All too conscious of the fact that she was fat and ugly and had straight hair that wouldn't curl . . .

"And what did the man do?" the lawyer shot.

"You know," she said.

"You must tell the court. What did he do?"

She squirmed. "The usher saw," she said.

"We have heard the testimony of the theatre manager, as well as of the usher," the lawyer said. "You must describe it now. What did the man do?"

She dropped her head, mumbling.

"Speak up," the lawyer shot.

"He put his hand on my leg," she said. Trying not to see the man, who sat at the bench.

"And what did he do then?" the lawyer shot.

She looked wildly around at the courtroom, begging with her eyes. Her mother and father sat in the front row, heavy, outraged. Her father's lips were sealed thin and tight. He was Postmaster of Salem then, and believed in government and law. Her mother's arms were folded, rolls of fat bulging stern.

"What did he do?"

She shook. "I can't say."

The Judge turning then. "Come here," he smiled, a finger beckoning. "You may show me, if you can't say."

It ended. It was past, gone. The man who owned the movie house gave her a year's free tickets, for herself, and for the three younger ones in the family. But she never ever went to the movies again. Nor could she ever erase the shamed figure at the bench, his long arms dangling, and the fleshy face loosened in fear . . .

"'Why are you requesting this extension of credit?'" She read from the form. To carry on, she thought. Somehow, to carry on. Yet, still not capable of moving pen to paper.

Clancy came bumping through the door, tearing a page, as he came, from *Boy's Life*. "Look at this, Hilda," he said, all excited. "I can go into business, selling birthday cards. There's gobs of money in it, see?" And he thrust the ad into her face.

"What in the world for?"

"To buy the orangoutang, of course. *That's* constructive, isn't it?"

She had gone to bed still undecided. And the morning was always a wild scramble against the clock. "Have you brushed your teeth, Clancy?" "Clancy, those jeans are filthy." "No, you can't have chocolate cake for breakfast." Or her last pair of stockings would snag and run, and she'd forgotten to pack their lunches. Or the sitter would call to say that she had the flu today, and couldn't Clancy go home with a friend till Hilda got back from work, and always that would be the day Hilda had an after-school conference.

Complications were part of the morning, dreaded, and expected. Shadow boxing with time in a second- or third-string bout that was only meant to whet the appetite for the big boys in the main affair. Yet there she was, morning after morning, back in the ring, repeating dully and thoughtlessly, the ingrained footwork, the sparring for some small hold.

This morning, it rained.

Clancy was up, and out, wading in the gutter, before she'd even opened her eyes. "Well, why didn't you put on your boots?" she said, deadening, thinking his shoes cost $9 a pair.

Then the car wouldn't start.

Clancy sat, his wet feet dripping over the guitar case, lost in a yellow slicker that she'd bought too large because she hoped it would "do" another year. "Try the choke," he said, unperturbed.

She glowered. "The starter's hung up." She pulled at it again, hopelessly.

"The man in the garage said you could unlock it if you shook the car back and forth, remember?"

"He weighed 200 pounds."

"You ought to get a new car," said Clancy.

"I expect," she said. Clancy's "debut" was scheduled for 9:15. She rolled down the window, as if the rain beating in against her face could get her started.

"Ask somebody for a push," said Clancy.

She stared through the rain at the busy morning traffic, all clearly headed somewhere. Who could she ask?

A vision of Flynn in a trenchcoat and, oddly, a blue beret came whistling through the slanted pellets of rain, skipping as Clancy sometimes did, to avoid the cracks in the pavement.

> . . . *And when it rains,*
> *it always rains,*
> *Pennies*
> *from heaven. . . .*

It had been a sticky, hot night in late August, but that was what he'd been wearing. A trench coat, with a blue beret. Like something left over that couldn't make up its mind whether to be a character out of Mickey Spillane, or a Bohemian free spirit.

Her last night in New York. She had wandered into some unknown bar in Greenwich Village because it had sawdust on the floor and seemed as remote as she could get from Salem. Sitting silent at a back booth, thinking that next month it would be Girls' High, and all the months after. She had got her education, like they insisted she should, cheap, at the State Teachers' College, it was a good, decent, upstanding profession for a woman, and besides, you got summer vacations. She'd had her month in New York, staying at the downtown YWCA, which was also decent—and clean. The train ticket back covered the hole in the red checkered tablecloth that blurred before her eyes.

He slid the beer across the table. "*. . . And when it rains . . .*" "Drown your sorrows," he said, "on me. I'm flush." He always spoke in a hit tune lingo that re-

minded her of the pink song sheets they sold in the five-and-dime on the square at home.

"Seamus Flynn's the name." She learned later it was really John. Seamus was something he'd picked up for "the profession." He was an actor, and he was "flush" because he'd just been paid for a bit part as a cabdriver in a documentary on the East Side. "Drivin' through the rain," he said, "with me back to the camera all the way." It was the only piece of acting she'd ever known him to be paid for. Underneath the trenchcoat, he was small and thin, with a pinched-in face that never smiled because his teeth were so badly decayed. She asked him about it once. "Started to get 'em capped," he said, "for the biz, you know. Couldn't take it. Man, that's worse 'n Brooklyn." His eyes were the best part of him. Small, but like two brilliants always dancing in the dark.

"Where you headed?" he'd asked in the bar, and shouting "Salem!" in the same breath, because he'd already read the ticket. "Massachusetts? . . . Where they fried all the witches . . ."

He made it sound like one of Hawthorne's haunted houses, with a sheeted face, hers, peering through brown bars.

"Me," he said, "I'm off to Hollywood in the mornin'." He bent his thumb over, and it practically hit his wrist. "Hitchin'."

A large, open road flashed before her. Narrow here, but widening and widening, with vistas beyond vistas, and the sun climbing over a hill. She went with him in the morning. And her father never spoke to her again. . . .

Clancy nudged her. "This man says he'll give us a push." A leather jacket topped by a red beer-parlor face and the mashed-in nose of a prizefighter grinned over the dash. "Put her in neutral," it said. They were rolling, and the rain parted like curtains on a first act. Flynn had disappeared round the bend. And pulling up, then passing was the fleeting face that had offered the push. He was driving a moving van, she noted, with a large drawing on its side of a black cat holding a baby kitten in its mouth.

"See," said Clancy, "all you got to do is ask."

She kept both hands on the wheel, tensely forward. The wipers weren't working too well, and the road was one long, gray, undistinguishable mass. Should she or should she not. If she traded this car in on another, something else was sure to go wrong. You never really got anywhere, you only kept on treading water till your feet gave out, or your lungs.

Clancy jumped on the seat beside her, knocking her hand off the wheel. "Gee, I almost forgot, Hilda," pulling an envelope from inside his slicker, next to the heart. "I gotta mail this letter 'bout the birthday cards. So's I can buy the orangoutang, you

know. I marked it 'VIA JET.' See. . . ." He thrust it under her nose. "There . . . there's a mailbox. . . . Stop, Hilda."

She screeched up to the curb.

He checked the pickup times on the front of the mailbox. His face shone wet and clean when he climbed back over the guitar. "I ought to be in business by Saturday."

Hilda said nothing. She didn't think he'd sell enough birthday cards to buy himself a package of bubble gum. But then, she didn't know, either. Clancy's world was blast-propelled, a direct line from here to there, like the two short words on the envelope, "VIA JET". . . . "I want, I can, I will. . . ."

"I been thinking about the program," he said, as they neared an intersection. "Suppose I should bow when they applaud." And, the other half answering before the words were fairly out, "Of course, I must bow." Practicing the gesture where he sat, one hand forward, one hand aft, the head brushing the dash, and the wide-brimmed hat flopping through the air.

The wheel was vibrating beneath her hand, and the car shook like an old man who'd suddenly taken a chill. Clancy's hat was still flopping when it exploded. One short, sharp boom . . . and a cloud of smoke rising. . . .

"Discipline, Mrs. Flynn, a little shaker of discipline is what we want." He was a good man, she supposed, only weak, like herself. Samuel Lemmons, principal of Redemption High. Always tiptoeing down the corridors as if two feet firmly placed weren't given to those heavenbound, being far too close to earth.

Her first year teaching. After Flynn had left.

It was a tough neighborhood and a tough school. But she'd been rather pleased about that, in the beginning. Teaching Freshman English to "the underprivileged"—a large unseen mass thirsty and eager—it had seemed then as if hers was the torch of knowledge to be borne high through one of Hugo's tortured mobs.

She had been reading from "A Midsummer Night's Dream." She didn't read well, and the class frightened her, which was why she clung to the book, and the desk, and the chair . . . reading into the page, the words limping softly, dimly, away.

Vernon, a big Negro boy who kept repeating year after year, and would until age released him, sat in the front row. Occasionally, she saw him mouthing the words after her.

The rest of the class was one large swatch.

When the thing exploded—in her mind, it was always a "thing," nothing more—she ran screaming to the coat closet.

"You hadn't ought to done that." Through the door, she could hear the scuffling. Ver-

non's voice booming. Laughter, pounding. An acrid smell sifting beneath the door sill, like the smell left by fireworks when the shooting's over, on the fourth of July. Cowering, defeated before she'd hardly begun.

And Samuel Lemmons, tiptoeing through, "Discipline, Mrs. Flynn, a little shaker of discipline . . . even Shakespeare can do with some seasoning. . . ."

Clancy was already out on the sidewalk, glaring at the engine. "Old pot," he blurted, his underlip thrust forward in belligerence.

He raced back to where she still sat behind the dead wheel. "I'll be late, Hilda," he shouted, shaking her.

But again she saw the desk, the classroom, and the coat closet.

He pulled her by the arm. "Let's walk," he said, insistently.

It had stopped raining. Hilda sat at the back of the classroom, removed, distant. The sun licked at the windows behind her, faintly beaming through. Her hands were folded on one of the children's desks, her legs cramped beneath, and she thought, vaguely, recalling Salem, it feels like church.

Clancy's classmates had formed a semi-circle, sitting Indian fashion on the floor at the front of the room, leaving an empty apron of eight or ten feet for the stage. To the right, Miss

Agnews—who seemed to Hilda very young, pretty, and un-touched—stood expectant. Occa-sionally, she turned to Hilda, as if to say, smiling across the rows of desks, "Aren't you proud? *Such a child!*"

Clancy, single, lone, facing them all, was having difficulty unpacking his guitar. He worked deliberately, but stiff, his face flushing in the consciousness that he was being watched. She hadn't realized before that he was wearing his best white shirt, starched, and buttoned tight al-most to the chin, with that awful red bow tie he'd traded some marbles for. His Billy the Kid jeans still wet at the ankles be-neath. He was her child, she thought, but foreign, she would never understand such total self-possession, already, at seven, a being apart.

The chrome folding stand he used for his music clicked into position. But the clasps were stuck on his case. "Excuse me," he said, turned, and ripped it open.

When it finally emerged, the guitar seemed ridiculously and overwhelmingly out of size.

He propped it on his knee, his foot steadied on the rung of a classmate's chair. "This," he said, "is a Spanish guitar," his round face serious and unsmil-ing. He plucked at a string. "This is the G chord." His fingers, she thought, were amazingly agile, and she remembered the way

Flynn's thumb had bent to the wrist that night in New York when he'd said, "hitchin'."

He straightened now, and like an actor who'd rehearsed his lines and that was the way he must say them declaimed, "For my first selection, I shall now play the well-known folk song, 'Shoo-Fly.'" His voice rose light and clear, with the quality of an old-fashioned recorder. Largely, he had taught himself—from books, and the ballads of Burl Ives—and listening, now, the sound plucked through to her heart, occasionally off-key, but pure. Oh, Clancy, she thought, that is the whole of it, the best of it, and nothing else matters. Did she only imagine it? Or was there, truly, a circle of light folding him round.

He bowed stiffly, as he had in the car. And of all who clapped, she was sure she clapped the loudest. Her hands burned with the ringing, and suddenly embar-rassed because she clapped on alone, she left off, but beaming still at her son, her boy, who sin-gular and lone had rent through all the gray and mired doubt and softly strummed a golden chord.

He went on, as he had planned, with his "selections," sturdy and impervious. "And for my third selection, I shall play. . . ."

Miss Agnews broke in. "Is there something that the class can sing along with you?"

Clancy stopped short. A

questioning shadow crossed the clear green eyes. "I haven't practiced . . ." There was fidgeting in the front row, a high broken-off giggle.

He continued, disregarding, *"I'm just a poor, wayfaring stranger*
trav'ling through
this world of woe, . . ."

A child coughed, blew his nose. "My big brother plays the guitar," he was whispering to his neighbor, but the words carried as if they'd been blown on a megaphone, "And he c'n sing better 'n Elvis Presley. . . ."

Miss Agnews motioned vigorously, clearly determined to avoid disruption at any cost. The group was obviously becoming restless.

"Let us sing you a song now," she ordered, hands already raised in the manner of a conductor, *"Nick, nack, paddy-wack, give a dog a bone. . . ."* She pulled the children along after her.

"No . . . !" said Clancy. And he stamped his feet.

Miss Agnews stopped mid-air.

Clancy's eyes bulged murderously. "That's not the way I planned it." A dead quiet had settled over the room. Suddenly Clancy was crying, without a sound, the tears rolling down over his pumpkin cheeks, staining the red bow tie at his neck.

Hilda ran forward, her arm around his shaking shoulders. She spoke very quietly. "He has

put a great deal of effort into this program," she said, "for you. Perhaps next week you can prepare a program for him." She felt treacherous and guilty, and not at all sure that she was doing the right thing, yet compelled somehow to defend his weakness, realizing suddenly that like herself, like Samuel Lemmons and Flynn and all the world that she had known, he *was* weak, and more . . . that he was a child, still no more than a child, and dependent—despite all appearances to the contrary—on whatever small strength she could muster. Yet, there were the sixty round, frightened eyes, of all these others before her. Children, too. And some innocence that she here was already burying; a guilt that was hers, of adult knowing, that harsh and cold could point and kill, to show what shouldn't yet be seen.

She stood off to a side now. "I'm sure Clancy would like to finish his program as he planned it."

Clancy was smiling when she left, a wide, toothless grin, all six of his songs played, as he had played them in his heart endless times before, to a victorious and applauding end. Still, she knew, and knew that he, too, would know that he had already tasted the sourest curd of all, and that his beginning, so proudly attempted, held within it all the bitter, shadowed portent of the "maybe not."

The credit office was cross-town, five, maybe six miles away. But she preferred to walk. The sky again was clouded, the air misty and gray.

And why? she thought. Why? What pot of gold at the end of what rainbow could possibly efface all the blackness between. To stand, as she must, beside him, a living promise that the quicksand and the quagmire were worth the folly of the struggle, when a single voice lifted high and pure was all it ever came to.

And she remembered the moment when she had first discovered life within her . . . .

"Feel," she had said to Flynn, a trembling inside, a thumping that, even only watching, rippled the skin over her belly.

They had been months on the road, and still no further than Alabama. Hot, dusty months, turning slowly to the orange chill of November and the snows of December.

His hand was ice across her middle. Unbelieving, looking still to the technicolor promise of Hollywood.

"We'll have to get married," he had said. An end, not a beginning.

So they had wandered through the streets of that town in Alabama. She no longer remembered the name, but only the lean-to look of it, the slush in the gutters, and the tobacco-stained snow. Turning in to the first YMCA they came to, an entrance for men on one side, an entrance for women on the other. Burrowing in torn pockets for a quarter to bathe, as if to wash clean all the dirt and the dust, before facing the justice, who would join together what was already rent asunder.

Then the farmhouse at the far edge of town. "Name's McCallum, he's an old fat Scot what kills hogs, got a green sign on the road what says J. P." Waiting for the butchering to be done. "C'mon on out and watch." Hot blood steaming up from hard, packed ice underneath a hangman's tree.

"Flynn," she had said, "Flynn, you don't have to." Standing there and watching the knife slit down the midline. "Call it a flip of the coin," wry little words tossed at the air in the song sheet grammar she knew he understood.

Flynn beating his arms against his chest cross-wise, like a man who would never again be warm. "He wants a name, don't he." Trapped.

The whiskey-soaked eulogy. ". . . And do you take this man . . ." A package of home-made pork sausage wrapped in brown paper stuffed into their arms at the door. "Call it a wedding present from the Missus." Beaming still hot from the blood of the kill.

Yet she had thrilled to the life that she bore. And if the road grew weary as the months wore on, and if Flynn's eyes no longer danced to the dream beyond, even so, the heart that pumped within leaped with every step, beating every minute stronger as each, in turn, they fell weaker.

He was a sentimental man. And he'd cried when the child was born. "Give him a good Irish name," he'd said, "a four-leaf clover like Clancy." And that, too, was the best of it. . . .

The steps of the credit office loomed out of the dusk. There was a pounding at the base of her head, a cudgel swung and vibrating with a dull, low whack. And when the hammering left off, it was answered by an eerie, high whine centered forward and above. Should she or should she not? The mist had darkened, she hardly saw at all. The steps seemed grained with marble, leading up and up. Above, an elevator with open grillwork, washed in blue.

"Which floor, Miss?" said the attendant. And when he turned to face her, she saw with horror, Clancy's face, and Clancy's hopeful eyes.

She stumbled out, began to run.

All along the corridor were doors. But locked. Every one. She ran and she pulled, she pulled and she ran, her hair strung out behind, soaked in sweat, like the wrung end of a mop. Tripping, falling, running on, another door! Locked. Shoving hard against it now, all the weight of her body hitting and hitting. Kicking with her feet. "Let me in . . . !

Blackness, finally, as she plummeted through, a high counter catching her, breathless, at the chest. Standing there, hands on the desk, shaking in short, sharp sobs.

A woman in white stood politely before her.

"What are you here for?" she said.

Hilda straightened, Her breathing was better now, and the darkness was clearing. She met the other's questioning look head-on.

"Why, Clancy wants an orangoutang, of course." So simple.

DISCUSSION

We have no test scores for Clancy, but much of what goes on in this story suggests that Clancy is a gifted child. When Hilda says Clancy "was altogether too much," she refers to his many ideas, his will to pursue them, and his mind that stores and associates information. Clancy is certain of his objectives and has a need to be recognized, which culminates in a project for his class. He seems to have all the details worked out: what the program will look like, where he will post it, how he will take his bows, and the proper attire for the occasion. His enthusiasm, inventiveness, and curiosity are unquenchable.

The author could not have provided us with a more specific example of one of the qualities of giftedness than the incident in which Hilda uses the word "constructive," which is unfamiliar to Clancy. He demonstrates that he quickly assimilates its meaning and can use the word correctly in another context. When Clancy comes forth with an idea to sell Christmas cards, he terms it a "constructive" way to earn money. Hilda, who is overwhelmed by her everyday concerns for survival, finds Clancy with his whirlwind of ideas and drive for completion a mixed blessing. Gifted children like Clancy are usually not docile and compliant because they have many ideas that they must pursue *now*. Yet Clancy's resourcefulness, self-sufficiency, and imagination are sources of strength for Hilda, too.

Although Clancy's teacher appreciates his creativity, she must be responsive to all of her students, who become restless as they listen to all of Clancy's repertoire. Hilda is sensitive to Clancy's feelings and takes care of his emotional needs when she insists that the children permit him to finish his program as planned. Despite his giftedness in thinking, he is still a little boy who cries when his plans go awry. This incident highlights the gifted child's need for support. Because he has interests and ideas not always shared by a majority of his peers, his self-esteem may suffer. Other children may tease him with terms like "egghead" or chastise him for using big words. Clancy is fortunate that the adults in his life recognize and show approval for his ability to achieve and to think divergently.

SPRINGBOARDS FOR INQUIRY

1. The following list of behaviors are usually associated with gifted children. Check off those behaviors that apply to Clancy, relating them to incidents in the story whenever possible.

   Learns easily and rapidly   Wide interest and abilities
   Large vocabulary; verbal profi-   Unusual power of observation
      ciency   Creative or unusual ideas
   Interest in problem solving   Long attention span
   Ability to generalize informa-   Self directing in work and
      tion   study
   Retentiveness: wide fund of   Advanced ability and interest
      knowledge   in reading

Intellectual curiosity   Power of critical thinking
Comprehension in abstract   Advanced specialized interest
  areas
Alertness and eagerness

2. Using the research listed in the footnotes in this chapter, discuss whether there is a difference between giftedness and creativity.

3. Comment on the instruments presently used to assess giftedness and creativity.

4. Read about curriculum for the gifted and plan a lesson in language arts or social studies appropriate for gifted children. Specify the grade level.

5. What are some of the classroom problems Clancy may encounter because of his giftedness?

6. What qualities should teachers who wish to work with gifted children possess?

CHAPTER FOUR

The Learning Disabled and Neurological Dysfunction

In a small school district in California, the school psychologist and special education teacher presented a filmstrip and cassette tape about children with learning disabilities because a class for children with learning disabilities was to be located in the school building.[1] While the class was listening to the cassette and watching the filmstrip, several students turned to each other and said, "Say, that must be what's wrong with David." The children were referring to a student in their own class who was considered "weird" and a "class clown," but whose obvious intelligence had kept him from being referred to a learning specialist. The fifth grade teacher found that the film brought into perspective her concerns for David. She subsequently referred him to the school psychologist for further evaluation. Table 4–1 lists (1) five of David's behaviors, (2) the labeling he was given by classmates and previous teachers, and (3) the actual terminology that should have been applied to David had his learning and behavioral problems been accurately diagnosed.

Students like David, because they appear to be bright, are often mislabeled as lazy, unmotivated, and spoiled, when actually they have undiagnosed learning disabilities. David, his parents, his classmates, and his teachers could have been spared a lot of anguish had he been

[1]B. Chester, *A Walk In Another Pair of Shoes* (California: California Association for Neurologically Handicapped Children, 1972).

Table 4-1
David, Ages 10-14

(1) Behavior	(2) Peer and teacher mislabels	(3) Accurate[a] diagnosis
1. Always in motion and out of his seat; does not complete assignments	Busybody, showoff, poor work habits	Hyperactive, distractible, short attention span
2. Has outbursts of temper and displays frustration	Spoiled	Low threshold for frustration
3. Refuses to participate in games	Egghead; not interested in sports	Poor gross motor coordination; poor eye-hand coordination
4. Cannot put ideas on paper; spelling severely below grade level; handwriting illegible	Lazy, unmotivated	Poor small motor coordination; difficulty in sequencing letters; visual perceptual disturbance
5. Asks to have instruction repeated after teacher has given directions	Inattentive	Poor short term memory

[a]For a description of each of the terms in the column "accurate diagnosis," see Sam D. Clements, "The Psychologist and Case Finding" in *Learning Disabilities: Introduction to Educational and Medical Management,* ed. Lester Tarnapol (Springfield, Ill.: Charles C. Thomas, Publisher, 1970), pp. 175-76.

referred for help earlier. Sometimes a student like David is retained because he is considered immature and not working at grade level, but retention does not remediate specific learning disabilities. The more effective approach is for a multidisciplinary team to diagnose the problem and to follow their recommendations.[2]

David was referred by the school psychologist to the child study unit of the local university hospital. Their multidisciplinary team included a pediatrician, neurologist, psychologist, speech and language specialist, educational diagnostician, and a psychiatrist, each of whom made a differential diagnosis in the areas of mental retardation, emotional disturbances and learning disabilities.[3] Identifying the primary

[2]The case for a multidisciplinary diagnostic evaluation for children with learning disorders is discussed in Stanley W. Johnson and Robert L. Morasky, *Learning Disabilities* (Boston, Mass: Allyn & Bacon, Inc., 1977), pp. 192-208.
[3]Some authorities in the field of learning disabilities object to attempts to separate the categories of learning disabilities, mental retardation, and emotional distur-

problem helps in formulating educational and behavioral goals. After a careful history and a neurological examination, the pediatrician and neurologist found that the reason David was unable to stay in his seat or complete assignments was not that David was a "busybody" or "unmotivated" but that he was hyperactive and distractible. His short attention span and low frustration tolerance were part of the hyperkinetic syndrome.[4] The diagnostic procedure and the diagnosis itself were palliative experiences for David and his family. For years David's parents were emotionally and physically exhausted by their unpredictable and difficult child. They had blamed each other for poor parenting when David was in constant motion at home and in company. Later when he began to bring home bad reports from school about his behavior and achievement, they shifted responsibility to the school and blamed poor teachers for David's problems. Now the doctor recommended a course of medication for David, requesting reports from home and school to document any side effects and definite indications of improved concentration.[5]

The psychologist and educational therapist administered a series of psychological and educational tests to measure David's in-

---

bance. They prefer to define "learning disabilities" broadly to include these three groups that have so much in common. Daniel P. Hallahan and James M. Kauffman contend that the new field of learning disabilities has its roots in the pioneering efforts of the leaders in the fields of mental retardation and emotional disturbance. They also see an overlap in the need for similar services and educational planning for the three types of children. See Daniel P. Hallahan and James M. Kauffman, *Introduction To Learning Disabilities: A Psycho-Behavioral Approach* (Englewood Cliffs, N.J.: Prentice-Hall, Inc., 1976), pp. 26–29. Patricia Myers and Donald D. Hammill do not deny that many mentally retarded children may have learning disorders, but they consider their learning disorders secondary to the more serious handicap of mental retardation. These authors state that if the child's outstanding learning disorder were corrected, the child would still be functioning only at his mental age in that ability. See Patricia Myers and Donald D. Hammill, *Methods For Learning Disorders*, 2nd ed. (New York: John Wiley & Sons, Inc., 1976), p. 6.

[4]For a discussion of the hyperkinetic syndrome, see Helen Gofman, "The Physician's Role in Early Diagnosis and Management of Learning Disabilities" in *Learning Disabilities: Introduction to Educational and Medical Management*, ed. Lester Tarnapol (Springfield, Ill. Charles C. Thomas Publisher, 1970), p. 122.

[5]The use of drug therapy for the hyperkinetic child has been under attack. The Department of Health Education and Welfare called together a panel of experts to discuss the use and misuse of amphetamine drugs for school children with hyperkinetic behavioral disturbance problems. They issued a seventeen-page statement that included the following highlights: (1) use of such medication in treating hyperkinetic behavior disturbance improves the child's attention, learning, and social abilities; (2) there is no need for sensational alarm about the health or safety of the individual child under carefully supervised treatment (*HEW News* [Washington D.C.: United States Department of Health Education and Welfare, March 10, 1971], pp. 1–3).

tellectual ability and to gain insights into his patterns of learning.[6] The psychologist administered the Revised Wechsler Intelligence Scale for Children, a test with ten subtests that reflect the child's ability to solve problems verbally and manually. David was found to be of above average intelligence with a vocabulary test age several years above his chronological age. He was able to respond superiorly to questions involving social judgment and abstract reasoning. His low score in short-term memory and his need for repetition of questions correlated with his difficulty in following a series of directions in school. Low scores on subtests involving visual motor perception explained his difficulty in accurately reading and copying assignments from the textbook and chalkboard. The Bender Gestalt Test of Visual Motor Perception and the Frostig Test of Visual Perception pinpointed David's visual-perceptual deficiencies as well as his poor small motor coordination, which made writing long assignments so arduous. The diagnostic teacher administered the Wide Range Achievement Test and found that David was above grade level in arithmetic but two years below grade level in reading and three years below grade level in spelling. With problems in reading, writing, and spelling, it was evident why David did not complete his work in school. He was the class "busybody" instead. His awareness of the discrepancy between what he could understand and what he could satisfactorily produce contributed to his frustration and bouts of temper.

The educational specialist and psychologist suggested that David spend two hours a day in the resource room provided by his school district for children with specific learning disabilities. In this resource room, a teacher trained in methods and materials to remediate learning disabilities worked with children individually and in small groups. She used the data given to her about David by the psychologist and educational therapist to devise an educational plan for David. It involved a multisensory approach to learning to read and spell new words. This approach is described by Grace Fernald.[7] David was to trace, then copy, and finally produce from memory those words that he had chosen to learn. The word lists were kept short to allow David to feel successful. He received postitive feedback from the teacher for complete and accurate work. David was permitted to tape oral reports in the resource room to substitute for written science and social science reports, and he learned to type, a skill that allowed him to produce neater, if not always more accurate, work.

[6]A discussion of the most frequently used standardized tests for diagnosing learning disabilities is found in Janet W. Lerner, Children With Learning Disabilities: Theories, Diagnosis, and Teaching Strategies (Boston, Mass.: Houghton Mifflin Company, 1971), p. 54–59.

[7]Grace M. Fernald, Remedial Techniques in Basic School Subjects (New York: McGraw-Hill, 1943).

David's story ended successfully. He went on to junior high school feeling much better about himself and became a student who was recognized for his abilities rather than for his misbehavior and lack of achievement. There are millions of children like David. Although Congress has recently legislated money for learning-disabled children, it has restricted funds to only 2 percent of the entire school population. Many educators feel that the number of children who cannot succeed in school without some individualized attention to their special learning needs far exceeds this 2 percent figure.[8]

The term *learning disabilities* is relatively new to the field of special education. In the last decade there has been a surge of research in the disciplines that have contributed to this new field. This research has been in the fields of medicine, psychology, education, physical therapy, and language and reading disorders and has made learning disabilities a fast growing, although often controversial, specialty. One area of diverse opinion is in the wide range of therapies advocated to remediate the various disturbances in learning-disabled children.[9] The most pervasive controversy, however, has surrounded the inclusion of organic impairment in the accepted definition of children with learning disabilities.

In November 1976 the National Advisory Committee for the Bureau of Education adopted the following regulations to define learning-disabled children as children

> who have a disorder in one or more of the basic psychological processes involved in understanding or in using language, spoken or written, which disorder may manifest itself in imperfect ability to listen, think, speak, read, write, spell, or do mathematical calculations. Such disorders include such conditions as perceptual handicaps, brain injury, minimal brain dysfunction, dyslexia, and developmental aphasia. Such terms do not include children who have learning problems which are primarily the result of visual, hearing, or motor handicaps, or mental retardation, of emotional disturbance or environmental, cultural, or economic disadvantage.[10]

By far the most prevalent learning disability is in the area of reading. The term dyslexia is often used to describe the child who is having difficulty reading. Samuel Orton suggests that this term should be reserved to describe only those children whose reading disability is

[8]For estimates of the prevalence of children who have learning disabilities, see Lerner, *Children With Learning Disabilities, p. 10.*

[9]The California Association for Neurologically Handicapped Children published in July 1976 a list of therapies and experimental approaches to helping children with learning disabilities. Their list had seventy-seven entries and covered therapies advocated in the fields of biology, psychology, biofeedback, nutrition, transactional analysis, and transcendental meditation.

[10]*Federal Register,* November 29, 1976, p. 52, 404.

particularly severe and caused by an organic dysfunction.[11] A great deal of research has been conducted in the area of reading. It is now known that some children learn best through the auditory channel and can use a phonics approach. For some children the visual, or look-say, approach is preferred, and for some a multisensory method using ear, eye, and tactile reinforcement is necessary. Teachers, therefore, are now advised to individualize their approach to the teaching of reading.

In the 1970s, there is a trend toward viewing learning disabilities in educational terms. Some authorities in the field of learning disabilities are using the term *specific learning disorders* (SLD) to narrow the difficulty in learning to specific problem areas.[12] There is also a movement away from a diagnostic approach that centers entirely upon the "in-child disorder." Beverly E. McKee stresses the importance of considering the characteristics of the environment and the specific task to be performed before deciding on specific approaches for educating children with learning disabilities.[13] Barbara Keogh and L. Becker state that the purpose of evaluation is not necessarily to identify only deficiencies but also to provide information useful in planning a program that a child can accomplish and to identify potential compensatory strengths.[14] J. M. Throne cites these five environmental considerations for improving the child's achievement in the regular classroom: (1) carefully specified goals; (2) contingent stimulation; (3) a consistent schedule or plan for reinforcement; (4) a responsible authority figure to direct learning; and (5) continuous evaluation and feedback.[15]

This interactional approach to educating the learning-disabled child conforms to the Education for All Handicapped Children Act that will prevail in special education in the 1980s. This act, which calls for the least restrictive environment for educating the handicapped child, will bring about great change in the role of the learning disabilities teacher. The latter will no longer be assigned all day to teach twelve children in a classroom often located far from the regular classrooms.[16]

[11]Samuel Orton, *Reading, Writing and Speech Problems in Children* (New York: W. W. Norton, 1937).

[12]Dean K. McIntosh and Lloyd M. Dunn, "Children With Major Specific Learning Disabilities" in *Exceptional Children in the Schools: Special Education in Transition,* 2nd ed., ed. Lloyd M. Dunn (New York: Holt, Rinehart and Winston, Inc., 1973), p. 585.

[13]Beverly E. McKee, "An Interactional Approach to Learning Disabilities," *Journal of Learning Disabilities,* vol. 9, no. 7 (August–September 1976).

[14]Barbara Keogh and L. Becker, "Early Detection of Learning Problems: Questions, Cautions and Guidelines," *Exceptional Child,* 40 (1973), 5–13.

[15]J. M. Throne, "Learning Disabilities: A Radical Behaviorist Point of View," *Journal of Learning Disabilities,* 6 (1973), 543–46.

[16]Barbara Aiello, "Up From The Basement: A Teacher's Story," *New York Times,* April 25, 1976, p. 18.

The distinction between the teacher of the "normal" and the "different" child will not be so evident in the physical organization of schools. This should result in a great deal more social acceptance for the learning disabled. The learning disabilities teacher will be a resource person, one who will be highly visible and will relate to many children and to many teachers. He or she will be expected to help students by translating their learning style and learning needs to the regular teacher. Optimally the learning disabilities teacher will provide the regular teacher with materials and methods that work with the child mainstreamed into the regular classroom. The special teacher will also be a resource for ideas for classroom management when the children with special learning needs are part of the regular classroom. The new role will call for tact, knowledge in methods and materials, and flexibility to play a variety of roles.

Federal law and new criteria for special teaching credentials cannot accomplish the human work that is necessary to translate these ideals into reality. The following questions need to be answered:

1. Is the move toward expecting the special educator to take over all aspects of diagnosis, teaching, and coordinating with parents and regular teachers, as well as acting as expert in classroom management, requiring too much of one person?
2. Should educational institutions eliminate the personnel who have traditionally handled some of the responsibilities outlined above, that is, the school psychologist, social worker, nurse, learning diagnostician, and administrator?
3. Will all classroom teachers be able to add even a few youngsters with a diversity of problems to their regular class load?
4. Should educational institutions discontinue referring children with learning disabilities to facilities that provide a multidisciplinary approach to learning problems and refer children only to an exclusively educational environment?
5. Is mainstreaming the answer for all children with learning handicaps?[17] Will children with serious emotional problems or excessively hyperactive behavior or with serious deficien-

---

[17]*Focus On Exceptional Children* (Denver, Colo.: Love Publishing Company) has devoted several issues to the concept of mainstreaming. The following three issues are particularly recommended: Jerry D. Chaffin, "Will the Real 'Mainstreaming' Program Please Stand Up (or . . . Should Dunn Have Done It?)," vol. 6, no. 5 (October 1974); Keith E. Beery, "Mainstreaming: A Problem and An Educational Opportunity for General Education," vol. 6, no. 6 (November 1974); and Barbara K. Keogh and Marc L. Levitt, "Special Education in the Mainstream: A Confrontation of Limitations?" vol. 8, no. 1 (March 1976).

cies in more than one learning channel (such as auditory and visual) be able to achieve their maximum potential in the regular classroom?

Sound educational policy for the child with learning disabilities dictates that those in positions of authority for special education be wary of changes that do not preserve the best kind of education for every child.

Gideon: A Boy Who Hates Learning

by Gladys Natchez

Gideon slouched way down in his seat. Now she can't see me, he thought. Now she doesn't even know I'm here! If I'm not here, she won't call on me. That's the way to beat the teacher.

• • •

"Gideon!" The shrill voice of the teacher shattered his dream. "Sit up in your seat and pay attention!" The other children sniggered, then there was silence.

Gideon shuddered. He squeezed his face into a series of furrowed lines. He could feel his forehead and his cheeks pressed together. It doesn't matter; I'm not here, he kept telling himself. She can't see me. I'm not here . . .

"Gideon, you must pay attention. You know you have a lot of catching up to do. Now kindly tell us, is squash a vegetable or a fruit?"

"A squash is a vegetable 'cause it has seeds," Gideon said, mixing up the answer he had carefully memorized the night before for homework. He knew that things with seeds were supposed to be fruit. His father had said that this wasn't true—that he should tell the teacher that vegetables could have seeds too. But he knew better than to argue with her. "I mean the other way 'round," he added.

"If you would stop daydreaming, Gideon, you might have an easier time," the teacher declared. Gideon wondered if a voice could be made of ice. That was it—Mrs. Mazur's was ice, or maybe snow with syrup on it. He remembered how he and his brother Kevin put maple syrup over snowballs in the winter. He licked his lips. But Mrs. Mazur would never taste good, he thought, not even as syrup over snow.

"I am not going to baby you. Remember you are a third grader now and you must begin to act like one."

Blah, blah, blah. Gideon shut her out and returned to his reverie.

• • •

At the end of the school day, everyone received his report card, the first of the school year. One look and Gideon felt arrows pierce his stomach. He had two straight failures, the first out-and-out failures he had ever had.

In a trance, he directed his feet home. Everything was sinking. His insides were upside down. Dad will shout. Mom will just pat my head and look sorrowful. What'll I do? The thunderous torrent in his chest gave no answer.

When he arrived home, he was relieved to find the house empty. Still stunned, he poured some milk and grabbed a mountain of cookies. He crammed them down and gulped his milk, but he couldn't finish. Sorrowfully he gave the surplus to his dog, whose name was Tuppence. He patted him and looked into his

eyes. "You're a good dog," he said with adoration. "Yes, you love me no matter what." He nuzzled up to his dog's head. "You won't get sad or mad at me because of a report card. For you, I'm just me."

Then he took the report card out of his pocket, handled it gingerly, and laid it on the hall table. He thought of changing the marks. I can't, I can't . . . I just can't! With an anguished sob, he turned and fled out of the house toward the woods.

• • •

During the conference with Mrs. Tobin, the teacher described Gideon as a careless, immature child who lacked discipline and proper work habits and dreamed away most of the day.

Mrs. Tobin argued that her son tried very hard, but that he got overtired doing his homework. "Why he spends as much as one to two hours a night on it!"

"It should never take him that long." Mrs. Mazur was truly surprised.

"My pediatrician claims that Gideon is a slow-growing child," Mrs. Tobin said with authority. "He feared that Gideon might have difficulty in schoolwork and told me to give him extra help and to be patient with him. He said that in time my son would outgrow it. I was hoping everything would be all right now that he's a little older."

"To tell you the truth, Mrs. Tobin, he should go back to second grade. Last year he had a very inexperienced teacher who was ill a great deal. As you know, she could not even return this year. Gideon in particular suffered because he couldn't catch on the way many of the other youngsters did. In fact, these children constitute one of the brightest groups that I've ever had. Most of them sail along beautifully, while Gideon trails far behind. If we only had more than one class for each grade the way larger districts do, it might be easier to find a better placement for him. We just don't have that choice."

"But what can we do about it?" asked Gideon's mother in a strained voice.

"I am going to try to help him. If he doesn't improve by the end of the year, we will just have to consider retaining him," answered Mrs. Mazur.

"Retaining him!" Fear swept through Mrs. Tobin's body. She stopped breathing. "That would be . . . " She swallowed the rest.

"Nothing drastic would happen," said the teacher coldly. How I hate these hysterical mothers, she thought. "In fact, that might be the best thing for him if we handle it correctly."

"Do you really know what *is* correct?" challenged his mother.

"To put him in a class where he can achieve properly." Mrs. Mazur was unyielding.

"That may be all well and good," Gideon's mother said, trying another tactic, "but in the meantime does he deserve to fail when he puts forth so much effort? He was so upset by those marks that he almost didn't come home after school." Mrs. Tobin was very agitated.

Mrs. Mazur was very firm. "Well, how would you like it if you did superior work and received the same recognition as someone who didn't? It just would not be fair." And if there's anything I pride myself on it's being fair, thought Mrs. Mazur.

• • •

The principal, Mr. Sagent, was a burly man with a pale face full of freckles. His bushy eyebrows shielded eyes that gave no hint of what he was thinking. His stance suggested that he was comfortable with himself. Indeed, his body seemed completely at home in his tweed jacket and slightly mussed trousers.

The Tobins heard Mrs. Mazur talking with him as they approached the office. She was saying, "This is one of the brightest third grades I've ever taught and that's what makes it twice as hard for Gideon." Mr. Sagent had no time to respond. He greeted the Tobins with a perfunctory, "Nice to see you." He was obviously uncomfortable and embarrassed.

"Look," said Mr. Tobin, "I'm a busy man and I say what I mean. I'm very upset with the way things are going for my son. He tries; we try. But he's still making no progress. Isn't the school supposed to assume responsibility for kids like him?"

"Of course, Mr. Tobin, of course. Gideon is a puzzle to us too. Mrs. Mazur," and he nodded his head toward her, "is one of our best teachers and she's doing a fine job in that class for most of the children. She is trying very hard with Gideon, too. But she can't devote all her time to your son, you know. Many of the pupils are reading at fifth, sixth, and higher grade levels. She is most patient and tolerant, considering the circumstances. She is strict, it is true," he added, smiling admiringly in her direction, "but she gets results."

Mr. Sagent continued after a pause. "Our staff has discussed Gideon's situation. We have thought of putting him back, but we never like to be drastic. We will watch him to see how he comes along. You do your part, Mr. Tobin, and we'll continue to do ours."

Actually what he says is true to a large extent, thought Mrs. Tobin. But how does that help? For Gideon, school is just plain torture.

"Look, it's a good explanation, Mr. Sagent," said Mr. Tobin,

"but it's not good enough. Something's got to be done. I appreciate that Mrs. Mazur is doing everything possible, but it's November already and Gideon's having too much trouble. What do you think is going to happen if we just wait and see? Is he the only one in this boat?" he said suddenly, jumping from question to question.

"Now, Mr. Tobin, we'll do our best for your son. But, really, if the truth be known, all but a few of the others are quite a bit ahead of him. We'll try to get him up in his work so that he can go on with the rest of his class. If not...," Mr. Sagent shrugged.

"If *not*?" boomed Mr. Tobin. "First you threaten putting him back; now there's a chance that he won't be promoted! Since when is putting him back or retaining him for a year any kind of enlightened educational solution?"

"Mr. Tobin," answered Mr. Sagent warily, "we have standards to uphold you know. It is much easier for a child to be retained in third grade than to flounder on indefinitely. He is bright and we have been hoping that he would catch up. So far he has not; in fact he has hardly moved. You see, he read at about middle-second grade level at the end of last year, and he has done little better than that so far this year. We are seriously concerned." He cleared his throat. "We will not make the decision lightly, I assure you. We are considering it from every angle, including the academic and the emotional."

• • •

In the meantime, Gideon's marks were a constant reminder that they had to do something. Mr. Tobin was still furious that the school did nothing. He weighed the alternatives—a tutor, this psychologist jazz, a private school. Private school was out of the question because of cost. His wife did not know any plain old-fashioned tutors— heaven forbid! No, it had to be some fancy psychologist who would make a big deal out of everything.

One night they finally talked it out. Mr. Tobin was adamant. "For heaven's sake, let's get it settled! Get a good old-fashioned tutor, O.K.?" He was very brusque. Despite his stand, he felt defeated somehow. Was he really right? Marion's uneasy expression disturbed him. Well, that's the way it had to be and that was all there was to it!

Mrs. Davis saw Gideon for several testing sessions.

He entered her office tentatively. It was so big! His mother had told him that someone was supposed to help him with his reading. He sat down in the chair and jiggled his knees up and down in short, jerky movements. He listened to Mrs. Davis explain that these tests were given to chil-

dren from six to sixteen years of age. Each part would start out simply and he might think it silly, but then it would become harder until, finally, he wouldn't be able to answer the questions at all, and they would know that was the place to stop.

"So you see, you won't be expected to know all the answers," she concluded. "Just do what you can. If anything bothers you as we go along, ask me about it."

Gideon couldn't listen to most of what she said. He felt too numb and cold. He submitted to her mutely. The whole thing made little sense to him and, outside of the reading tests, the rest of it certainly didn't seem to have anything to do with reading.

After he had finished all the testing, Mrs. Davis asked, "When did you lose your first tooth, Gideon?"

He looked at her wonderingly. He couldn't imagine what she was talking about. "I don't know."

"Well, do you remember when you first rode a two-wheeler?"

"Oh, I remember that! I tried and tried, but I kept wobbling and falling off. Everyone was doing stunts before I could. But I'm as good as they are now," he ended proudly.

"Well, I think that learning in school is going to be about the same way, Gideon. The children in your class learned to read more quickly than you, but you'll be able to catch up to them eventually, just like you caught up with bike riding, I imagine."

He was still puzzled. Reading had nothing to do with bikes.

"You see, you seem to grow more slowly than most children. That's why I asked you about your teeth. I bet that they came in late. And you were slow to learn to balance and move your legs properly on a bike. I would think that the slowness interfered with your learning to recognize words, too."

"Oh."

"So now you need some extra help in reading. What do you think about coming here and learning to read with me?"

"What time?"

She laughed. "Oh, I don't know. I must talk with your parents first to see if it's possible, but I wanted to know how you feel about it before I talked with them. What's the best time for you?"

"Not on Saturdays."

She laughed again. He liked her laugh.

"O.K., not on Saturdays." She noticed his face again. It still looked puzzled. "What's wrong?"

"Nothing." Gideon felt mixed up. He didn't know what to expect so how could he answer? Besides, he didn't like the idea of going after school if he wanted to play football or something. Suddenly he asked, "Will you always have cookies and soda like now?"

She laughed. "Sure. You can even tell me what kind you like best and I'll try to have them for you. But I have to talk first with your father and mother. Then we'll decide for sure. Afterwards I'll talk to you again. Then we can try to work it out."

. . .

Gideon started reading lessons with Mrs. Davis toward the middle of November. He was restrained and uneasy and answered her questions with a noncommittal "Yes" or "No." When she offered him a choice of books, he didn't care which one he read. When they played reading games, he let Mrs. Davis choose any one she wished. For the most part he sat through the lessons listless and indifferent. Why was he the only one in the class who had to come? What was the matter with him?

A few weeks after he started, they were reading a book. As was her custom, Mrs. Davis read one line, while Gideon read the next. He had always done this willingly enough, but in a mechanical fashion as if the words were far removed from him. Today he was equally stilted, but instead of reading his line he repeated each sentence that Mrs. Davis read. At first she thought that he had lost his place, so she pointed to where he should read. When this didn't work, she asked, "Gideon, is this the way you like to do it—by saying each sentence after me?"

He nodded.

Mrs. Davis was puzzled, but she decided to see what would happen. He continued repeating every sentence. Often he wouldn't even look at the book as he rattled it off.

Suddenly a thought struck her. "Gideon," she said, "do you think this book is too hard?" She knew it really wasn't but . . .

"No," he protested, vigorously shaking his head.

There was a long pause. Mrs. Davis just waited. I like the flat, skinny books, he thought, so you can get finished with them. They don't torture like a monster mountain, a monster mountain that you can't climb. Sit still, he told himself. Do what you're supposed to and sit still. Then you're safe.

"You just hate reading altogether, is that it?"

Gideon didn't answer. Now he was in turmoil inside.

• • •

Gideon burst into Mrs. Davis' the next day. "We have the craziest substitute. You should see her! She's a real monster! As soon as the first bell rang, two kids and me came into the class ahead of the others—two girls and then me—and she says right away, before we did *anything*, 'It's too noisy. Sit down and do twelve examples, nine para-

graphs, and two reading exercises.' I hate her. We don't even get inside the door and right away she's 'Do examples, do examples.'"

Just then Mrs. Davis was called to the telephone. Good, he could stuff his pockets with candy. She returned in the middle of his raid and he looked up sheepishly. She smiled. All she said was, "Take as much as you like, Gideon. It's for you, you know." He beamed. Then she read a story to him.

"Oh, look, they're catching lightning bugs," commented Gideon, looking at the picture in the book. "Hey, where do lightning bugs go in the winter?"

"I honestly don't know. I think they die off at the end of June. Should we look it up in the encyclopedia?" Thank goodness he's getting livelier, she thought.

He ignored the question. He was not going to wade through any encyclopedia. "What makes them light up?"

"I guess they have some chemical ingredient like phosphorus that glows in the dark. I never thought about it."

"Does it hurt when they light up? Do they get burned?"

"I'm sure they don't. And I'm sure it doesn't hurt. They just have something in them that glows in the dark."

"Like the numbers on a watch?"

"Yes. That's a good comparison. Let's look it up."

But Gideon quickly asked her to continue reading. Soon he interrupted. "You know," he said shyly, "I want to be a scientist when I grow up. But I'll have to learn to read if I want to be a scientist."

"I think you'd make an excellent scientist or anything you really want. Do you know why?"

"Why?"

"Because you ask sharp, penetrating questions. And you're observant. I never would have thought to question why lightning bugs light up. You've gotten me so curious that I'm going to see what I can find out about them later today. We can do experiments here, too, if you'd like."

"What's pene-something mean?"

"Penetrating means very thoughtful and smart." Mrs. Davis smiled.

A big grin suffused Gideon's face and he had a glow that would have matched that of any lightning bug.

• • •

As the days passed, Gideon came to know when it was Mrs. Davis time, as he called it. He even forgot to forget when to go. Mondays and Fridays he sat patiently in the car with his mother and wondered why she always looked so worried. She was forever rushing, too, always hustle, hurry, hustle, hurry. The lines on her face looked scary. He went back to thinking of Mrs. Davis. Although he still felt ashamed that he needed special help, a lot of the strangeness had disappeared. He even looked forward to some of the things that they did together. The games they played; they were the best. *Grab* was his favorite, *Word Bingo* next. He never tired of them but, he wanted to play more.

"Why can't we play them all the time?" he asked her.

"Well, playing games is good, but why do you come here, Gideon?"

"To read," he said, being compliant. At the same time he thought of how much he disliked it. Even here, yes, even here where it wasn't very icky.

"I'll do what I can to make the hard reading easier," she promised. "Games are one way, good stories another. Then we'll try harder things."

He began to feel creepy. That sort of icy feeling on the edges of his skin. He didn't know why.

"You like only easy things?"

He nodded gravely.

"O.K. Let's have 'easy' day today."

He looked at her, wishing it could be easy all the time.

• • •

Mrs. Davis and Gideon were playing *Grab* as he sipped his soda. She had the best candy and soda! While he drank, he looked at the pictures of the old cars that were printed on the glass. "Let's see," he mused, "this car says 1914 under it and this one 1915, right?"

"Yes."

"Then the 1915 car is older."

"No," said Mrs. Davis, "it might seem that way, but the later the year the newer the car."

"How come?"

"Well, for instance, the earlier the year in which you were born, the older you are. What year were you born, Gideon?"

"1975."

"What? This year?"

"What do you mean?"

"Well, if a baby is born this year, he is a very new baby. We can't call him a year old until a year has passed. What year will it be next year?"

"1976?"

"Yes. Some time in 1976 he'll be a year old. But if he were born in 1974, how old would he be?"

"Six?" replied Gideon, taking a wild guess.

"Where did you get the six from, Gideon?"

"It just sounded right. I don't know."

"Gideon, when you're mixed up, say so. Then I'll try to help you understand. How long would it be from 1974 to 1975?

"One year?" asked Gideon uncertainly.

"Yes, of course." Mrs. Davis went through a few similar examples until Gideon was certain. "Now, what year were you born, Gideon?"

Gideon added eight to 1975, wrote it down, and said, "There it is."

"You were born in 1983?

"That's what it says."

"Gideon, you're so used to just going through the motions, you're not bothering to think. Besides, the idea of now, the past, and the future—they all seem foreign to you. That can happen. Let's try again." Gideon practiced for a few minutes until he understood how to count the years backwards. He became more and more restless, but he obeyed each request. When Gideon understood the concept fairly well, Mrs. Davis said, "O.K., now I think you're ready to solve the problem that we started out with. If you are eight years old in 1975, what year were you born?" Gideon counted back eight years and said, "1967."

"Yes. Now, can you think of an easier way of figuring it out?"

They worked together until Gideon understood subtraction in relation to dates and time.

Whew! Thank goodness they were finished! he said to himself. Then he said hesitatingly, "Now can we go back to *Grab*?"

"Of course," chuckled Mrs. Davis. "We made a big detour, didn't we?" That's where a lot of the trouble is, thought Mrs. Davis. Sometimes he has such difficulty grasping certain concepts—particularly time and space and backwards and forwards. And the teacher hasn't time for him, I suppose, particularly if the class is galloping along at the speed she describes. Yet at other times the depth of his perception is astonishing. It's a shame . . .

"Oh boy, I love this!" Gideon exclaimed as they played the word game. "I wish it was work."

"Why isn't it work? It helps you practice the words you know."

"But it's too much fun."

"Don't you think that you can find fun in work?"

Is she crazy or something—fun in work? Work was "that place," that dark, dank, musty dusty place. "C'mon, let's play," was all he said, not bothering to answer her. He eagerly called out a word and grabbed it from Mrs. Davis' hand as soon as she proffered it.

That night he thought about Mrs. Davis. Somehow she made him smile. She was, well, so much fun. But that work thing she talked about, that was gooney. How could work be fun? Somehow in "that place" you were always wrong. Take today, when the teacher had some crummy poem she was discussing and she asked us "What rolled across the island?" I answered, "water," 'cause at camp rain pours on our island and rushes down the hills in huge rivers. All she said was, "No, Gideon, it is not water." And then she liked it so much just 'cause Phillip said "Fog." Humph! "Water" makes her growl but "fog" makes her glad. "No, Gideon, No, Gid-

eon"—that's all I ever hear. Someday there'll really be no Gideon. I'll burn down "that place"—and that's what will really be fun!

The next week when he came to see Mrs. Davis, he picked out a story about a blind toolmaker who "mended" boys. The Court sent the toolmaker youths who had dropped out of school and gotten into lots of trouble. When asked how he managed so successfully with them after everyone else had failed, he said that caring about them and teaching them a trade was all he did.

"If only teachers————" Gideon started to say when they had finished reading.

"What do you mean?"

There was a long pause. "Well, the blind man fixed boys after teachers messed them up." He was frightened by the boldness of what he had said.

"I agree," said Mrs. Davis simply, and Gideon felt relieved. He looked at her and was glad. He began to ask a question. He hesitated. His voice wavered. "Will I ever . . . will I get fixed?" he asked finally.

"I think so, Gideon," said Mrs. Davis gently. "In time. In time you'll get fixed. You see," she explained, "when you don't learn the way everyone else does, you get frightened that maybe you're dumb, even though deep down you know you're not. And then you get mixed up because you don't know whether you're really dumb or just that everybody thinks you are. The slowness, the fear, and the confusion all make it very tough."

But he wasn't listening. When I grow up, thought Gideon, setting his chin with determination, I'm gonna find ways of fixing things up so that nobody hates to learn. I'm gonna find those ways of fixing everything. All he said aloud was, "Someday. . . when I'm big, I'm gonna fix it all up."

"You mean you're going to change the schools?" guessed Mrs. Davis.

He nodded.

"Sometimes it's people just like you, Gideon, who really help. I'm with you!"

He liked the trueness of her voice. He liked the way she looked at him. It seeped in and made him feel as though he could do anything!

DISCUSSION

Dr. Gladys Natchez, the author of *Gideon: A Boy Who Hates Learning*, is a professor of education at the City University of New York, and she is well known for her books on reading disabilities. This story in some ways parallels the case study of David. Unlike David, who reacts to failure by assuming the role of class clown, Gideon withdraws from the classroom situation in an effort to go unnoticed by the teacher. Mrs. Mazur does not ignore Gideon and is concerned that he does not perform up to grade level. Her methods to help him, however, are not only ineffectual but are also destructive. She chides Gideon repeatedly for not paying attention or for daydreaming. She uses hackneyed comments such as, "Remember you are a third grader now and you must begin to act like one." Her remarks are typical of the programmed scoldings that teachers use and that are demeaning to the child and offer no guidelines for improvement.

Gideon's grades spell failure despite the fact that he has done his homework and classroom assignments. He is ashamed and bewildered by the failures. Gideon, like all children, wants to please his parents, and he is aware that his parents value success in school. Mrs. Mazur justifies the grades by comparing Gideon's work with that of the rest of the students, which is of much better quality than Gideon's. Teachers are frequently driven by the oughts and shoulds of being "fair" when assigning grades. Students in the class usually know at what level their classmates are working and are frequently less concerned than the teacher when she makes allowances in grading for slower learning students. The tyranny of letter grades has caused many schools to adopt conferencing with parents or writing descriptive comments about the child's work in lieu of the traditional report card. By giving Gideon failures on his report card, Mrs. Mazur may siphon off her anger at her inability to reach Gideon and in this way transfers the failure to her student.

In an attempt to solve the problem of Gideon's inability to keep up with his classmates, the principal suggests retention. Mr. Tobin, the parent and a layman in the field of education, realizes that retention is "not an enlightened educational solution." The school Gideon attends apparently has no resource personnel such as a school psychologist or learning specialist for help in analyzing Gideon's learning problems. Mr. Tobin must decide whether or not to seek help outside of the school.

When a psychologist is mentioned as a valuable resource for Gideon's learning problem, Mr. Tobin reacts with the fear and guilt that many parents experience when referred to a psychologist. The fear stems from the thought that something irremediable must be wrong with the child, and the guilt is associated with the parent's feeling that he must be at fault. The rest of this story reveals that a psychologist like Mrs. Davis can be reassuring and helpful rather than menacing and faultfinding. A psychologist uses standardized individual tests and interviews to pinpoint the nature of learning problems. In this case, Mrs. Davis is also an educational therapist and is able to assume remediation of Gideon's specific difficulties.

Mrs. Davis' testing reveals that Gideon is a bright child who has a reading problem that has created an unfavorable emotional response toward learning in general. Mrs. Davis also learns that Gideon's disability includes an inability to understand abstract concepts involving time and space. Her approach to learning is appealing. She is aware of Gideon's need for success after the discouraging excesses of failure he has suffered. She uses a graduated approach in introducing new material and is always alert to his need for more challenge. Mrs. Davis has to teach Gideon to ask when he doesn't know something rather than taking wild guesses. She takes Gideon seriously as a person with preferences and interests. She solicits his opinion about the materials she chooses for him.

It is obvious that Gideon will not be able to learn in his regular classroom unless the teacher is aware of the exact nature of his learning problem. He is receiving too much negative feedback to emerge as a person with self-respect in that environment. The Tobins would do well to remove Gideon from Mrs. Mazur's classroom. Sometimes it is necessary for parents to be their child's advocate and find a more receptive school environment for him, particularly when he has special needs.

Gideon's story is not an isolated one. Parents and professionals should work together to see that the schools do more for learning-disabled students from entry to school through the college level. Assigning labels is not the answer. Schools should provide services for remediating as well as diagnosing learning disabilities. Until recently there has been much variation in the availability and extent of services in this area, but the present federal legislation for the handicapped carries with it provision for identification and appropriate education for the learning-disabled child in every community.

SPRINGBOARDS FOR INQUIRY

1. What would you do if you were a parent of a child like Gideon and your child was in a class with a teacher like Mrs. Mazur?

2. Select a standardized reading test and list all of its subtests. After each describe the aspect of reading it attempts to identify and give an example.

3. Read a chapter in a book describing learning disabilities, describe a problem in reading, handwriting, or spelling, and indicate the methods used for assessment and remediation of the problem. Two suggested books are Donald D. Hammill and Nettie R. Bartel, *Teaching Children With Learning and Behavior Problems* (Boston, Mass.: Allyn & Bacon, Inc., 1975) and Annabelle Most Markoff, *Teaching Low Achieving Children Reading, Spelling and Handwriting* (Springfield, Ill.: Charles C. Thomas, Publisher, 1976).

4. Write some of your thoughts about the following terms: learning disabilities, hyperactivity, distractibility, dyslexia, remedial reading, learning modalities, and perceptual-motor training.

CHAPTER FIVE

The Speech
and Language Impaired

Discussions of exceptionality that used to focus on a speech-hearing disability now include these under the rubric of language disorders.[1] M. F. Berry broadens the speech-hearing base and refers instead to children with disorders of verbal communication.[2] Schools still treat basic speech disorders, although the speech-language (bonding) relationship is recognized. Charles Van Riper's definition of a speech defect is the most widely recognized: "Speech is defective when it deviates so far from the speech of other people that it calls attention to itself, interferes with communication, or causes its possessor to be maladjusted."[3] Nearly 2.5 million children in the United States have speech problems. Some of these are typified by the letters Van Riper reprints in his text:

> I am a country school teacher in a two-room school. In my room there is a little boy in the third grade with a kind of funny voice. I mean he doesn't talk like other children.

[1]Frank Hewett, *Education of Exceptional Learners* (Boston, Mass.: Allyn & Bacon, Inc., 1974), p. 100. A particularly concise guide to the role of the classroom teacher in the amelioration of all speech impairments may be found in Phyllis P. Phillips, *Speech and Hearing Problems in the Classroom* (Lincoln, Neb.: Cliff Notes, Inc., 1975). For further techniques in treating articulatory disorders, see Harris Winitz, *From Syllable to Conversation* (Baltimore, Md.: University Park Press, 1975).

[2]M. F. Berry and Jon Eisenson, *Speech Disorders* (New York: Appleton-Century-Crofts, 1956).

[3]Charles Van Riper, *Speech Correction*, 4th ed., (Englewood Cliffs, N.J.: Prentice-Hall, Inc., 1963), p. 16.

I have an impediment or something in my mouth. Sometimes I talk all right but not always. I open my mouth and words won't come out right.[4]

Speech defects may be classified into a number of major categories:[5]

1. *Disorders of articulation* involve the unacceptable production of speech sounds.[6] Classroom teachers are aware of more articulatory speech problems than any other type. Phyllis P. Phillips contends that "articulation disorders make up three-fourths of all speech problems."[7] Disorders of articulation involve substitution, that is, the speaker accepts one sound for several. For example, a child using a "t" for the "k" sound may not really be substituting but interpreting the "k" as a "t" because of the similarities of the two sounds.

2. *Disorders of voice* include problems in vocal quality, vocal pitch, and vocal intensity. Many children who have extreme voice disorders also have articulatory problems. While the nature of the relationship is unclear, teachers working with articulatory-voice problems need to be aware of the frequency of linkage of the two problems. Samuel A. Kirk writes, "Instead of speaking of the *formation* of sounds, one is concerned with the *production* of sounds in the larynx, with the selective transmission of that sound . . . with the pitch level and intonation pattern . . . and with the loudness or softness of vocal production."[8]

3. *Stuttering* is a disorder of rhythm or fluency.[9] Yet dysfluency does not adequately describe stuttering. Van Riper states that "the stutterer shows breaks in the usual time sequence of utterance. These are conspicuous oscillations and fixations, repetitions and prolongations of sounds and syllables . . . one of the prime features of stuttering is that it seems to be more of a communicative disorder than one of speech. Most stutterers can sing without difficulty. . . . Most of them can speak perfectly when alone."[10]

[4]Ibid., pp. 14–15.
[5]Hewett, *Education of Exceptional Learners*, p. 100.
[6]Phillips, *Speech and Hearing Problems in the Classroom*, p. 45.
[7]Ibid.
[8]Samuel A. Kirk, *Educating Exceptional Children* (Boston, Mass.: Houghton Mifflin Company, 1972), p. 84.
[9]Hewett, *Education of Exceptional Learners*, p. 101. Also, Phillips lists fifteen "agreed on facts" about stuttering; see Phillips, *Speech and Hearing Problems in the Classroom*.
[10]Van Riper, *Speech Correction*, p. 23.

4. *Delayed speech development* refers to children who "have failed to acquire normal speech as a usable tool. They have been slow in speech mastery. Their 'tool speech' (the use of speech to fulfill the person's communicative needs) . . . is so deviant from normal standards that listeners often cannot understand [it]."[11]

5. *Cleft palate-associated defects* are due not to cerebral dysfunction but to "structural deficiencies caused by the failure of the bone and tissue of the palates to fuse during the first thirteen weeks of pregnancy."[12] The typical characteristics of cleft palate speech are hypernasality, nasal emission, and misarticulation.

For a child, a speech problem is essentially a communication problem. His connections to the world around him depend upon being understood and understanding the world. The school has become the place where communication disorders such as speech impairment are remediated. In a real sense the school focuses on one and all communication problems and provides specific help for children whose speech does not fulfill their need to be understood. Though specialists are increasingly assuming the role of those who intervene, even the general classroom teacher becomes an important adult in the life of the speech-impaired child.

Recent discussions of exceptionality in the area of learning have focused on the child's language processing. "Language is composed of numerous tasks involving several modes of reception and expression including the more complicated tasks of integration, storage and retrieval."[13] Disturbances in any of these task areas may result in dysfunction in reading, memory, and interpretation of ideas. A number of investigators are attempting to devise tests and remediation procedures that identify the specific area of disability.[14] The language disability is ordinarily in any one or more of three language areas. These are the areas of

---

[11]Ibid., p. 103.

[12]Kirk, *Educating Exceptional Children*, p. 93.

[13]Stanford Lamb, "The Illinois Test of Psycholinguistic Abilities: Implications for Diagnosis and Remediation," in *Learning Disabilities: Introduction to Educational and Medical Management*, ed. Lester Tarnopol (Springfield, Ill.: Charles C. Thomas, Publisher, 1969), p. 256.

[14]For information on tests, see Samuel A. Kirk, J. J. McCarthy, and Winifred D. Kirk, *The Illinois Test of Psycholinguistic Abilities, Revised* (Urbana, Ill.: University of Illinois Press, 1968); and Charles H. Lindamood and Patricia C. Lindamood, *Auditory Discrimination in Depth* (New York: Teaching Resources, 1969). For information on remediation procedures, see Hortense Barry, *The Young Aphasic Child: Evaluation and Training* (Washington, D.C.: Alexander Graham Bell Association for the Deaf, 1961); Lloyd M. Dunn, James O. Smith, and Kay Horton, *Peabody Language Development Kits, Levels 1, 2, 3, and P* (Circle Pines, Minn.:

receptive language, expressive language, and the intermediate processes that link the two. In other words, the visual-auditory input (receptive language) a child gets from his world needs to be assimilated, stored, and subject to retrieval at will in order for the learner to produce vocal or motor responses known as expressive language. A breakdown in any one or combination of these facets of language development is termed an aphasia.

Jon Eisenson, a leading authority in the field of childhood aphasia, views the child's auditory-perceptual abilities as the central factor underlying the impairment. He describes the developmentally aphasic child as "brain different" or "perceptually different" because he or she is unable "to organize sensory-auditory events (speech) even though 'received,' to hold the events in mind, and to scan them and compare them with others stored by the central nervous system."[15] These children for whom language is not intelligible obviously have concomitant difficulties in verbal expression that become evident between two and three years of age. According to Eisenson, the developmentally aphasic child's expressive difficulty is linked to his or her auditory perceptual disturbance, whereas the child with a purely expressive disability probably has oral apraxia, that is, a motor disturbance in which the child cannot control the articulators (tongue, lips, and so on). Children who are developmentally aphasic need a concentrated language program initiated in the preschool years, and public school programs for children with delayed speech usually accept children as young as three and one-half years old. In the past, the parents of a child whose language was delayed in developing were often advised to wait six months or a year for the child to start talking in sentences. This advice is not substantiated by recent research. Doris Johnson and Helmer Myklebust write, "In rare instances this might occur; however, experience indicates that prognosis for language development is better when proper training is begun early."[16]

Because language and thought are so closely related, children with a subtle disability in the area of language (particularly reception and association-assimilation of language) manifest learning problems in

---

American Guidance Services, 1965, 1966, 1967, 1968); Siegfried Engelmann and E. C. Bruner, *Distar Reading I and II: An Instructional System* (Chicago, Ill.: Science Research Associates, Inc., 1969); Samuel A. Kirk and Winifred D. Kirk, *Psycholinguistic Learning Disabilities: Diagnosis and Remediation* (Urbana, Ill.: University of Illinois Press, 1971); and Robert E. Valett, *The Remediation of Learning Disabilities* (Palo Alto, Calif.: Fearon, 1967).

[15]Jon Eisenson, *Aphasia In Children* (New York: Harper & Row Publishers, Inc., 1972), p. 30.

[16]Doris Johnson and Helmer Mykelbust, *Learning Disabilities: Educational Principles and Practices* (New York: Grune & Stratton, Inc., 1967), p. 85.

school. Teachers in the primary grades need to be alert to the child who does not participate in class discussions, whose remarks are not related to the topic under discussion, or who misinterprets assignments and directions. It is easy to mislabel this behavior as daydreaming or lack of motivation. School personnel such as the school psychologist and the speech and language specialist work together to use the many diagnostic techniques available to ascertain whether a learning problem is linked to a language disability.

The following are some of the tests frequently used to explore the child's language functioning in order to identify specific areas of disability:

Wechsler Intelligence Scale for Children, Revised.   A comparison of scores achieved in the verbal and performance sections of this test of intellectual functioning identifies depressed language functioning. The vocabulary test indicates word knowledge and facility in expressive language.[17]

Peabody Picture Vocabulary Test.   It assesses the child's receptive vocabulary. This nonverbal test requires that the child point to one of four pictures that best represents the definition for the word asked by the examiner.[18]

Wepman Test of Auditory Discrimination.   This test is used to determine auditory perceptual ability. The child is asked to indicate whether a pair of words spoken by the examiner are the same or different. Of the forty single-syllable word pairs, thirty differ by a single phoneme (speech sound), for example, bum-bun, while ten are identical, for example, ball-ball.[19]

Goldman-Fristoe Test of Articulation.   This test determines the child's ability to reproduce phonemes and blends in response to a series of pictures. Articulation is also studied as the child repeats two stories told to him by the examiner.[20]

Language Sampling Analysis and Training.   This is one of the few tests that examines a sampling of the child's natural speech in order to analyze the rules the child has acquired to

[17]David Wechsler, *Wechsler Intelligence Scale for Children, Revised* (New York: The Psychological Corporation, 1976).

[18]L. M. Dunn, *Peabody Picture Vocabulary Test* (Circle Pines, Minn.: American Guidance Service, 1959).

[19]J. M. Wepman, *Auditory Discrimination Test* (Chicago, Ill.: Science Research Associates, 1958).

[20]Goldman, R. Fristoe, M. *Goldman-Fristoe Test of Articulation* (Circle Pines, Minn.: American Guidance Service, 1969).

form sentences. The linguistic analysis assists the language teacher in determining the content for a teaching program for the language-handicapped child. Behavioral procedures are outlined to provide an effective and efficient teaching model.[21]

Illinois Test of Psycholinguistic Abilities (ITPA).   This test has received the most discussion in the field of learning disabilities because its twelve subtests provide a profile of assets and deficiencies of the individual child in both psychological and linguistic abilities considered basic to academic achievement. In addition to pinpointing intra-individual psycholinguistic differences in children, the test scores can be used as a guideline for remediation of deficiencies in any of the psycholinguistic processes tested.[22]

Because of the wide use of the ITPA, the following is an amplification of the subtests and the processes that the child is asked to demonstrate:

1. *Auditory reception* is the ability to understand auditory symbols such as verbal discourse. For example, the student responds yes or no to, "Do ponies shave?"
2. *Visual reception* is the ability to gain meaning from pictures of objects. For example, S is shown a picture of a can on one page and then is asked to point to another picture of a different type of can included with three picture "decoys" on another page.
3. *Auditory association* is the ability to relate concepts presented orally. For example, "Grass is green; sugar is _____."
4. *Visual association* is the ability to relate concepts presented visually. For example, S is asked to point to one of four pictures that goes with the central stimulus picture, such as the dog goes with the bone.
5. *Verbal expression* is the ability to elaborate on concepts. For example, S is shown an actual nail and is asked to tell the examiner all about it.
6. *Manual expression* is the ability to express ideas manually. For example, S is asked to demonstrate manually the use of a pictured hammer.

[21]Dorothy Tyack and Robert Gottsleben, *Language Sampling, Analysis and Training* (Palo Alto, Calif.: Consulting Psychologists Press, 1974).
[22]Kirk, McCarthy, and Kirk, *Illinois Test of Psycholinguistic Abilities*, Revised.

7. *Grammatical closure* is the ability to make use of the redundancies of oral language in acquiring automatic habits for handling syntax and grammatic inflections. For example, S is shown a plate with one bed pictured on one side and two on the other and is asked to complete the statement, "Here is a bed; here are two _____."

8. *Visual closure* is the ability to identify a common object from an incomplete visual presentation. For example, S is shown a picture of a busy construction scene and is asked to point to as many partially exposed hammers as possible in thirty seconds.

9. *Auditory sequential memory* is the ability to repeat digit series of increasing length when they are presented orally. For example, "Listen, say 3–7–4–2."

10. *Visual sequential memory* is the ability to reconstruct sequences of nonmeaningful figures from memory after a visual presentation of the series. For example, S is shown a picture of a series of geometric designs and is asked to reproduce them from memory in order, using plastic chips on which these same geometric designs have been imprinted.

The following two tests are supplementary:

11. *Auditory closure* is the ability to recognize words presented orally in units when one or more of the units is omitted. For example, S is to say "bottle" when he or she hears "bo/le."

12. *Sound blending* is the ability to blend sounds presented orally into whole words with and without picture clues. For example, S is to say "dog" when he or she hears the two speech sounds "d---og" presented orally with a pause between each.

Since its publication, the ITPA has received wide acceptance because it is an assessment technique that leads to a remedial program. Samuel A. and Winifred D. Kirk acknowledge that the test in itself cannot be the entire basis for building a language program. They make the following suggestions for sound language teaching practices:

1. Teachers should continue to test as they teach. Tests monitor a child's performance, and the teacher plans instructional alternatives as a result of observations.

2. Remedial programs should aim to stimulate low functioning areas. Attempts should even be made to remediate deficiencies that are highly resistant to amelioration.

3. Assets are important in the process of remediation. In many

situations a child can acquire knowledge through his or her stronger channel.

4. A multisensory approach provides an opportunity for children to gain information through their best modality. At times unisensory stimulation is essential; for example, if a child has difficulty in sound blending, remediation should be presented through the auditory channel without reliance on visually presented letters.

5. The most basic deficiency should be remediated first. If a child does not talk because he or she does not understand oral language, auditory reception should be the first area for remediation. In other words, a child should be taught to understand speech before expecting him or her to be able to converse.

6. Good teaching makes use of feedback. The child needs to monitor his or her own responses in order to recognize errors and correct them. A child can learn a list of words more efficiently if they are vocalized than if they are not.

7. In training a specific ability, it is preferable to utilize training that is usable. If a child has difficulty in visual-sequential ability as evidenced by poor spelling, it is better to learn to sequence letters in words than to sequence circles and squares.

8. Remedial programs should be started early before the child experiences repeated failure in school.

9. Remedial methods should be tailored for the individual child.[23]

Although they emerge from the field of language disabilities, the teaching model and instructional systems derived from such tests as the ITPA and Language Sampling Analysis and Training have applicability for *any* child who is having difficulty in learning. The field of special education gains from a fusion of ideas from various areas of specialization.

---

[23]The list of good teaching practices is adapted from Kirk and Kirk, *Psycholinguistic Learning Disabilities: Diagnosis and Remediation*, pp. 119–32; and Patricia L. Myers and Donald D. Hammill, *Methods for Learning Disorders* (New York: John Wiley & Sons, Inc., 1976), pp. 233–35.

A Walker in the City

by Alfred Kazin

All my early life lies open to my eye within five city blocks. When I passed the school, I went sick with all my old fear of it. With its standard New York public-school brown brick courtyard shut in on three sides of the square and the pretentious battlements overlooking that cockpit in which I can still smell the fiery sheen of the rubber ball, it looks like a factory over which has been imposed the façade of a castle. It gave me the shivers to stand up in that courtyard again; I felt as if I had been mustered back into the service of those Friday morning "tests" that were the terror of my childhood.

It was never learning I associated with that school: only the necessity to succeed, to get ahead of the others in the daily struggle to "make a good impression" on our teachers, who grimly, wearily, and often with ill-concealed distaste watched against our relapsing into the natural savagery they expected of Brownsville boys. The white, cool, thinly ruled record book sat over us from their desks all day long, and had remorselessly entered into it each day—in blue ink if we had passed, in red ink if we had not—our attendance, our conduct, our "effort," our merits and demerits; and to the last possible decimal point in calculation, our standing in an unending series of "tests"—surprise tests, daily tests, weekly tests, formal midterm tests, final tests. They never stopped trying to dig out of us whatever small morsel of fact we had managed to get down the night before. We had to prove that we were really alert, ready for anything, always in the race. That white thinly ruled record book figured in my mind as the judgment seat; the very thinness and remote blue lightness of its lines instantly showed its cold authority over me; so much space had been left on each page, columns and columns in which to note down everything about us, implacably and forever. As it lay there on a teacher's desk, I stared at it all day long with such fear and anxious propriety that I had no trouble believing that God, too, did nothing but keep such record books, and that on the final day He would face me with an account in Hebrew letters whose phonetic dots and dashes looked strangely like decimal points counting up my every sinful thought on earth.

All teachers were to be respected like gods, and God himself was the greatest of all school superintendents. Long after I had ceased to believe that our teachers could see with the back of their heads, it was still understood, by me, that they knew everything. They were the delegates of all visible and invisible power on earth—of the mothers who waited on the stoops every day after three for us to bring home tales of our daily triumphs; of the glacially remote Anglo-Saxon principal, whose very name was King; of the incalculably important Superintendent of

Schools who would someday rubberstamp his name to the bottom of our diplomas in grim acknowledgment that we had, at last, given satisfaction to him, to the Board of Superintendents, and to our benefactor the City of New York—and so up and up, to the government of the United States and to the great Lord Jehovah himself. My belief in teachers' unlimited wisdom and power rested not so much on what I saw in them—how impatient most of them looked, how wary—but on our abysmal humility, at least in those of us who were "good" boys, who proved by our ready compliance and "manners" that we wanted to get on. The road to a professional future would be shown us only as we pleased *them. Make a good impression the first day of the term, and they'll help you out. Make a bad impression, and you might as well cut your throat.* This was the first article of school folklore, whispered around the classroom the opening day of each term. You made the "good impression" by sitting firmly at your wooden desk, hands clasped; by silence for the greatest part of the live-long day; by standing up obsequiously when it was so expected of you; by sitting down noiselessly when you had answered a question; by "speaking nicely," which meant reproducing their painfully exact enunciation; by "showing manners," or an ecstatic submissiveness in all things; by outrageous flattery; by bringing little gifts at Christmas, on their birthdays, and at the end of the term—the well-known significance of these gifts being that they came not from us, but from our parents, whose eagerness in this matter showed a high level of social consideration, and thus raised our standing in turn.

It was not just our quickness and memory that were always being tested. Above all, in that word I could never hear without automatically seeing it raised before me in gold-plated letters, it was our *character*. I always felt anxious when I heard the word pronounced. Satisfactory as my "character" was, on the whole, except when I stayed too long in the playground reading; outrageously satisfactory, as I can see now, the very sound of the word as our teachers coldly gave it out from the end of their teeth, with a solemn weight on each dark syllable, immediately struck my heart cold with fear—they could not believe I really had it. Character was never something you had; it had to be trained in you, like a technique. I was never very clear about it. On our side *character* meant demonstrative obedience; but teachers already had it—how else could they have become teachers? They had it; the aloof Anglo-Saxon principal whom we remotely saw only on ceremonial occasions in the assembly was positively encased in it; it glittered off his bald head in spokes

of triumphant light; the President of the United States had the greatest conceivable amount of it. Character belonged to great adults. Yet we were constantly being driven onto it; it was the great threshold we had to cross. *Alfred Kazin, having shown proficiency in his course of studies and having displayed satisfactory marks of character* . . . Thus someday the hallowed diploma, passport to my further advancement in high school. But there—I could already feel it in my bones—they would put me through even more doubting tests of character; and after that, if I should be good enough and bright enough, there would be still more. *Character* was a bitter thing, racked with my endless striving to please. The school—from every last stone in the courtyard to the battlements frowning down at me from the walls—was only the stage for a trial. I felt that the very atmosphere of learning that surrounded us was fake—that every lesson, every book, every approving smile was only a pretext for the constant probing and watching of me, that there was not a secret in me that would not be decimally measured into that white record book. All week long I lived for the blessed sound of the dismissal gong at three o'clock on Friday afternoon.

I was awed by this system, I believed in it, I respected its force. The alternative was "going bad." The school was notoriously the toughest in our tough neighborhood, and the dangers of "going bad" were constantly impressed upon me at home and in school in dark whispers of the "reform school" and in examples of boys who had been picked up for petty thievery, rape, or flinging a heavy inkwell straight into a teacher's face. Behind any failure in school yawned the great abyss of a criminal career. Every refractory attitude doomed you with the sound "Sing Sing." Anything less than absolute perfection in school always suggested to my mind that I might fall out of the daily race, be kept back in the working class forever, or—dared I think of it?—fall into the criminal class itself.

I worked on a hairline between triumph and catastrophe. Why the odds should always have felt so narrow I understood only when I realized how little my parents thought of their own lives. It was not for myself alone that I was expected to shine, but for them—to redeem the constant anxiety of their existence. I was the first American child, their offering to the strange new God; I was to be the monument of their liberation from the shame of being—what they were. And that there was shame in this was a fact that everyone seemed to believe as a matter of course. It was in the gleeful discounting of themselves—what do we know?—with which our parents greeted every fresh victory in our savage competition for "high averages," for prizes, for a few condescending words of official praise from the principal at assembly. It was in the sickening invocation of "Americanism"—the word itself accusing us of everything we apparently were not. Our families and teachers seemed tacitly agreed that we were somehow to be a little ashamed of what we were. Yet it was always hard to say why this should be so. It was certainly not—in Brownsville!—because we were Jews, or simply because we spoke another language at home, or were absent on our holy days. It was rather that a "refined," "correct," "nice" English was required of us at school that we did not naturally speak, and that our teachers could never be quite sure we would keep. This English was peculiarly the ladders of advancement. Every future young lawyer was known by it. Even the Communists and Socialists on Pitkin Avenue spoke it. It was bright and clean and polished. We were expected to show it off like a new pair of shoes. When the teacher sharply called a question out, then your name, you were expected to leap up, face the class, and eject those new words fluently off the tongue.

There was my secret ordeal: I could never say anything except in the most roundabout way! I was a stammerer. Although I knew all those new words from my private reading—I read walking in the street, to and from the Children's Library on Stone Avenue; on the fire escape and the roof; at every meal when they would let me; read even when I dressed in the morning, propping my book up against the drawers of the bureau as I pulled on my long black stockings—I could never seem to get the easiest words out with the right dispatch, and would often miserably signal from my desk that I did not know the answer rather than get up to stumble and fall and crash on every word. If, angry at always being put down as lazy or stupid, I did get up to speak, the black wooden floor would roll away under my feet, the teacher would frown at me in amazement, and in unbearable loneliness I would hear behind me the groans and laughter: tuh-tuh-tuh-tuh.

The word was my agony. The word that for others was so effortless and so neutral, so unburdened, so simple, so exact, I had first to meditate in advance, to see if I could make it, like a plumber fitting together odd lengths and shapes of pipe. I was always preparing words I could speak, storing them away, choosing between them. And often, when the word did come from my mouth in its great and terrible birth, quailing and bleeding as if forced through a thornbush, I would not be able to look the others in the face, and would walk out in the silence, the infinitely echoing silence behind my back, to say it all cleanly back to myself as I walked

in the streets. Only when I was alone in the open air, pacing the roof with pebbles in my mouth, as I had read Demosthenes had done to cure himself of stammering; or in the street, where all words seemed to flow from the length of my stride and the color of the houses as I remembered the perfect tranquillity of a phrase in Beethoven's "Romance in F" I could sing back to myself as I walked—only then was it possible for me to speak without the infinite premeditations and strangled silences I toiled through whenever I got up at school to respond with the expected, the exact answer.

It troubled me that I could speak in the fullness of my own voice only when I was alone on the streets, walking about. There was something unnatural about it; unbearably isolated. I was not like the others! I was not like the others! At midday, every freshly shocking Monday noon, they sent me away to a speech clinic in a school in East New York, where I sat in a circle of lispers and cleft palates and foreign accents holding a mirror before my lips and rolling difficult sounds over and over. To be sent there in the full light of the opening week, when everyone else was at school or going about his business, made me feel as if I had been expelled from the great normal body of humanity. I would gobble down my lunch on my way to the speech clinic and rush back to the school in time to make up for the classes I had lost. One day, one unforgettable dread day, I stopped to catch my breath on a corner of Sutter Avenue, near the wholesale fruit markets, where an old drugstore rose up over a great flight of steps. In the window were dusty urns of colored water floating off iron chains; cardboard placards advertising hairnets, Ex-Lax; a great illustrated medical chart headed THE HUMAN FACTORY, which showed the exact course a mouthful of food follows as it falls from chamber to chamber of the body. I hadn't meant to stop there at all, only to catch my breath; but I so hated the speech clinic that I thought I would delay my arrival for a few minutes by eating my lunch on the steps. When I took the sandwich out of my bag, two bitterly hard pieces of hard salami slipped out of my hand and fell through a grate onto a hill of dust below the steps. I remember how sickeningly vivid an odd thread of hair looked on the salami, as if my lunch were turning stiff with death. The factory whistles called their short, sharp blasts stark through the middle of noon, beating at me where I sat outside the city's magnetic circle. I had never known, I knew instantly I would never in my heart again submit to, such wild passive despair as I felt at that moment, sitting on the steps before THE HUMAN FACTORY, where little robots gathered and shoveled the food from chamber to chamber of the body. They had put me out into the streets, I thought to myself; with their mirrors and their everlasting pulling at me to imitate their effortless bright speech and their stupefaction that a boy could stammer and stumble on every other English word he carried in his head, they had put me out into the streets, had left me high and dry on the steps of that drugstore staring at the remains of my lunch turning black and grimy in the dust.

DISCUSSION

The preceding selection is an excerpt from Alfred Kazin's autobiographical novel about growing up in Brooklyn, New York, just before and during the depression. The author's memories of his early school years are filled with fear, dread, and humiliation. The large brick school building is an impersonal institution. His life in school is characterized by endless striving to please and to conform to the unfamiliar Anglo-Saxon standard that the teachers and principal represent. Kazin is a serious and sensitive child who is painfully aware of his parents' immigrant status. Early in life he realizes that there is a relationship between speaking refined, "correct" English and success and stability in the new culture. Through parental pressure and self-induced anxiety about his "foreign" ways, Kazin is driven to liberate himself from the stigma of not being sufficiently "American." His striving meets catastrophe because he stutters; the fluency he values so dearly is not his.

The cause of stuttering still has not been identified, but psychological factors are one consideration. Certainly Kazin's identification of well-spoken English as the key to his future success makes spoken language a logical target for his stress. In retrospect, Kazin's impression of his early years was the oppressive need to achieve in order to please authority figures—at home and at school. His stress seems unrelieved either from wholesome relationships with peers or from a friendly relationship with an adult outside of his household.

Kazin describes the ordeal of the young stutterer in school. He was considered lazy and stupid because he never volunteered to answer in class. When he finally stood up to speak, he involuntarily repeated the small word he could not get past. Knowledge that the other children were laughing at him added to his distress. Kazin's discomfort is not surprising. By the middle grades, any very pronounced problem in oral communication is embarrassing for a child. When children become angry, they are quick to use any disability as a means of hurting each other. The author felt alone and different because of his speech disability. When he must leave school every Monday at noon, he felt "expelled from the great normal body of humanity." It is doubtful that Kazin was helped by the clinic because the psychological factors surrounding his attendance were so negative. Also, he was seen in a group of children, each of whom had a different speech problem.

Kazin's experience took place in the 1920s. Today, schools and clinics are much more concerned with the emotional factors involved in a program of speech and language therapy. In many school districts therapy is done by an itinerant teacher so that children need not leave school grounds. Parents and children are more involved in the process of decision making regarding time and place for evaluation and therapy. There are increasing numbers of programs being initiated, particularly in the areas of assisting children in the reception, expression, and understanding of language. The job being done in both identification and remediation of these problems is constantly improving.

SPRINGBOARDS FOR INQUIRY

1. Was Kazin's response to his handicap realistic, or do you think he had other problems?

2. What would you do if you had a student in your class who stuttered badly?

3. Choose a speech or language problem and write a paragraph about methods used today to remediate the disability. Refer to a textbook in the footnotes in this chapter.

4. What are the advantages and disadvantages of using outside agencies, such as a speech clinic, as a support system for the schools?

5. Which agency or agencies in your geographical area conduct language and speech evaluations and therapy?

6. Look up the word aphasic. Role play a discussion between a teacher and a language therapist regarding a boy the teacher thinks may be aphasic. Give the child's age and describe the classroom behavior that leads the teacher to believe the child has a language disability.

CHAPTER SIX

The Orthopedically Handicapped and the Multiply Handicapped

"What is this darkness like?" asks Louis Michaux, a victim of cerebral palsy. His reference is to the darkness of being physically handicapped. Michaux reflects upon a lifetime of being handicapped and is particularly concerned because "the stings of the darkness are accentuated by the fact that there are many people who relegate [the] main role [of the handicapped] in life to being mere spectators, never entering into life's mainstream, and there are the stares and the rejections."[1] Those who study somatopsychology (body image concept) consider the "stings of darkness" to be part of the orthopedically handicapped person's body image concept. There are two aspects of this concept: "the individual's ideal (desired) body image and the actual body image." Although this body image concept may be a simplistic conceptualization, it does "portray the crux of psychological adjustment to disability."[2]

The greater the resemblance between the two images (desired and actual body image), the better the psychological adjustment of the person. The usual defense mechanisms associated with all exceptionality that calls attention to itself are used by the orthopedically handicapped person facing his or her personal and exterior worlds. When

---

[1]Louis Michaux, *The Physically Handicapped and the Community* (Springfield, Ill.: Charles C. Thomas, Publisher, 1970), p. 11.
[2]Richard E. Hardy and John G. Cull, *Mental Retardation and Physical Disability* (Springfield, Ill.; Charles C. Thomas, Publisher, 1974), p. 6.

reality is harsh, it is often unacceptable. Thus it is necessary to defend one's self unconsciously (if conscious, the defenses would be ineffective) against pain and suffering. Students of special education, especially those who are preparing to teach and counsel the orthopedically handicapped, need to be aware of these readily identifiable mechanisms:[3]

> *Denial.*   Immediately after the onset of a disability, the individual frequently rejects the fact of disability by denying it.[4] After the existence of the incapacity can no longer be denied, this is often continued by substituting denial of the permanency of the disability.
>
> *Withdrawal.*   When a patient wishes to reduce interaction with others in which he or she is continually forced to face the disability, the individual reduces his or her tension by moving away from interpersonal reactions.
>
> *Regression.*   This is a defense mechanism that occurs after withdrawal and after the person's handicap becomes evident to him or her. The individual reacts more consciously to the stress of being handicapped by returning to an earlier prehandicapped stage of life. The person may adopt the speech, dress, and mannerisms appropriate to the age level to which he or she is regressing; the individual may model his or her behavior to conform with younger people of the present; or the person may return to a behavior pattern that was once part of his or her own life.
>
> *Repression.*   Repression means forgetting events leading to the disability. If a person's attitudes toward the disability are very negative, he or she must repress them in order to further his or her psychological adjustment.
>
> *Reaction Formation.*   When a person's attitude toward his or her handicap creates exceptional guilt, tension, or anxiety, he or she unconsciously adopts behavior typical of the opposite attitude. Thus, a paraplegic may choose to participate

---

[3]Adapted from Hardy and Cull, *Mental Retardation and Physical Disability*.

[4]The film *The Other Side of the Mountain* in which Olympic skiing candidate Jill Kinmont crashes on skis and becomes a quadraplegic demonstrates this denial vividly. In one of the most striking scenes in the film, a friend who is a polio victim observes the denial by Kinmont and turns to her and says, "You mean the accident that ended your skiing career, don't you?" This was her way of forcing Jill to face her quadraplegia more realistically.

in activities atypical of, and even dangerous to, his or her condition. The excessive behavior characterizes reaction formation.[5]

Fantasy.   As a person starts to adjust to a new body image and a new role in life, he or she may daydream and fantasize. This is an attempt to try out a variety of life-roles.

Rationalization.   A paraplegic patient once rationalized the advantages of his disability by saying that since many of his family died from coronaries because of overactivity, he was spared this fate by an incapacity that severely curtailed his active life. A *rationalization* is generally an explanation that is more acceptable to the person than the actual truth, although a rationalization is in itself not a lie.

Projection.   Many of the feelings of a disabled person are unacceptable to him or her. The individual feels inferior and lacks a sense of self-respect, but he or she would prefer to blame others for these feelings. In order to survive this personal pain, the individual projects these feelings onto society in general: "they" feel he or she is not capable; "they" think he or she is inferior.

Identification.   In order to adjust to a disability, a person makes a very strong identification with a larger group, such as a veterans' group or a handicapped persons' organization. Identification is a healthy type of adjustment because it does away with the need to deny, withdraw, and regress.

Compensation.   To reduce self-criticism, a handicapped person turns to whatever activities bring success. When the individual identifies and compensates, he or she is well on the way to adjusting to a new body image and a new role in life.

---

[5]Though these defense mechanisms spring from Freudian psychology, behaviorally oriented practitioners need not be skeptical of using them since they fit the behavioral model, that is, they produce behavior that is clearly observable. In and of itself none of these defenses is bad. The therapy implied by these mechanisms is helping patients to observe their behavior and to keep in touch with their environment by slowly coming to grips with their defenses so that they may evaluate their behavior. The ultimate aim of any therapy is to assist the handicapped to behave interdependently with the environment rather than independently of it. Further resolution of the medical as opposed to the psychological model may be found in James M. Kauffman and Daniel P. Hallahan, "The Medical Model and the Science of Special Education," *Exceptional Children*, vol. 41, no. 2 (October 1974), 91–102.

The child who is orthopedically handicapped is morally and now legally due an education.[6] (See John A. Downey and Niels L. Low's book for a complete definition of what constitutes an orthopedic handicap. They list seventeen categories of disability.[7]) Instructional programs for children who are handicapped are urgent. Frances P. Conner outlines the steps necessary to the clarification of the educational problems for each child:

1. a basic screening test inventory
2. analysis of test results
3. a task analysis curriculum and evaluation
4. diagnostic or prescriptive teaching[8]

Before going into the specific details of these steps, Conner's warning should be noted:

> In educational planning, these children have the same basic requirements all other children have. As a result of their disabilities, they have additional needs. . . . Since education must be part of the child's total program, it requires intensive integration to help him develop intellectually, socially and emotionally as well as physically.[9]

In the basic screening approach, the teacher samples the child's function in specific areas. Such things as the child's listening vocabulary, nonverbal intelligence, gross motor ability, speech production, hearing, auditory memory, visual functioning, and discrimination need to be recorded. Achievement tests plus the assessments just noted are prerequisites for the planned educational intervention for each child. When the results of the screening battery are carefully and critically shared with the teacher, there should be enough cues available so that a program plan for each exceptional child can be designed. Thus it becomes possible to define learning objectives with almost pinpoint accuracy. A

---

[6]The provisions of the Education for All Handicapped Children Act (November 1975) were called by the *New York Times* the "quiet revolution" (Sunday, April 25, 1976).

[7]John A. Downey and Niels L. Low, eds., *The Child with Disabling Illness: Principles of Rehabilitation* (Philadelphia, Pa.: W. B. Saunders Company, 1974).

[8]Frances P. Conner, "Education for the Handicapped Child," in *The Child with Disabling Illness*, Downey and Low, p. 582.

[9]Frances P. Conner, "The Education of Crippled Children," in *Education of Exceptional Children and Youth*, ed. William M. Cruikshank and G. Orville Johnson (Englewood Cliffs, N.J.: Prentice-Hall, Inc., 1967), pp. 446–47. Sleep-in summer camps are one way of providing for these additional needs; see Susan S. Dibna and Andrew S. Dibna, *Integration or Segregation for the Physically Handicapped Child?* (Springfield, Ill.: Charles C. Thomas, Publisher, 1973), chapter 8.

profile of the step-by-step school tasks to be performed by each child in his educational program is then laid out. These tasks need to be clearly written, the child's previous knowledge carefully noted, and the specific activities within the child's range of ability duly outlined. Once accomplished, it is virtually impossible for teachers to start their instruction at any level beyond the child's ability. For example, if a child needs to "clarify his body image, to improve spatial organization, and to establish laterality and directionality, very specific school activities can be designed and prescribed to upgrade function."[10]

Abraham J. Tannenbaum offers some sound advice relative to the development of specific strategies of instruction for each handicapped child. These principles follow:

1. Teachers should respond to the behavior of individual children, developing lessons that capitalize on their strengths and interests, rather than have a preconceived program for children with a diagnosed learning disability.
2. The teacher should know that understanding the child is not synonymous with understanding how to teach him or her.
3. The teacher must engage the child's attention before instruction can proceed.
4. The teacher, aware that each learner has a favorite receptive style, must ascertain the most comfortable and receptive stimuli for future instruction for that learner.
5. The teacher's instructional role should be to achieve a good match between the pupil's functional capacity and preferred learning style and the organization of content and strategy. This match is individualized instruction.[11]

The ultimate goal, however, is to move the pupil from individualized to personalized instruction. Individualization implies the identification of the best mode of understanding between the teacher and the pupil, while personalization involves the improvement of understanding in an increasing number of ways. This new taxonomic approach takes into

---

[10]Conner, "Education for the Handicapped Child," in The Child with Disabling Illness, Downey and Low, p. 585. Ogden Lindsley's concept of precision teaching described in numerous articles in the late 1960s and the 1970s is of particular relevance here; see especially the spring 1971 issue of Teaching Exceptional Children.

[11]Abraham J. Tannenbaum, "The Taxonomic Instruction Project: A Manual of Principles and Practices Pertaining to the Content of Instruction" (report to the United States Office of Education, 1969, revised 1973).

account the teacher's function in organizing content, in transmitting instructional stimuli through any of the pupil's receptive sensory modalities, in eliciting responsiveness through any of the pupil's expressive channels of communication, and in mastering the total range of instructional modes (styles) and methods (pupil grouping arrangements) available.

Physically handicapped children experience the same needs for recognition, security, and self-esteem that normal children do. Physically disabled children more frequently exhibit behavior that would be considered maladjusted if it were exhibited by physically nonhandicapped children. It needs to be understood, however, that "at best 'to have something wrong'—the very expression, so commonly used—implies some guilt or blame."[12] The growing awareness of being different casts a heavy burden upon children who are fully aware of their differences. Gerald Caplan reports that "where a thousand new children a year attend for physical handicaps . . . all . . . have some form of emotional complications, and many . . . have explicit psychiatric symptomatology."[13]

The orthopedically handicapped child may need few, if any, special materials to aid in learning. This contrasts with usual needs of the multiply handicapped. "We are only now [1971] beginning to discover the multiply handicapped child; although he has been with us for a long time, we have not recognized his existence. We have become accustomed to think in terms of the blind child, the crippled child, the cerebral palsied child, the deaf child."[14] While children may be labeled as having one handicap, a careful study of the child uncovers an array of disabilities, multiple handicaps that are not easily subsumed under one simple rubric. Mia K. Pringle writes, "it is comparatively rare now to find a child with a single handicapping condition. This is partly due to greater diagnostic skill and awareness; also to greater recognition of the importance of emotional factors; and partly to advances in medical knowledge."[15]

A discussion of the multiply handicapped must confront the issue of labeling and classification. As parents attempt to adjust to the initial diagnosis of their child's condition, professionals often add addi-

---

[12]Joan K. McMichael, *Handicap* (Pittsburgh, Pa.: University of Pittsburgh Press, 1971), p. 76.

[13]Gerald Caplan, *An Approach to Community Mental Health* (London: Tavistock Publishing, 1961), as quoted in McMichael, *Handicap*, p. 79.

[14]Regina Schattner, *An Early Childhood Curriculum for Multiply Handicapped Children* (New York: The John Day Company, Inc., 1971), p. 17.

[15]As quoted in Stanley Segal, *No Child is Uneducable* (Oxford: Permagon Press, 1974), p. 343.

tional labels to describe the child's handicap. Table 6–1 reproduces the results of a questionnaire sent to parents of 500 multiply handicapped children, asking them to indicate the label or labels given their child: "only 215 of them received only one label, 130 had received two labels, 86 had received three and 64 had received four or more . . . some had received as many as six."[16] Multiple labels may create concern and confusion for parents. Professionals, however, find single labels are often inaccurate and oversimplistic. A child with one label, both legally and educationally, will be the recipient of only those services relevant to the label, despite the fact that other behaviors indicate the importance of multiple types of services. Kathryn A. Gorham and her collaborators conclude that "the label oversimplifies a complex and unique child. . . . even worse, the label can consign him to a track . . . or a teacher who expects little from 'such children'. . . . for these young people labels are tickets to storage rooms."[17]

Services are almost nonexistent for the multiply handicapped child, such as the deaf-blind, deaf-retarded, cerebral palsied–deaf or blind, and the blind-retarded, despite the fact that they are recipients of more than one label. Because of their combined disabilities, these multiply handicapped children are usually considered severely and profoundly retarded and are frequently placed in state residential institutions. Burton Blatt and his colleagues cite the exclusionary language traditionally used by public school systems to reject a multiply handicapped child:

> This child is an exceptional child among exceptional children. She just doesn't fit any category of student in our schools.
>
> Your child is too severely disabled.
>
> We need at least ten of them with the same disability before we can set up a specialized program.
>
> We do not have a program at that level.[18]

These same authors are in the forefront of the movement to close large residential institutions and to provide services for all handicapped individuals in the community. They advocate a range of community residences offering long- and short-term facilities and a variety of educa-

---

[16]Kathryn A. Gorham et al., "Effects on Parents," in *Issues in the Classification of Children: A Sourcebook on Categories, Labels, and Their Consequences* (San Francisco, Calif.: Jossey-Bass, Inc., Publishers, 1975), vol. II, p. 160.

[17]Ibid., p. 169.

[18]Burton Blatt et al., "From Institution to Community: A Conversion Model," *Educational Programming for the Severely and Profoundly Handicapped*, ed. Ed Sontag (Reston, Va.: The Division on Mental Retardation, The Council for Exceptional Children, 1977), p. 45.

Table 6–1.
Children Receiving Two or More Labels

Label considered "most accurate" by parents, and number of children with this label	Other labels received by children																	
	Normal, will outgrow	Autistic	Aphasic	Brain-damaged, minimal brain dysfunction, neurologically impaired	Perceptually handicapped	Hyperactive	Learning-disabled	Emotionally disturbed, mentally ill	Childhood schizophrenia	Mentally retarded	Cerebral palsy	Spastic	Epileptic	Deaf, hearing-impaired	Multiply handicapped	Slow learner	Dull	Vegetable
Autistic (30)	4	—	3	10	0	5	1	13	4	26	1	1	0	5	1	1	0	0
Brain-damaged, minimal brain dysfunction, neurologically impaired (76)	23	8	3	—	5	16	6	17	4	34	5	1	9	3	1	9	2	2
Cerebral palsy (13)	2	0	1	3	0	1	2	1	0	8	—	0	3	1	2	0	0	0
Deaf, hearing impaired (11)	3	1	3	1	0	0	2	1	0	3	0	0	0	—	0	1	0	0
Aphasic (6)	1	3	—	4	0	0	1	1	0	2	0	0	0	1	0	1	0	0
Emotionally disturbed, mentally ill (10)	1	4	0	3	1	2	1	—	3	3	0	0	0	0	1	0	0	0
Learning-disabled (63)	16	3	1	31	8	14	—	17	1	14	1	0	2	2	0	13	0	0
Mentally retarded (48)	7	6	2	22	2	3	1	3	0	—	11	0	4	2	0	8	0	2
Slow learner (9)	3	1	0	2	0	0	2	0	0	5	0	0	0	1	0	—	0	0
Multiply handicapped (5)	0	0	0	5	0	1	0	2	0	4	3	0	2	1	—	0	0	0
TOTALS (280)	60	26	13	81	16	42	16	55	12	99	21	2	20	16	5	33	2	4

TOTAL NUMBER OF LABELS = 803

Source: Nicholas Hobbs, ed., *Issues in the Classification of Children: A Sourcebook on Categories, Labels, and Their Consequences* (San Francisco, Calif.: Jossey-Bass, Inc., Publishers, 1975), vol. II, p. 161. Reprinted by permission of the publisher.

tional programs based on the needs of children with particular disabilities.

There is new concern in the field of special education for providing education within the public school system for the severely and profoundly handicapped. Previously there was no dispute that the institution was the appropriate setting for the severely handicapped. The financial and philosophic investment in institutions made the consideration of a community-based alternative unthinkable. In the late 1970s, however, institutionalization versus community services is a controversial issue. In the winter of 1975, the *Journal of Special Education* announced, "It is with pleasure that we introduce a new series which will provide current information regarding the severely and profoundly handicapped, one of the most critical areas in special education."[19]

The quest for appropriate education for this extremely heterogeneous group has been a catalyst for restructuring ideas regarding special education. Floyd McDowell and Ed Sontag take issue with the prevailing system of using IQ scores and specific behavioral characteristics as the basis for defining special education categories:

> For example, the severely handicapped may be "defined" as having IQ's between 20 and 35, and as being characterized by self-stimulation, self-mutilation, aggression toward others, severe sensory or physical defects, poor communication skills, and so on, while profoundly handicapped may be described as having IQ's of less than 20, and having only a few reflexes, extreme feeding problems, inability to sit in an erect position, numerous associated physical disorders, and the like. Because such definitions lack relevance for educational programming, and because they are conducive to false negatives and false positives when placement occurs, our intellectual and practical struggle with them is now leading to the questioning of static definitions in all areas of special education.[20]

Ed Sontag, Judy Smith, and Wayne Sailor describe a plan for special education that would create three instructional areas: early childhood education, general special education, and severely handicapped education.[21] Early childhood education would provide for children in the preschool years who enter the school system at the age of three. Children, regardless of handicap, who require instruction in basic

[19]Norris G. Haring, "Educational Services for the Severely and Profoundly Handicapped", *Journal of Special Education,* vol. 9, no. 4 (1975), 425.

[20]Floyd E. McDowell and Ed Sontag, "The Severely and Profoundly Handicapped as Catalysts for Change," in *Educational Programming for the Severely and Profoundly Handicapped,* Sontag, p. 3.

[21]Ed Sontag, Judy Smith, and Wayne Sailor, "The Severely/Profoundly Handicapped: Who Are They? Where Are We?" *The Journal of Special Education,* vol. 11, no. 1 (January 1977), 5–11.

skills (self-help, motor, perceptual, social, and communication skill development) would be placed in a program for the severely handicapped; those requiring academic instruction would enter a program of general special education. The goal would be to move students gradually from severely handicapped education to general special education and then into the mainstream of regular education. Teachers would teach in the areas in which they have specific competencies, for example, in basic self help, in severely handicapped education, or in preacademic or academic instruction (general special education). In this way delivery of service would be a need-centered model rather than one based on categories of disability.

Special educators who advocate community-based education acknowledge the monumental task of working within the mainstream of education to raise the potential of severely and profoundly and multi-handicapped children. To help meet the needs of these children, paraprofessionals will need to be trained to keep an optimum ratio of adult to child of approximately one to three. Fuller use must be made of resource personnel such as occupational, physical, and speech therapists. Specialists trained in deafness, blindness and other specialty areas will also be needed to enhance the educational program. In the short time that recognition of the needs of the multiply handicapped and the severely and profoundly handicapped have been recognized, a small and devoted group within special education has made observable progress. Much more needs to be done.

Little Baseball World

by Robert Lowry

Helen turned it on very low so that nobody else in the house would know she was listening (she'd sworn before them all never to listen again, because they'd kidded her about it), and then as soon as she heard the score she turned it off and sat staring at the back yard.

The score was five to two in favor of the Cubs and it was only the last half of the third inning with the Reds at bat—who was batting? Lombardi? Lombardi was a good hitter, you couldn't tell what they were going to do now. Of course the Reds would lose eventually, they always lost, they were so dumb, they did so many dumb things just when they got you all excited about how good they were, then somebody did something so dumb you wanted to throw the radio out of the window. Who was batting anyhow? She turned on the radio again, very softly, and listened, leaning forward in her rocker.

"Lombardi on second, Harry Craft at bat with one ball and two strikes ———" Lombardi on second! She leaned forward to listen.

They were so dumb though, they'd never do anything right, they'd lose this one too. "All right," said the announcer. "Bill Lee is ready ———". And the black-eyed buxom girl rocked back and forth in the rocker before the radio; she was ready too, it was evident; she was waiting for whatever was sure to come. She just had no faith at all in the Reds any more, they lost yesterday and they'd lose today, they weren't going to be leading the

League for much longer. . . . Like what happened yesterday, they were winning until the first of the ninth, then that dumb Johnny Vander Meer let the bases get full by walking so many, and Hartnett came in to pinch-hit and made a home run, and that was the end of your old ball game. That was the way they always did—got you all worked up then betrayed you.

". . . hits a long fly ball into right field—and he's *out!*"

"Oh my God," Helen said, and snapped the radio off.

She went to the kitchen, got herself a glass of water, and came back into the dining room. She sat stiffly in her rocker, staring out at the back yard. She wouldn't turn it on for ten minutes, then she'd see what happened. Not that she expected anything good to happen.

But all the radios up and down Gorker Street were blaring forth the game, and before three minutes were up she couldn't resist, she turned it on very low.

"—— and the Reds are out in front again! Now let me turn you over to Dick Bray who has a few words to say about the Breakfast of Champions . . ."

She'd missed the best part—the score and everything. That silly Dick Bray was talking away in his tenor voice about Wheaties, the Breakfast of Champions—he wouldn't tell it.

"Shut up about your Wheaties and tell us the score," she said out loud. "We know all about your Wheaties, just shut up and tell us something we want to know."

But no, he never would. Finally Red Barber came on to announce the first half of the fourth, and she found out the Reds were leading to six to five.

Well, that was better than nothing—she rocked away in her rocker. They'd lose it anyhow, though. They always did something good, then went ahead and lost it anyhow. They didn't care how hard you rooted.

She'd certainly done her part—been here by radio since the opening game in spring, shouting at the announcer, getting angry when the Reds fumbled, furious when the Giants or Cards or Phillies made a run. Anyhow the Reds were leading the League, even if they wouldn't win the pennant. It was the last of July, everybody else on that street was sure they were going to be champions and play in the World Series, but she laughed at that, you never could depend on them just when you thought they were so good. That was when they always lost.

"Well, the Reds are out in front now with that one-run margin," Red Barber said, "but don't forget we still have six-long-innings to go and ——"

"Six long innings is true," Helen said right back. "And don't kid yourself that plenty can't happen between now and then."

She knew enough about it,

this was her second year listening and they'd made plenty of mistakes in that time. Of course she *wanted* them to win—stayed tuned in even on Sundays when the club officials wouldn't let the game be broadcast because it hurt attendance. She read the *Ladies' Home Journal* or *Liberty* in front of the radio then and waited for the pause in the recorded music when Red Barber gave the runs, hits, and errors at the end of each half-inning.

Seven days out of the week she was here, but she didn't care. People could just leave her alone to sit here, they could mind their own business. Her mother never told her to go out and get a job or anything, but she knew that was what they were all thinking she should do, and she didn't care. Her brother Tom would make some remark to her, and she'd tell him off. Just let me alone, just go away and never speak to me.

She didn't care if she *never* went out of the house again. She almost never did either, except to go downtown to the library. She hated clothes, she hated getting all dressed up. She felt so conspicuous on the streetcar. Wearing those silly gloves.

They didn't understand, nobody else had anything wrong with them. They didn't have to wear silly gloves when they went out. Tom thought he was smart and could do anything he wanted, go anywhere he wanted. He was a boy seventeen, two years younger than she was—she'd wanted a sister anyhow.

Well, yesterday she'd told her mother off, all right. Her mother had said, "Why don't you ever go out any more? Why don't you and some of your girl friends go to the movies? She'd told her mother then. "Because of my hand, that's why. Because I'm crippled," she'd said right out. Her mother had begun crying and Helen hadn't even felt sorry. "Now you know, so just stop crying. I'm not ever going anywhere again, so just don't bother me. I'm not ever going to go out and get all dressed up and wear those silly gloves again."

They could all just leave her alone, she was perfectly happy. She was glad she was all through with high school—glad she had no friends—glad she didn't have anything to do but listen to the baseball game—glad she was crippled. If anybody didn't like it they could just not look at her, that was all. She knew she was ugly and they could just all stay away.

Baseball was more interesting anyhow. She'd never seen a game but that didn't matter, she didn't want to. She knew all the players, she read the papers and listened to all the sports broadcasts and she liked the players better than any people she knew. Paul Derringer was the best of them—he was tall and slender and always going out to the night clubs so sometimes he couldn't play the next day. She liked little Eddie Joost too—he was like a grade-school boy, always doing something crazy like fumbling the ball when it was an easy play. Ernie Lombardi supported a lot of his relatives out in California and she felt he played awfully serious—not like Frank McCormick who was good-looking and so sure of himself.

Her mother asked once how could she know what a ball game looked like if she'd never seen one, and she'd got mad and told her mother she didn't *want* to know. But she knew all right— she could picture Harry Craft "shifting his chaw of tobacco from the left side of his mouth to the right and stepping up to the plate" or Whitey Moore "pounding his fist in the palm of his glove and glancing over at first." Red Barber was a really good announcer, he could say funny things about the players and make it all humorous. Of course he made a lot of mistakes too, sometimes got so excited he forgot what he was saying and you had to wait till he calmed down to find out if it was a hit or an out.

Well, here we go into the first of the ninth, she thought. Cubs at bat. The Reds better watch out with their old one-run lead— they usually were leading up to the last inning and then threw the game away by making errors. Who was batting anyhow?

"Quit talking about last inning and tell us who's batting,"

she said to Red Barber, and he answered by saying: "Whambo! It's a *hard* bouncing ball to Joost at third—and Joost *fumbles!* He picks up the ball and makes the throw to first—but too late!—and Wilson is tucked away there safely with ———"

"Did you do those dishes?"

She turned scarlet and whirled around on her mother standing in the doorway. "Let me alone!" Helen shouted. "Can't you see I'm listening?"

"If you're not going to do them *I* will," her mother said. "They've been around here all afternoon and I'm sick of seeing them."

Her face was toward her mother but her plump body was bent eagerly toward the radio.

"Just tell me," her mother began again, but Helen really turned on her then: "Now you made me miss who was next at bat! Don't bother me! I'll do them! Just let me alone now!"

It was a long fly ball—that dumb Craft would never catch it—going back, back, the sun in his eyes—oh, he caught it! She looked around then, and her mother was gone.

The rest of the inning was nothing, a ground ball and a strikeout, so the Reds won and they were lucky they did. She turned the radio off and rocked away. She had to admit that she *wanted* them to win even if she didn't really believe in them— days they won she felt so good.

Her brother came into the room from outside. "What'd they do today, lose?"

She felt her hand clench. "Well, they almost did but they didn't," she said. "It was a crazy game—the Cubs got five runs in the third inning, then the Reds got three more runs and it was six to five. So the Cubs couldn't do anything till the first of the ninth and Wilson got on first—that crazy Eddie Joost had a ground ball and he fumbled it. The next batter up hit a long fly and I thought Craft would never catch it; he had to go all the way back to the stands. So they won all right—but I bet they're still shaking in their boots!"

"That's all right," Tom said, "just so they won. It won't be long till they have the pennant clinched, if they just keep winning."

"Well, they better do better than they're doing if they're going to beat out St. Louis," Helen said. "All the fumbles they've been making. Wait'll the series next week when they meet the Cards. Johnny Mize made two home runs yesterday."

"That don't mean anything," Tom said. "How about Lombardi yesterday? He made a home run and a double."

"Yes, he has to hit a home run or not get anything, he's so slow! Red Barber said that double yesterday would have been a triple if Bill Werber or Craft had hit it. The other team makes fumbles and everything and they still get old Lombardi out."

"How about Goodman?" Tom asked. "He made a triple yesterday."

"Goodman!" she shouted. "Don't talk to me about Goodman! Today when he came up to the plate in the first inning the crowd was clapping and everything because of that triple, and all he did was just stand there while Bill Lee whizzed three of them over, and he went back to sit down. The crowd was so stunned it didn't know what to say. All Red Barber said was, 'Well, that's the way it goes' —Red Barber says such dumb things sometimes."

She was feeling all warmed up, the way she always did whenever she talked about baseball. Her brother was the only one in the family who really knew anything about it. He'd played on the Turkey Bottoms Blues when he'd been in grade school, so she always liked to hear what he had to say. Sometimes she would even flatter him by asking his opinion on something.

"I feel like going sometime," Tom said. "I haven't seen them play all this season."

"It costs too much," Helen said. "It costs a dollar and ten cents just for regular seats."

She felt him looking at her intently, but she wouldn't look back at him—she never did know what he was thinking. "Let's get tickets and go the World Series if the Reds win," he said.

Helen's hand clenched up tight against her breast and the color all drained out of her face. She couldn't answer: maybe he was making fun of her because she just sat here all day. She looked at one of the Aimsley fox terriers smelling at something in the back yard.

"I think Cokie Myers's father can get me tickets, he works at the park," Tom said. "Should we go if I can get them?"

"You can't get them," she said loudly. "So just don't bother me!"

"I can get them."

"Just don't bother me!" she said. "You can't get them so just don't even talk to me about it!"

"I tell you I *can* get them!" he said, getting mad too. "Will you go if I get them?"

She jumped up from the chair, her face white, her hair all mussed. "Just leave me alone!" she shouted at him. "Just quit bothering me and leave me alone!" And she went out into the kitchen and turned on the hot water for the dishes.

At supper table that night she got so mad, her mother and her brother were so optimistic about the Reds' chances and they didn't know anything about it. When they said some of the things they did, she just couldn't help shout-

ing at them. They *always* thought the Reds were going to win.

"They're not going to win tomorrow," she shouted. "They always lose on Friday. Joe Aston in the sports page yesterday analyzed how many times they lost on Friday and it turned out to be eight out of ten times."

"That doesn't mean anything," Tom said, breaking a piece of white bread and mopping up gravy with it. "They're in a winning streak now and they're going to keep on going. I bet you they win tomorrow."

She just got furious, she waved her hand and could hardly speak, he made her so mad. "Why? Why?" she demanded, leaning forward, her black eyes jumping out of her head, her hair falling around her face. "How can you say they're going to win tomorrow?"

"Because of Derringer, that's why."

"Yeah, yeah, Derringer!" Helen stopped eating altogether and sat back in her chair. "Look what he did in his last game—got knocked out of the box in the second inning by the Boston Bees! Derringer! Don't talk to me about Derringer!"

"Well, Derringer *is* good," her mother put in innocently. "He's a good pitcher," she added.

Helen turned on her mother with a fixed expression of horror, her right hand clenched in close to her and her left thrown out as if to defend herself. "Good pitcher! Yes! Good pitcher! He pitches good when he wants to, but that's only about twice a month! I know him!"

For five minutes there was silence while her mother and brother ate, but she could hardly eat anything, they made her so mad. Then she turned on Tom suddenly when he was just about to put a forkful of peas into his mouth and said: "You should have heard the booing the crowd gave Joost today when he dropped that bunt! Boy!"

She liked to sit in the dark like this: the kitchen light was on but it didn't shine on her rocker by the radio at all. The Sports Round-Up program had been a disappointment; Dick Bray and Red Barber hadn't had time to do anything but give their opinions on the Reds' pennant chances, and she already knew what *their* opinions were, they were so optimistic.

There was just dance music now and she didn't feel like dialing around. She was tired, she'd been so keyed up all day. She was glad her mother was taking a nap upstairs and her brother was out to Ray's Place. Sometimes she just didn't want to be with anybody at all, she just wanted to be alone. She only felt natural when she was alone, and they didn't like her anyhow. She didn't care,

they could just leave her alone if they didn't like her.

Well, her father would be down soon—she heard her mother stirring around now, waking him. "Come on, William get up. It's ten o'clock."

She went out to the kitchen and poured herself a glass of milk. She began to feel better, thinking about the day's game —wait till her father heard what almost happened in the ninth inning!

"Hello, Helen," he said— still a little sleep-dazed so that she felt he hardly saw her out of his eyes. It was funny, he always seemed about a foot smaller in the evening, when he got up, than when he came home from work in the morning. A small man with a pot belly and arms too thin and long for his body, he was dressed in a blue workshirt buttoned at the collar and brown whipcord pants. She always felt strange with him, maybe because he didn't really look like her father. His face was altogether different from hers: he had a strong nose with a little bend in it and small gray eyes under gray eyebrows. A kind of bony face. She looked like her mother—round like her mother, with large brown eyes and full lips.

"Old Bucky Walters thought he was so good today!" she said as he went to the icebox and brought out a large plate of sliced tomatoes and cucumbers and a bottle of beer. "He had to go and let the Cubs get three hits in the first inning and everybody thought the Reds were sunk."

He sprinkled huge amounts of salt and pepper over the salad and opened the beer. "Yeah?" he said, sitting at the table.

"Then they got two more runs in the second, and we got two runs. That made it five to two. You should have heard the crowd booing the umpire when he called Frey out at third in the fourth inning! That was when Werber singled and it looked like we were going to get some runs. The umpire was the only guy who believed old Frey was out. Red Barber said it was the worst booing he'd heard in years."

He drank the beer and wiped the foam off his mouth. He was always so quiet when he was sleepy—he only really talked a lot when he came home from Ray's Place in the afternoon.

"Well, who won?" he asked finally.

"Oh, we won," Helen said, hating to tell him the end of the game first. "But it's a wonder. Red Barber almost threw a fit when Joost fumbled in the ninth inning and the Cubs had Wilson on first. We were only leading by one run—six to five. But then Craft did something good for a change: he made a one-handed catch all the way back to the

stands with the sun in his eyes and, boy, the crowd really cheered then, I thought the radio was coming apart. Then there was a ground ball and a strike-out and that was all. Oh, I forgot to tell you, they put in Gene Thompson to pitch in the eighth inning."

"Gene Thompson?" he said. "I didn't know he was playing with the Reds any more."

"Sure he is. They always talk about trading him but they never do. He did pretty good too, except for that last inning. If Craft hadn't been awake for a change, Thompson would just have another loss on his record."

She followed him out in the hall, where he put on his blue work coat. "Tomorrow the Giants come to town, then we'll see! Carl Hubbell is supposed to pitch—and after what he did to the Reds last time, they better be lying awake tonight thinking about it."

She followed him back into the kitchen, where he stuffed a handful of kitchen matches into his pockets for his stogies. She watched him, trying to think of something else to say, as he took out his gold pocket-watch and noted the time. She always felt desperate when he was leaving in the evening—she never got to tell him half of what had happened.

"Ten-forty," he said. "Got to get down there."

Following him to the front

door, she said, "Everybody's so sure they're going to win the pennant, but I'm not so sure. If they can take two games out of three from the Giants they'll be all right."

"Oh, they'll win," he said. "Good night."

She watched him through the window as he stopped to light a stogie on the front porch, and then she turned and went upstairs. She didn't feel tired now, she felt all excited again. But she thought she might as well go to bed anyhow—there was nothing else to do.

She went right on through August with them, never missing a game, and she never gave them the benefit of the doubt but they kept winning anyhow, doing plenty of things wrong but somehow pulling through. She still wouldn't believe they were going to be champions even when they were within two games of clinching it. They'll do something dumb, she kept thinking, they always do. And besides, Johnny Vander Meer has a sore arm and can't pitch.

But then they took a game from Philadelphia and they were only one game away from the pennant and she was so nervous the next day because they didn't play, they were on their way back to Cincinnati to meet St. Louis, and that was the hardest team of them all—St. Louis had all the

batters, Johnny Mize, Enos Slaughter, all of them. She didn't talk back to Red Barber very much during that St. Louis game, she just sat there with her heart high in her chest and both her hands clenched, listening hard to every play. The radio wasn't turned off once during the game, and she got wildly irritated between innings when Dick Bray talked about Wheaties.

It was the last half of the ninth and Frey was on second, the score was still nothing to nothing and she wasn't making a sound. Jimmy Ripple was coming up to the plate and Red Barber gave a minute description of everything he did—dusted his hands with dirt, picked up the bat, stepped over to the plate, dug in his right toe. She was leaning forward, her head almost touching the radio, her teeth clenched together, when suddenly the scream of the crowd hit her full in the face ———

"It's a smashing line drive into left field and Frey is rounding third ———"

He was scoring, he was scoring! She couldn't sit down, she jumped up and walked around the room, her mouth open, her eyes blazing, her hand clutched in tight against her breast.

"——— and the Cincinnati Reds are now ———"

All of Gorker Street was screaming, Mrs. Must next door

was screaming to her husband Allen who was out in the back yard: "Allen, Allen, they did it —————"

She stood very still in the middle of the room, no longer hearing the radio, her body full and free, all her doubts gone. Should I go up and wake him? she thought, but instead she ran out on the front porch where her mother and Tom had been sitting in the swing.

"They —————" she said, but they already knew, they were both standing up shouting something at Mrs. Tellmacher across the street and here came Mrs. Aimsley up the walk.

"What's the matter?" Mrs. Aimsley asked.

"The Reds just won the pennant," Tom said.

"My God, I thought war was declared or something."

Helen's mother was beaming, "Tom's going to get tickets and take you," she said.

"What?" Helen asked, looking from Tom to her mother.

"Tom's getting tickets from Mr. Myers to one of the World Series games and he's going to take you."

She felt like crying—she hated them, they were always making fun of her. "You leave me alone," she said, the tears popping into her eyes. She began to scream: "All of you just leave me alone, I'm happy the way I am, so just leave me alone!" She ran off

the porch around to the back yard.

"I don't care!" she said, "I'm not going!"

Tom had the tickets in his hand. "You want me to tear them up?" he asked. "Just say tear them up and I'll do it right now."

She didn't know what to say. But she knew why he'd gone and got them: just because she didn't want him to. He was always making fun of her, she listened to the game all the time and he thought she was silly. That's why he'd got the tickets, just to show her up.

"You can go by yourself!" she shouted and ran out on the front porch. She just wanted to get away from all of them, she hated them.

But they were at her day and night, they acted as if they couldn't understand why she wouldn't go. As if she wanted to get all dressed up and wear those silly gloves!

Her mother kept pounding away at her till she thought she'd go crazy. "It would be so nice for the two of you to go out together once in a while," her mother said, and that almost made her burst a blood vessel.

"Nice!" she said. "Nice! Do you think I want to go out with *him*? He doesn't like me and I know it! He can just go out by himself whenever he wants to."

"Why don't you go with Tom?" her father said one evening while he was eating his snack. "He got those tickets and now you won't go with him."

Somehow she never really got angry with her father, he didn't talk at her like her mother did. But now she felt so emotional she couldn't answer him, and she left the room. They were all the same—none of them understood. None of them would leave her be, they all had to keep picking on her.

The day before the game she came into the kitchen where her mother was pressing her blue dress.

"You can do all that you want," Helen said, "but I'm not going!"

Her mother didn't answer her—just went on pressing. And Helen sat down and watched her mother working, wishing she'd argue. "Tom doesn't want to take me anyhow—he just did it because you made him." But still her mother didn't answer and finally Helen got up and left the room.

The sun wasn't even up! She looked at the alarm clock beside her bed: five-twenty. And then she remembered, this was the day! Today we'll see, she thought. Today we'll know whether they're any good or not. Derringer was going to pitch— she wished it were Bucky Walters. Derringer was more bril-

liant sometimes, but Bucky could really be depended on more.

She wondered if Tom would try to make her go. Well, she wasn't going, that was all; he could put that in his pipe and smoke it. All of them could try to make her go, but she wouldn't.

She couldn't stay in bed, she was too excited. She'd never been so excited about anything in her life before. She got up and dressed and went downstairs. There were some sliced peaches in the icebox so she ate them and drank a glass of milk. Then she went out on the front porch and Gorker Street looked so strange, the air smelled good and the street was quiet, deserted. Just Mr. Timpkins's car parked down the street, but none of the kids who were always around. Wait a minute—here came Mr. Daugherty up the street. She ducked back into the house, she didn't want him to see her.

At eleven she was sitting on the front porch reading the *Ladies' Home Journal* but not really getting anything out of the story because she was so excited, when Tom came out. She wouldn't look up at him but he came over to her anyhow.

"You better get dressed," he said.

She still didn't look at him, there was a strange feeling in her chest. She surprised herself when she jumped up. "All right then, I will." And she went into the house and up the stairs.

When she was all dressed, she stared at herself in mirror. I don't look so fat when I'm dressed up, she thought. She wore her blue dress with the little white collar, and on her head was the hat she'd got last spring—a white, off-the-face hat with a black bow on it. She hadn't been out for three months, she'd almost forgotten how it felt to be all dressed up. . . .

"You can wear your new gloves," her mother said when she arrived down in the kitchen. And she didn't get mad, she just took the gloves from her mother and started working the right one on. She had a hard time, the hand always persisted in clenching up hard whenever she wanted to do anything with it, but finally she succeeded and then worked the left one on by using the edge of the table. Tom and her mother did not watch her: Tom was looking out the back door and her mother was washing a skillet at the sink.

She wished her mother wouldn't come out on the porch with them, but she didn't say anything. She felt so strange all dressed up, she just knew that people were looking out of their windows at her as she came down off the porch steps behind Tom. For a moment she almost decided to dash back into the house, but then they were on their way, going past Mrs. Must's. Tom turned once at the top of the street and waved to his mother, but she didn't. She didn't even want to look at that house, besides it was silly to wave.

They climbed the footbridge over the railroad tracks and then they were standing side by side at the car stop on Eastern Avenue. She couldn't resist looking at Tom as they stood there—he did look handsome in his brown suit and his tie. She got car tickets out of her purse. "Here, drop these," she said, as the trolley came swaying toward them from the end of the line. And then they were on the car, bumping against each other as they sat on the straw seat.

Part of a swarm, she moved forward toward the high wall that was the ball park, Tom somewhere behind her, but she didn't look around. She felt that life had caught her and was dragging her along toward something she must know. . . something so inevitable she could not escape now even if she struggled. She was carried in through a doorway cut in the green wall, Tom was handing over the tickets, then they were free again, going up the ramp into the grandstand. And suddenly she thought: Is this the day I've been waiting two years for? The battle she had put up against coming certainly did seem ridiculous now that she was here. Nobody even noticed her, they all just rushed along, nobody stopped and laughed at her and stared at her gloved hands.

They were following an usher down to their seats and she was so busy watching her step she didn't get a good look at the field till she sat down—and then she looked, and she couldn't believe it. It was so little! It was a dozen times smaller than she'd expected! She looked at the centerfield wall over which Lombardi had hit so many home runs, and it hardly seemed any distance at all. She looked at the diamond itself—the distance between the bases was so short! And she hadn't known about the signs out there surrounding the outfield—signs advertising insurance, loans, suits of clothes, ham. They made it all seem so commercial.

Tom bought two bottles of Coke and gave her one. "Did they really charge you fifteen cents each for these?" she asked. Everywhere were men in white suits selling things to the crowd—popcorn, Crackerjacks, score cards, souvenir pins. Red Barber had never mentioned the way they hit you over the head to buy things.

But the players don't have anything to do with it, she thought. These are just a lot of people trying to make money

out of the game, they don't really care about baseball. . . . Well, it wouldn't be long now, the groundkeepers were smoothing out the infield. She watched them, trying to feel the same excitement she'd always had at home just before the game, but she couldn't: two men on her left were discussing Florida and in front of her a Spanish-looking fellow was pressing kisses on the cheek of a little blonde. Wasn't anybody interested in the game?

"Where's the broadcasting booth?" she asked Tom.

"It's up above us, you can't see it," he said. "But look down there, there's Dick Bray interviewing people."

"Fans in the Stands," she said—but Dick Bray was lost in a knot of people, she couldn't see him.

Then the band was playing —The Star-Spangled Banner— and everyone was standing. Why did she always feel so silly standing—feeling everyone would turn and look at her? "There's the Reds!" Tom said, nudging her.

She started, she strained toward them, even bending forward a little. They came stringing out on the field from their dugout, tiny loping men, each one like the other way down there—and she didn't know them!

She didn't know a single one

of them. Had she been foolish enough to think they would be bigger than life, that she would actually recognize each one? They were all alike in their white suits with the big numbers on the back, just miniature men who seemed to have nothing to do with her or the rest of the crowd. And here came Derringer out to the mound—but it wasn't really Derringer at all, Derringer was taller than Gary Cooper, Derringer was nonchalant, masterful, and this was just a tiny man in a white suit, far away.

The game was starting—Derringer threw to Wilson. But she couldn't see the ball. She realized, as the first inning progressed and Detroit had men on base, that the game itself was just like the park: it was all in miniature, it wasn't like the game she'd imagined at all. They were just a lot of little men down there standing around, and she didn't know any of them. Even when the ball was hit, nobody seemed to do very much—one man out in the field ran around a little and then there was someone on first; Derringer had the ball again and was throwing to the plate.

The Tigers were making runs, but she didn't care. She didn't know any of those people down there, she didn't care what they did. The crowd was screaming because Detroit was scoring again but she felt disgusted, she felt unclean. It isn't mine at all,

she thought. It belongs to everybody. It isn't anything.

The second inning had come along, but she wasn't even watching any longer, she wasn't even *trying* to identify the players. Instead of looking at them, she studied the ads on her score card, reading all about Pepsi-Cola and then about Chesterfields, They Satisfy. Her stomach was swimming in her, she felt she would drown if she had to stay the whole game, her head was bursting. Just to get out of here, to run away from here she didn't care where. . . . "Tom," she said, but he didn't hear her, he was shouting something down at the players.

She stood up and someone behind her pushed her shoulder and said, "Sit down!" but she kept on going, stumbling over people as she headed for the aisle.

Just as she got to the exit, Tom appeared at her side. "Where you going?" he asked. She didn't answer, she walked on. "You can't leave now ———"

She saw the sign, LADIES REST ROOM, and she rushed toward it, not even looking around at him. Nobody inside at all, that was good. She slumped down in an armchair: it was over. The crowd was screaming out there but she didn't care. She didn't care whether the Reds won or lost.

And suddenly she saw herself as she had been—wearing that sloppy house dress and sitting by the radio for two years. It was a dream, she thought, it wasn't real. I made it all up myself. There is no such person as Paul Derringer. Bucky Walters and Lonnie Frey and Bill Werber —they are all just people I made up. No one has ever seen them but me.

I have just told lies, that's all, she thought. I lied to myself every day of the week. It's really a silly game, with nothing important happening in it, but I made it the most important thing in the world. I acted as if they were playing for me alone, and here they weren't really playing for anybody. They wouldn't know me if they saw me, and I didn't know them. Really it was just something I dreamed. Just a silly dream.

Thinking this she began to feel better. She'd been sick, that was it. And after you'd been sick for two years you wanted to wash yourself clean and never be sick again.

These silly gloves, she said to herself, working off the right one. These silly gloves that I've been wearing all my life. . . . She had to use her mouth to pull off the left one. Then she pushed up her sleeves and began. She washed her crippled hand last and most thoroughly.

Finished, she dried with a paper towel. So it's all over, she thought. It wasn't real and I don't want it. Now I will just have to change, that's all. I will have to be someone different.

She picked up her handbag and started to reach for the gloves, then turned quickly and hurried to the door.

DISCUSSION

Helen is at a period in her life when her peers are entering the world of work and enjoying the social relationships that precede intimacy and marriage. Because of her negative attitude toward her disfigured hand, Helen has chosen to sit in a rocking chair in front of the radio seven days a week. As a substitute for a normal life, she has made the world of baseball the focal point of her existence. She knows the details of the player's personalities and habits much like people know about the traits and mannerisms of their friends and associates at work. At the beginning of this story, the family seems resigned to Helen's baseball world. Any attempt to get her to leave the house is met with Helen's shouts and reminders that she is a cripple. Helen's behavior reduces her mother to tears. Her mother has never dealt with her feelings about Helen's deformity; she has instead given in to feelings of guilt and shame that make her defensive about Helen's handicap. Helen is encouraged by her mother to wear gloves to hide her hand from view, but the gloves are more conspicuous than Helen's clenched hand. Helen's view of herself is influenced by her mother's attitude, that her hand is ugly and disgusting to others. It is not surprising that Helen believes that everyone sees her hand as the most important aspect of her. Even the normal sibling rivalry that occurs in a family is viewed by Helen in terms of her handicap. She feels envious of Tom and projects her own angry feelings onto him. She appeases her anger, bred by jealousy, by fuming, "He doesn't like me and I know it!" Helen fantasizes that others have nothing wrong with them. All of her energy is bound up in angry, hostile feelings about herself that she cannot accept. It is more acceptable for her to assume that she is disliked by everyone around her than to examine her self-destructive feelings. It is not unusual for individuals like Helen, who are consumed by self-pity, to develop negative attitudes toward everything and everyone. It is, however, very difficult to help someone whose self-concept has become as entrenched as Helen's.

It is fortunate that the family is able to get Helen out to the ballgame. This experience helps her to realize that in the last two years she had centered her life around baseball, a game that she did not even understand. She becomes aware of the distortion she has created and is ready to make changes in her life. The ending of this story is somewhat idealistic, an attitude that has been as long standing as Helen's usually does not reverse itself with one positive experience. An individual like Helen needs counseling to help her consolidate a new and more positive attitude toward herself and her capabilities. A source of counseling are the state departments of rehabilitation, agencies that help the handicapped when they leave school and wish to get a job. They provide testing and counseling in the area of job training and job opportunities. As is true of the population at large, individual ability, personality, and attitudes contribute greatly to the eventual adjustment of the physically disabled person.

SPRINGBOARDS FOR INQUIRY

1. Should the family have confronted Helen about her fantasy baseball world earlier? What are some realistic next steps for Helen now that she has taken a step into the real world?

2. Have you personally known a person with an obvious physical defect? How has it effected him or her socially?

3. Have you ever felt sensitive about some aspect of your physical appearance? In what ways have you permitted your sensitivity

to affect your own life? Name two community resources that you could turn to for help. What might each of these resources offer you?

4. What are some of the realistic concerns an orthopedically or multiply handicapped person has toward the end of his or her high school career? How can the schools be of assistance?

5. Choose a book from the suggested readings in the area of a physical handicap and discuss its emotional impact upon you as someone who may be considering work in the field of exceptionality.

Cannery Row

by John Steinbeck

Frankie began coming to Western Biological when he was eleven years old. For a week or so he just stood outside the basement door and looked in. Then one day he stood inside the door. Ten days later he was in the basement. He had very large eyes and his hair was a dark wiry dirty shock. His hands were filthy. He picked up a piece of excelsior and put it in a garbage can and then he looked at Doc where he worked labeling specimen bottles containing purple Velella. Finally Frankie got to the work bench and he put his dirty fingers on the bench. It took Frankie three weeks to get that far and he was ready to bolt every instant of the time.

Finally one day Doc spoke to him. "What's your name, son?"

"Frankie."

"Where do you live?"

"Up there," a gesture up the hill.

"Why aren't you in school?"

"I don't go to school."

"Why not?"

"They don't want me there."

"Your hands are dirty. Don't you ever wash?"

Frankie looked stricken and then he went to the sink and scrubbed his hands and always afterwards he scrubbed his hands almost raw every day.

And he came to the laboratory every day. It was an association without much talk. Doc by a telephone call established that what Frankie said was true. They didn't want him in school. He couldn't learn and there was something a little wrong with his co-ordination. There was no place for him. He wasn't an idiot, he wasn't dangerous, his parents, or parent, would not pay for his keep in an institution. Frankie didn't often sleep at the laboratory but he spent his days there. And sometimes he crawled in the excelsior crate and slept. That was probably when there was a crisis at home.

Doc asked, "Why do you come here?"

"You don't hit me or give me a nickel," said Frankie.

"Do they hit you at home?"

"There's uncles around all the time at home. Some of them hit me and tell me to get out and some of them give me a nickel and tell me to get out."

"Where's your father?"

"Dead," said Frankie vaguely.

"Where's your mother?"

"With the uncles."

Doc clipped Frankie's hair and got rid of the lice. At Lee Chong's he got him a new pair of overalls and a striped sweater and Frankie became his slave.

"I love you," he said one afternoon. "Oh, I love you."

He wanted to work in the laboratory. He swept out every day, but there was something a little wrong. He couldn't get a floor quite clean. He tried to help with grading crayfish for size. There they were in a bucket, all sizes. They were to be grouped in the big pans—laid out—all the three-inch ones together and all the four-inch ones and so forth.

Frankie tried and the perspiration stood on his forehead but he couldn't do it. Size relationships just didn't get through to him.

"No," Doc would say. "Look, Frankie. Put them beside your finger like this so you'll know which ones are this long. See? This one goes from the tip of your finger to the base of your thumb. Now you just pick out another one that goes from the tip of your finger down to the same place and it will be right." Frankie tried and he couldn't do it. When Doc went upstairs Frankie crawled in the excelsior box and didn't come out all afternoon.

But Frankie was a nice, good, kind boy. He learned to light Doc's cigars and he wanted Doc to smoke all the time so he could light the cigars.

Better than anything else Frankie loved it when there were parties upstairs in the laboratory. When girls and men gathered to sit and talk, when the great phonograph played music that throbbed in his stomach and made beautiful and huge pictures form vaguely in his head, Frankie loved it. Then he crouched down in a corner behind a chair where he was hidden and could watch and listen. When there was laughter at a joke he didn't understand Frankie laughed delightedly behind his chair and when the conversation dealt with abstractions his brow furrowed and he became intent and serious.

One afternoon he did a desperate thing. There was a small party in the laboratory. Doc was in the kitchen pouring beer when Frankie appeared beside him. Frankie grabbed a glass of beer and rushed it through the door and gave it to a girl sitting in a big chair.

She took the glass and said, "Why, thank you," and she smiled at him.

And Doc coming through the door said, "Yes, Frankie is a great help to me."

Frankie couldn't forget that. He did the thing in his mind over and over, just how he had taken the glass and just how the girl sat and then her voice—"Why, thank you," and Doc—"a great help to me—Frankie is a great help to me—sure Frankie is a great help—Frankie," and Oh my God!

He knew a big party was coming because Doc bought steaks and a great deal of beer and Doc let him help clean out all the upstairs. But that was nothing, for a great plan had formed in Frankie's mind and he could see just how it would be. He went over it again and again. It was beautiful. It was perfect.

Then the party started and people came and sat in the front room, girls and young women and men.

Frankie had to wait until he had the kitchen to himself and the door closed. And it was some time before he had it so. But at last he was alone and the door was shut. He could hear the chatter of conversation and the music from the great phonograph. He worked very quietly—first the tray—then get out the glasses without breaking any. Now fill them with beer and let the foam settle a little and then fill again.

Now he was ready. He took a great breath and opened the door. The music and the talk roared around him. Frankie picked up the tray of beer and walked through the door. He knew how. He went straight toward the same young woman who had thanked him before. And then right in front of her, the thing happened, the co-ordination failed, the hands fumbled, the panicked muscles, the nerves telegraphed to a dead operator, the responses did not come back. Tray and beer collapsed forward into the young woman's lap. For a moment Frankie stood still. And then he turned and ran.

The room was quiet. They could hear him run downstairs, and go into the cellar. They heard a hollow scrabbling sound—and then silence.

Doc walked quietly down the stairs and into the cellar. Frankie was in the excelsior box burrowed down clear to the bottom, with the pile of excelsior on top of him. Doc could hear him whimpering there. Doc waited for a moment and then he went quietly back upstairs.

There wasn't a thing in the world he could do.

DISCUSSION

John Steinbeck, who has won the Nobel Prize for Literature, writes with sympathy of the oppressed and the misfits in our society. He often includes a mentally retarded person in his stories. This excerpt from *Cannery Row* introduces Frankie, who is multiply handicapped in that he is mentally retarded, neurologically damaged, and emotionally disturbed. When Doc phones school, he learns that the school system cannot provide education for Frankie. In many communities the compartmentalization of special education makes a boy like Frankie hard to place. He could not keep up with children in a class for the retarded because of his overall poor coordination. His problem with fine motor coordination would make handwriting and cutting and pasting activities particularly difficult. Frankie's deficient gross motor coordination means that he could not participate freely with other children in outdoor activities. He does not have the intellectual ability to be placed in a class for physically disabled students with birth defects or cerebral palsy, and he would not be suited to a class with acting-out emotionally disturbed children. Since he needs modifications of his program and special help in the areas of his deficiencies, Frankie requires educational opportunities that are designed for the multiply handicapped student. In the last few years, the fields of medicine, psychology, and education have contributed better methods of diagnosing the multiply handicapped. In the coming decade, a nationwide effort will be made to seek out and to serve handicapped children like Frankie who fall through the cracks of hard and fast categories of special education.

Doc's laboratory is a safe place for Frankie to spend the day. It is some respite from his sordid and uncaring home life. Despite good intentions, however, Doc does not have the time, training, or commitment to meet Frankie's needs. Frankie responds to Doc with feelings of love and slavish loyalty. He delights in mimicking Doc and in pleasing him. Like all young people, Frankie enjoys social situations and tries to fit in at parties in the laboratory by laughing when he sees others doing so, even if he does not understand what they are laughing about.

Doc relates to Frankie in a consistently interested manner, but his concern does not measure up to that of a highly motivated parent. Doc does not know how to help Frankie who has a low threshold for frustration. He gives him little verbal feedback that would enable Frankie to learn new ways to adapt to social and learning situations. They have few conversations because of Frankie's limited interests and the demands of Doc's work. Frankie needs more experience with words and concepts in order to gain self-confidence. Frankie is also missing a great deal by not associating with other children of his age and learning from their example.

Frankie's well-meaning plan ends with failure because of his damaged central nervous system function. The party atmosphere adds the extra stress that incapacitates him at the critical moment. If Doc had been able to advise Frankie, he may have suggested that he serve one drink on a tray at a time. In a subsequent chapter in *Cannery Row*, Frankie once more carries out a plan without adult input that reveals poor judgment. He gets into trouble with the police and is sent away to an institution.

SPRINGBOARDS FOR INQUIRY

1. Which of Frankie's disabilities are most restricting in school, in social settings, for vocational training, and for independent living?

2. If you were a social worker assigned to Frankie, what interventions would you plan for him for his present and future?

3. Discuss whether you feel Doc's supervision is preferable to residential placement for Frankie.

4. List other combinations of multiple handicaps and indicate what special needs students with these combined disabilities need during the school years.

CHAPTER SEVEN

The Hearing Impaired

"Deafdead?"

What was the difference? The two words were alike. A person who was deaf might as well be dead. Aunt Harriet said so.

"What's the matter—cotton in your ears?"[1]

Add to that an observation of your mother's. Out in town with you (and invariably with a handicapped friend of yours along as well) she knows what sort of looks you will all get. . . . Staggered by your bird call . . . the hoipolloi actually lose a second or two while standing to stare and then pout their troughing slots to hold back the offensive word. . . . Their eyes they tighten up as if to eliminate you from sight altogether.[2]

Both excerpts are illustrative of emotional responses to the handicap of the hearing impaired. The first are a deaf person's personal reactions that border upon anguish and despair. The second is a beautifully expressed stream-of-consciousness that reveals the pent-up fury of the father of a deaf child. Each is in sharp contrast to the less emotional, clinical definitions of deafness. For example, Helmer R. Myklebust defines deafness as follows:

The implications of an auditory impairment vary. . . . [It is] difficult to define rigorously what is meant by terms such as *hearing loss, deaf* and

[1]Frances Warfield, *Cotton in My Ears* (New York: The Viking Press, Inc., 1948), pp. 146–47.
[2]Paul West, *Words for a Deaf Daughter* (New York: Harper & Row, Publishers, Inc., 1970), p. 175.

hard of hearing. One of the longstanding, useful definitions of deafness was given by the Committee on Nomenclature of the Conferences of Executives of American Schools for the Deaf. This committee defined the deaf as "those in whom the sense of hearing is non-functional for the ordinary purpose of life." They classified the deaf into two groups. . . .

    a. *The congenitally deaf.*. Those who are born deaf.

    b. *The adventitiously deaf.* Those who are born with normal hearing but in whom . . . hearing becomes non-functional later through illness.[3]

Samuel A. Kirk notes that "because of the multi-dimensional nature of the problem, any classification is incomplete unless it takes into account all variables, such as (1) degree of hearing loss, (2) age at onset, and (3) type of hearing loss."[4] Frederick S. Berg and Samuel D. Fletcher have sharply delineated the hard of hearing child and the deaf child and contrasted these persons with the normal hearing child:

    The *hard of hearing* child is a hearing impaired individual who can identify through hearing and without visual reception communication enough of the distinguishing features of speech to permit at least partial recognition of the spoken language. With the addition of visual receptive communication such as speech reading, he may understand even more language provided the vocabulary and syntax are a part of his linguistic code.

    The *deaf* child is a hearing impaired person who can identify through hearing at best only a few of the prosodic and phonetic features of speech and then not enough to permit auditory recognition of sound or word combinations. He relies mainly or entirely upon speech reading or some other form of visual receptive communication for the perception of the spoken or manual form of language.

    The *normal hearing* child, in contrast to either a hard of hearing or deaf child, can recognize all the distinguishing features of speech under good listening conditions and without the aid of speechreading or some other visual form of receptive communication.[5]

Frances P. Conner and her colleagues identify three distinct, but not mutually exclusive, types of hearing impairment:

    (1) A conductive-hearing loss implies an obstruction to sound transmission through the sound-conducting apparatus of the ear as a direct result of a lesion to the external or middle-ear mechanisms. (2) If damage

---

[3]Helmer R. Myklebust, *The Psychology of Deafness* (New York: Grune & Stratton, Inc., 1960), p. 3.

[4]Samuel A. Kirk, *Educating Exceptional Children*, 2nd ed. (Boston, Mass.: Houghton Mifflin Company, 1962), p. 240.

[3]Frederick S. Berg and Samuel G. Fletcher, *The Hard of Hearing Child* (New York: Grune & Stratton, Inc., 1970), p. 7.

occurs to the nerve endings of the inner ear (cochlea) or to the auditory nerve that permits transmission of sound to the brain, the resulting hearing loss is classified as sensory-neural. (3) The term *central dysacusis* refers to a lesion in the central auditory nervous system and the auditory area of the cortex.[6]

Conner and her colleagues conclude with the following statement that will serve as a guideline in this discussion of hearing impaired children: "Although the generic terms *deaf* and *partially hearing* appear to be inadequate, since they fail to recognize the many different types and degrees and consequences of auditory dysfunction, no substitute terminology has emerged."[7]

Language in humans (and in some animal species) is learned, imitated.[8] "Deaf children," write Joseph Rosenstein and Walter H. Mac-Gintie, "typically develop language slowly, even with intensive and intelligent application of the most advanced techniques."[9] Freeman McConnell contends that "the greatest single handicap that results from sensory deprivation of hearing from the prelingual years is the barrier to language learning, which in turn is the main reason for the educational

---

[6]Frances P. Conner et al., "Physical and Sensory Handicaps," in *Issues in the Classification of Children: A Sourcebook on Categories, Labels, and Their Consequences*, vol. 1 (San Francisco, Calif.: Jossey-Bass Inc., Publishers, 1975), p. 243.

[7]Ibid., p. 244.

[8]In the sense used here, we refer to *language* in other than humans as being the ordinary sounds animals *learn* to make from birth that may or may not (depending upon your scientific predisposition) be considered language. (Robert A. Hinde, "Intraspecific Communication in Animals," in *Disorders of Communication*, ed. David M. Rioch and Edwin A. Weinstein [New York: Hafner Publishing Co., Inc., 1969], pp. 62–84, cites numerous studies of communication between and among animals.) The 1973 conference entitled "The Role of Speech in Language," sponsored by the Growth and Development Branch of the National Institute of Child Health and Human Development (NICHD), produced a volume entitled *The Role of Speech in Language*, edited by James F. Kavanegh and James E. Cutting (Cambridge, Mass.: MIT Press, 1975). In this volume, the work of Peter Marler shows that animals use sounds to communicate, and that if song sparrows are reared in acoustical isolation or become deaf early in youth, they develop song, but the "singing will be highly abnormal" (Peter Marler, "On the Origin of Speech from Animal Sounds," in *The Role of Speech in Language*, ed. Kavanegh and Cutting, p. 25). Marler concludes his discussion with special reference to the development of speech and sounds in infants and children. He suggests that for certain speech sounds infants, like birds, need templates (models): "This result [referring to Peter D. Eimas et al., "Speech Perception in Infants," *Science*, 171 (1971), 303–306] showed that one- and four-month-old infants were able to discriminate the acoustic cue underlying the adult phonemic distinction between the voiced and voiceless stop consonants /b/ and /p/" (p. 303).

[9]Joseph Rosenstein and Walter H. MacGintie, *Verbal Behavior of the Deaf Child: Studies of Word Meanings and Associations* (New York: Teachers College Press, 1969), p. xii.

handicap."[10] Before a child can learn to speak, he or she must hear language used. If the child hears complex language, he or she learns to speak with linguistic complexity. Frank M. Hewett, analyzing the essence of the deaf child's problem, focuses on three aspects of the deaf child's language deficit: "One of the most difficult communication areas for the deaf is developing abstract language skills. Although the normal child may come to imitate adult language forms more . . . more subtle forms of language, different shades of meaning of the same word and complex grammatical functions may have to be systematically taught to the deaf child."[11] The following vignette is an excellent example of the errors in word order, morphology, and sense inherent in a student profoundly deaf from birth:

What America Means to Me

America mean to me for Freedom and not be slaves to the people. America have to be to right speech and insult. American look like the people like Freedom. American will complain about the slave, the American won't become Freedom. American right the worship. American is our business and we can't error with the people. Our American is Freedom of Speech.[12]

Charles K. Ogden and Ivor A. Richards, speaking of the English language, indicate that, "one word has to serve functions for which a hundred would not be too many."[13] The vignette just cited shows unique, simplistic dependence upon what may be termed "one-word, one-meaning" linguistic ability. A sharply limited vocabulary results in the misuse of words because their isolated definitions do not give the deaf person facility with these words in different contexts.

It is appropriate to include dissenting points of view in this discussion of the language deficiencies of the hearing impaired. Donald M. Morehead's[14] chapter in Sadanand Singh's[15] volume cites William

---

[10]Freeman McConnell, "Children with Hearing Disabilities," in *Exceptional Children in the Schools*, 2nd ed., ed. Lloyd M. Dunn (New York: Holt, Rinehart and Winston, Inc., 1973).

[11]Frank M. Hewett, *Education of Exceptional Learners* (Boston, Mass.: Allyn & Bacon, Inc., 1974), p. 98.

[12]Dunn, *Exceptional Children in the Schools*, p. 377.

[13]Charles K. Ogden and Ivor A. Richards, *The Meaning of Meaning* (London: Routledge, 1949), p. 130.

[14]Donald M. Morehead, "The Study of Linguistically Deficient Children," in *Measurement Procedures in Speech, Hearing and Language*, ed. Sadanand Singh (Baltimore, Md.: University Park Press, 1975).

[15]Ibid., p. 19.

Stokoe,[16] Donald F. Moores,[17] Jean Piaget,[18] Ursula Bellugi and Edward Klima,[19] and Hilde Schlesinger and Kathryn P. Meadow[20] as evidence that deaf children develop early language in a way very similar to hearing children. There is a sharp contrast between the findings of the latter authorities and the allegations in this chapter regarding the eventual language deficiencies of deaf children. Nevertheless, there seems to be agreement that eventually deaf children are less able to use language with the same kind of sophistication that normal children can.

Because of the nature of the impairment, the education of the hearing impaired child must start very early. Other children, even the blind, at least learn language in the normal way. Unlike a physically restricted child who learns to walk on his or her own as time passes, a child with hearing impairment cannot learn speech in a natural way. Since language acquisition is the basis for all further education, the importance of auditory stimulation and aural training has been emphasized for years. Grace M. Harris feels that

> the language element must be given priority over any other in the training of the deaf child, especially the *young* deaf child. . . . It would be a great error to restrict our concept of the term "language" to the spoken form or to the printed form. Understanding . . . the spoken word, and, much later, the printed word, is essential to the deaf child, and steps must be taken from the earliest possible moment.[21]

Alexander and Ethel Ewing emphasize education for a deaf child under five:

> [Parents need to] cheer on his efforts to say correct words, respond to him when he tries and when he succeeds, read to him and provide him with what experts call "corrective feedback." In this kind of rich, verbal environment a child's vocabulary grows and his ability to use sentences develops. . . . He uses words as tools of thought.[22]

---

[16]William Stokoe, *Semiotics and Human Sign Language* (The Hague: Monton, 1972).
[17]Donald F. Moores, "Nonvocal Systems of Verbal Behavior," in *Language Perspectives—Acquisition, Retardation and Intervention,* ed. Richard Schiefelbusch and Lyle Loyd (Baltimore, Md.: University Park Press, 1974).
[18]Jean Piaget, *Play, Dreams and Imitation* (New York: W.W. Norton & Company, Inc., 1962).
[19]Ursula Bellugi and Edward Klima, "The Roots of Language in the Sign Talk of the Deaf," *Psychology Today* (June 1972), 61–64.
[20]Hilde Schlesinger and Kathryn P. Meadow, *Sound and Sign: Childhood Deafness and Mental Health* (Berkeley, Calif.: University of California Press, 1972).
[21]Grace M. Harris, *Language for the Preschool Deaf Child,* 3rd ed. (New York: Grune & Stratton, Inc., 1971), pp. 17–18.
[22]Alexander and Ethel Ewing, *Hearing Impaired Children Under Five* (Washington, D.C.: The Volta Bureau, 1971), p. 85. In this particular quote they are, in fact, quoting Joan Beck, *How to Raise a Brighter Child* (London: Fontana Collins, 1962).

It seems to be generally agreed that deaf children need a curriculum that emphasizes language.[23] Yet there is much debate about what methodology for stressing language should be used. There is great bitterness among those who favor certain exclusive methods of teaching the deaf to communicate. The most commonly used terms in relation to methodology follow:[24]

Oralism is a point of view that requires all communication with deaf children to be done exclusively by means of speech and speech reading. Proponents of this form of communication contend that the use of fingerspelling and the language of signs retard speech development. They also insist that all deaf children can acquire good oral skills.[25]

Manualism is a system of communication that stresses use of the manual alphabet (fingerspelling) and the language of signs as a means of instruction in the classroom and as a form of communication between deaf persons[26] Since no educational programs in the United States practice manualism as it was conceived in the nineteenth century, the term is outmoded and often used erroneously to refer to an educational program that uses manual communication in any form.

Total communication is a theory of communication that embraces the concepts of oralism and manualism into a single and all-inclusive procedure of communication. It stresses the right of the teacher and the deaf child to use all forms of communication to develop language competencies. These forms include child-devised gestures, amplifica-

---

[23]McConnell says, "The curriculum (after the pre-school years) should be essentially the same as that recommended for normal-hearing children, including a balance of content directed at language and speech development, intellectual including perceptual-motor and conceptual development, and personal-social development." (McConnell, "Children with Hearing Disabilities," in *Exceptional Children in the Schools*, 2nd ed., Dunn, p. 396.)

[24]Lee Katz, Steve L. Mathis, III, and Edward C. Merril, Jr., *The Deaf Child in the Public Schools* (Danville, Ill.: The Interstate Printers & Publishers, Inc., 1974), pp. 16–17.

[25]The vast majority of deaf children can, through appropriate environmental impact (early identification, amplification, and so on), acquire good skills.

[26]Ameslan is an anacronym for American Sign Language, "ASL" or "Sign." It is a "legitimate language in and of itself," is not based upon English, and is a spatial language. There are no articles (the, a, an); the verb "to be" does not exist; and there are no tenses in Ameslan. For further information read Gallaudet College's journal, *Gallaudet Today* (Winter 1974–75), particularly Louie Fant's article "Ameslan."

tion, speech, lipreading, fingerspelling, formal signs, reading, and writing.

The Rochester method is a communication procedure that stresses oralism while emphasizing use of the manual alphabet. This alphabet consists of the letters "a to z" formed by certain fixed positions of the fingers of one hand. Its use enables one to spell words, phrases, and sentences with the same speed and ease as spoken words.

Cued speech is a procedure designed to reduce the degree to which the deaf child differs from the hearing child in acquiring and using language. Sounds that cannot be perceived upon the lips are recognized through cues that are formed by positions of the hand near the lips, neck, and shoulder. The cues consist of hand movements to indicate vowels, diphthongs, and consonants. This procedure seeks to promote lipreading skills through the recognition of cues for sounds that cannot be seen on the lips and to strengthen speech production by recognizing, combining, and producing appropriate sound elements.

The force of the controversy may be put into perspective by a close reading of Gary Nix's article. It shows that the studies offered in support of the *total communication* point of view are replete with research errors that weaken the position of *total communication* adherents.[27]

Methodology aside for the moment, table 7–1 points up the seriousness of the deficiency in educational achievement of deaf children. The data represents the results of tests administered to nineteen thousand hearing-impaired children enrolled in two hundred ninety different special education programs. It is reliably reported that the reading vocabulary of many deaf students at age eighteen may be as much as eight to nine years retarded.

Again, without appearing to choose a methodology, we offer figure 7–1, which finally puts us into a camp. Regardless of how hearing-impaired children are taught language, the idea of educating them with normal children intrigues us. Carl W. Asp's integration model seems to epitomize the problem:

> If a deaf child receives the proper training, he can function more like a hard-of-hearing child and possibly be integrated into a regular public

[27]Gary Nix, "Total Communication: A Review of the Studies Offered in Its Support," *The Volta Review*, vol. 77, no. 8 (November 1975).

Table 7-1

Weighted Mean Grade Equivalents Attained from Stanford Achievement Tests
 Administered in Annual Survey of Hearing Impaired Children and Youth,
 1970-71.

Subject	N	Mean grade equivalent	Range of means by test battery	Grade-level expectancy for normal children
10-Year-Old Students				
Arithmetic Computation	1277	2.5	1.8 - 5.1	5
Total Arithmetic	1269	2.4	1.8 - 6.2	5
Paragraph Meaning	1290	2.2	1.8 - 6.4	5
Total Reading	1277	2.3	1.9 - 6.4	5
14-Year-Old Students				
Science	554	4.7[a]	4.2 - 8.0	9
Social Studies	442	5.3[a]	4.9 - 8.0	9
Spelling	532	6.3[a]	5.6 - 9.3	9
Arithmetic Computation	1560	4.5	1.9 - 7.9	9
Total Arithmetic	1550	4.0	1.9 - 8.2	9
Paragraph Meaning	1566	3.2	1.8 - 7.9	9
Total Reading	1566	3.1	2.0 - 7.9	9
18-Year-Old Students				
Science	629	5.3[a]	4.2 - 7.5	13
Social Studies	629	5.9[a]	5.0 - 7.7	13
Spelling	973	6.4	6.0 - 9.6	13
Arithmetic Computation	973	6.4	1.9 - 9.2	13
Total Arithmetic	972	5.6	1.9 - 8.6	13
Paragraph Meaning	974	4.3	1.9 - 7.4	13
Total Reading	974	4.3	2.0 - 7.4	13

Source: *Annual Survey of Hearing Impaired Children and Youth* (Washington, D.C.: Personal
 Communication, 1972). As reprinted in Lloyd Dunn, ed., *Exceptional Children in the
 Schools* (New York: Holt, Rinehart and Winston, Inc., 1973), p. 378. Reprinted by
 permission of the Office of Demographic Studies.

[a]Approximately one-third of the fourteen-year-old students were judged unable to take the
 intermediate I battery or higher of the science, social studies, and spelling subtests;
 the total mean, therefore, represents the more advanced two-thirds of the fourteen-
 year-old students taking the tests. About one-third of the eighteen-year-old students
 were judged unable to take the Intermediate I battery or higher of the science and
 social studies and subtests.

school classroom. On the other hand, if the proper training is not provided, a hard-of-hearing child may regress and function like a deaf child.[28]

The concept of mainstreaming has been touched on elsewhere in this volume. *Standard mainstreaming* is the approach in which hearing-impaired children are instructed for all or part of the school day with hearing peers in the regular classroom under the direction of a regular classroom teacher. Grant B. Bitter introduces two variations of the term that appear to be particularly relevant in discussing the education of the hearing impaired:

> *Cross-mainstreaming* is a teaching arrangement similar to a team-teaching concept which involves the regular classroom teacher and the teacher of the hearing impaired. . . . However, in cross-mainstreaming, the teachers do not occupy the same room. The regular classroom teacher may take one or more of the members of the special class into her own room for a period or periods of instruction. As a reciprocal measure, the teacher of the hearing impaired includes one or more children from the regular class in one or more periods of instruction in his/her classroom with hearing impaired children.
>
> *Reverse mainstreaming* refers to the strategy of bringing one or more hearing children into the classroom with the hearing impaired for one or more periods of instruction each day.[29]

Even in special schools for the deaf, the idea of mainstreaming has its special educational significance. Leo Conner describes the significance

[28]Carl W. Asp, "Measurement of Aural Speech Perception and Oral Speech Production of the Hearing Impaired," in Sadanand Singh, ed., *Measurement Procedures in Speech Hearing and Language* (Baltimore, Md.: University Park Press, 1975), p. 193.

[29]Grant B. Bitter, "Whose Schools: Educational Expediency/Educational Integrity," in *Mainstream Education for Hearing Impaired Children and Youth,* ed. Gary W. Nix (New York: Grune & Stratton, Inc., 1976).

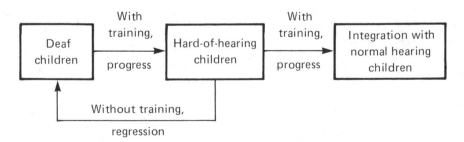

Figure 7–1 An integration model for training deaf and hard-of-hearing children for integration with normal hearing children

of this and defends the concept of mainstreaming in a school (the Lexington School for the Deaf) originally designed only for the hearing impaired:

> The Lexington School's main purpose in educating deaf and hearing children together is to mainstream the special school. We will continue to integrate or mainstream individual deaf children by transfers to regular schools. But we also have an explicit objective to insure that every deaf child must live and learn together with hearing children. This does not mean that all deaf children must leave a special school and attend a regular class. This does not mean that all deaf children must or can get by with itinerant teachers or resource rooms. We have seen too many young deaf children placed in ordinary nurseries and kindergarten classes before they have appropriate speech, language, auditory and speechreading skills. We will not accept the mainstreaming concept that every deaf child should be experimented with by "being placed in the least restrictive setting" until he fails. We do not believe that the lessons learned over the past one hundred years in United States education about the values and achievements of special classes, special schools, and special teachers should be ignored.
>
> The Lexington School considers itself a realistic but innovative school in that its aim is to be sure that all deaf and hearing people live and learn together. That means again that every deaf child in the Lexington School will be exposed to hearing children on a daily, continuous full time basis and that they must learn and live together for the entirety of their educational careers. We are saying that special schools can remain special but should be a part of the mainstream. We are proving that parents of hearing children will send their children to a special school if it's good enough. We are showing that teachers of the deaf are excellent teachers of normally hearing children and that whether judged by critical observers, standardized tests and/or clinical analysis that deaf and hearing children can be helped educationally in an open and project-oriented curriculum environment that also involves the recreational, social, and cultural aspects of their lives.[30]

Anthony van Uden, Department of Psychology and Research, Institute of the Deaf, Saint Michielsgestel, the Netherlands, has developed a program of integrating the prelingually deaf into the hearing society.[31] First he defines this integration: "Two or more groups, al-

---

[30]Leo Conner, "Deaf and Hearing Children at the Lexington School for the Deaf, or Mainstreaming the Special School," in *Mainstream Education*, ed. Nix, pp. 214–25. Also see Winifred H. Northcott, *The Hearing Impaired Child in a Regular Classroom: Preschool, Elementary and Secondary Years* (Washington, D.C.: The Alexander Graham Bell Association for the Deaf, 1973); and Grant Bitter, *Review of the Literature: Integration of Exceptional Children into Regular School Classes* (Salt Lake City, Utah: Project Need, October 1973).

[31]We are indebted to Dr. Grant Bitter, Department of Special Education, University of Utah, for the text of an address by van Uden.

though different from each other, accept each other, as comembers of one overall society so that an arising of subcultures within secluded groups is prevented." Referring to the overall concept of the integration of the deaf into the world around them (mainstreaming), he contends that integration into the family, that is, conversation with both parents and all siblings, must precede integration anywhere else:

> A second important [factor] . . . in the education of the deaf is that we should bring deaf children to insight. Now insight is a technical, psychological term, and means that a person should be aware of his own possibilities and impossibilities. . . . There's always a big danger if we educate our children too much together, the deaf with the deaf; then they will not sufficiently come to that insight, because they have other children on the same level in some way. They do not have a partner. But if they are educated with hearing, every day they have that partner. . . . We say a deaf child should be educated to openness to the hearing. The heart open to the hearing; trustfulness, confidence . . . .

The deaf child's first contact with the hearing world is generally with his family. The impact of the deaf child upon his family starts with their first inkling of the existence of the child's disability. This awareness of the child's deafness most frequently appears first to the mother who realizes that she must "read" the child's nonverbal utterances to satisfy his or her needs rather than to hear his or her problems. Since parents ordinarily communicate their expectations through conventional speech, the deaf child must depend upon learning the "house rules" by analyzing his environment. Thus, if the child correctly interprets his or her mother, who is most often the child's constant companion during the first year of life, the child still has to make sense of the father's demands.[32] Eugene D. Mindel and McCay Vernon write, "Ambiguity in communication is one of the deaf child's greatest problems in the home."[33]

Upon discovering their child's deafness, it is not at all unusual for parents to go through a series of adaptive mechanisms described in the chapter on the exceptional child in the family. To the child, deafness (if it is not congenital) is a profound loss that, unlike a crippling handicap, "alter[s] the nature of the child's contact with the world."[34] Information that is filtered through one's sense of hearing is lost, leading to deficiencies in subsequent psychological and social development. A

---

[32]Arthur van Uden, A World of Language for Deaf Children, Part I, Basic Principles (Rotterdam: Rotterdam University Press, 1970).

[33]Eugene D. Mindel and McCay Vernon, They Grow in Silence (Silver Spring, Md.: National Association for the Deaf, 1971), p. 11.

[34]Ibid., p. 18.

profound hearing loss excludes the child from the earliest and probably the most important contacts with the mother.[35] The human voice is the child's first affective contact with the adult world and conveys the tenderness felt by that world for the child. The isolation of deafness hinders the child's development of language and general knowledge. With the recent and increasing emphasis upon mainstreaming the exceptional child in education, one must consider that deaf children are "acutely sensitive to their difficulty and to the lack of understanding of their difficulties by well-meaning hearing people. This is especially true when they are placed in situations which require that they conform to classroom and social activities geared to those who have no hearing loss."[36]

Because of psychological adaptation to their child's deafness, parents of deaf children rarely realize that their child's progress will be severely limited by deafness; this is due in part to the fact that most deaf children look like normally hearing children and that, up to the age of eighteen months, their play patterns and vocal utterances are similar to the sounds and play patterns of hearing children. The shift from an illusory view of their child to one that relinquishes fantasies of perfection and normal development is exceedingly difficult to make. Until about the age of five, parents not only tolerate but also exult in the meager acquisition of vocabulary and by so doing deceive themselves further. As the child matures, the differences between him or her and hearing children widen, and parental anxiety, guilt, and fear are renewed. Current professional opinion holds that the earlier parents resolve their feelings about their child's impaired hearing, the better progress the child (and the parents) makes in his or her education and integration into the world.

It is probably true that most deaf people in America today have joined the deaf club; that is, they have secluded themselves from the hearing society. Nonetheless, the promise of the future for deaf children is very bright. With techniques for early identification, amplification, and more effective teaching strategies and with increased involvement of parents and the community, the challenge of teaching the deaf is becoming one that will test the ingenuity and intelligence of all who are deeply involved in this facet of exceptional education.

[35]See, for example, Burton White, *The First Three Years of Life* (Englewood Cliffs, N.J.: Prentice-Hall, Inc., 1975).
[36]Mindel and Vernon, *They Grow in Silence*, p. 19.

And Sarah Laughed

by Joanne Greenberg

She went to the window every fifteen minutes to see if they were coming. They would be taking the new highway cutoff; it would bring them past the south side of the farm; past the unused, dilapidated outbuildings instead of the orchards and fields that were now full and green. It would look like a poor place to the new bride. Her first impression of their farm would be of age and bleached-out, dried-out buildings on which the doors hung open like a row of gaping mouths that said nothing.

All day, Sarah had gone about her work clumsy with eagerness and hesitant with dread, picking up utensils to forget them in holding, finding them two minutes later a surprise in her hand.

She had been planning and working ever since Abel wrote to them from Chicago that he was coming home with a wife. Everything should have been clean and orderly. She wanted the bride to know as soon as she walked inside what kind of woman Abel's mother was—to feel, without a word having to be said, the house's dignity, honesty, simplicity, and love. But the spring cleaning had been late, and Alma Yoder had gotten sick—Sarah had had to go over to the Yoders and help out.

Now she looked around and saw that it was no use trying to have everything ready in time. Abel and his bride would be coming any minute. If she didn't want to get caught shedding tears of frustration, she'd better get herself under control. She stepped over the pile of clothes still unsorted for the laundry and went out on the back porch.

The sky was blue and silent, but as she watched, a bird passed over the fields crying. The garden spread out before her, displaying its varying greens. Beyond it, along the creek, there was a row of poplars. It always calmed her to look at them. She looked today. She and Matthew had planted those trees. They stood thirty feet high now, stately as figures in a procession. Once—only once and many years ago—she had tried to describe in words the sounds that the wind made as it combed those trees on its way west. The little boy to whom she had spoken was a grown man now, and he was bringing home a wife. *Married. . . .*

Ever since he had written to tell them he was coming with his bride, Sarah had been going back in her mind to the days when she and Matthew were bride and groom and then mother and father. Until now, it hadn't seemed so long ago. Her life had flowed on past her, blurring the early days with Matthew when this farm was strange and new to her and when the silence of it was sharp and bitter like pain, not dulled and familiar like an echo of old age.

Matthew hadn't changed much. He was a tall, lean man, but he had had a boy's spareness

then. She remembered how his smile came, wavered and went uncertainly, but how his eyes had never left her. He followed everything with his eyes. Matthew had always been a silent man; his face was expressionless and his body stiff with reticence, but his eyes had sought her out eagerly and held her and she had been warm in his look.

Sarah and Matthew had always known each other—their families had been neighbors. Sarah was a plain girl, a serious "decent" girl. Not many of the young men asked her out, and when Matthew did and did again, her parents had been pleased. Her father told her that Matthew was a good man, as steady as any woman could want. He came from honest, hard-working people and he would prosper any farm he had. Her mother spoke shyly of how his eyes woke when Sarah came into the room, and how they followed her. If she married him, her life would be full of the things she knew and loved, an easy, familiar world with her parents' farm not two miles down the road. But no one wanted to mention the one thing that worried Sarah: the fact that Matthew was deaf. It was what stopped her from saying yes right away; she loved him, but she was worried about his deafness. The things she feared about it were the practical things: a fall or a fire when he wouldn't hear her cry for help. Only long after she had put those fears aside and moved the scant two miles into his different world, did she realize that the things she had feared were the wrong things.

Now they had been married for twenty-five years. It was a good marriage—good enough. Matthew was generous, strong, and loving. The farm prospered. His silence made him seem more patient, and because she became more silent also, their neighbors saw in them the dignity and strength of two people who do not rail against misfortune, who were beyond trivial talk and gossip; whose lives needed no words. Over the years of help given and meetings attended, people noticed how little they needed to say. Only Sarah's friend Luita knew that in the beginning, when they were first married, they had written yearning notes to each other. But Luita didn't know that the notes also were mute. Sarah had never shown them to anyone, although she kept them all, and sometimes she would go up and get the box out of her closet and read them over. She had saved every scrap, from questions about the eggs to the tattered note he had left beside his plate on their first anniversary. He had written it when she was busy at the stove and then he'd gone out and she hadn't seen it until she cleared the table.

The note said: "I love you dearest wife Sarah. I pray you have happy day all day your life."

When she wanted to tell him something, she spoke to him slowly, facing him, and he took the words as they formed on her lips. His speaking voice was thick and hard to understand and he perceived that it was unpleasant. He didn't like to use it. When he had to say something, he used his odd, grunting tone, and she came to understand what he said. If she ever hungered for laughter from him or the little meaningless talk that confirms existence and affection, she told herself angrily that Matthew talked through his work. Words die in the air; they can be turned one way or another, but Matthew's work prayed and laughed for him. He took good care of her and the boys, and they idolized him. Surely that counted more than all the words—words that meant and didn't mean—behind which people could hide.

Over the years she seldom noticed her own increasing silence, and there were times when his tenderness, which was always given without words, seemed to her to make his silence beautiful.

She thought of the morning she had come downstairs feeling heavy and off balance with her first pregnancy—with Abel. She had gone to the kitchen to begin the day, taking the coffeepot down and beginning to fill it when her eye caught something on the kitchen table. For a minute she looked around in confusion.

They had already laid away what the baby would need: diapers, little shirts and bedding, all folded away in the drawer upstairs, but here on the table was a bounty of cloth, all planned and scrimped for and bought from careful, careful study of the catalogue—yards of patterned flannel and plissé, coat wool and bright red corduroy. Sixteen yards of yellow ribbon for bindings. Under the coat wool was cloth Matthew had chosen for her; blue with a little gray figure. It was silk, and there was a card on which was rolled precisely enough lace edging for her collar and sleeves. All the long studying and careful planning, all in silence.

She had run upstairs and thanked him and hugged him, but it was no use showing delight with words, making plans, matching cloth and figuring which pieces would be for the jacket and which for sleepers. Most wives used such fussing to tell their husbands how much they thought of their gifts. But Matthew's silence was her silence too.

When he had left to go to the orchard after breakfast that morning, she had gone to their room and stuffed her ears with cotton, trying to understand the world as it must be to him, with no sound. The cotton dulled the outside noises a little, but it only magnified all the noises in her head. Scratching her cheek caused a roar like a downpour of rain; her own voice was like thunder. She knew Matthew could not hear his own voice in his head. She could not be deaf as he was deaf. She could not know such silence ever.

So she found herself talking to the baby inside her, telling it the things she would have told Matthew, the idle daily things: Didn't Margaret Amson look peaked in town? Wasn't it a shame the drugstore had stopped stocking lump alum—her pickles wouldn't be the same.

Abel was a good baby. He had Matthew's great eyes and gentle ways. She chattered to him all day, looking forward to his growing up, when there would be confidences between them. She looked to the time when he would have his own picture of the world, and with that keen hunger and hope she had a kind of late blooming into a beauty that made people in town turn to look at her when she passed in the street holding the baby in the fine clothes she had made for him. She took Abel everywhere, and came to know a pride that was very new to her, a plain girl from a modest family who had married a neighbor boy. When they went to town, they always stopped over to see Matthew's parents and her mother.

Mama had moved to town after Pa died. Of course they had offered to have Mama come and live with them, but Sarah was glad she had gone to a little place in town, living where there were people she knew and things happening right outside her door. Sarah remembered them visiting on a certain spring day, all sitting in Mama's new front room. They sat uncomfortably in the genteel chairs, and Abel crawled around on the floor as the women talked, looking up every now and then for his father's nod of approval. After a while he went to catch the sunlight that was glancing off a crystal nut dish and scattering rainbow bands on the floor. Sarah smiled down at him. She too had a radiance, and, for the first time in her life, she knew it. She was wearing the dress she had made from Matthew's cloth—it became her and she knew that too, so she gave her joy freely as she traded news with Mama.

Suddenly they heard the fire bell ringing up on the hill. She caught Matthew's eye and mouthed, "Fire engines," pointing uphill to the firehouse. He nodded.

In the next minutes there was the strident, off-key blare as every single one of Arcadia's volunteer firemen—his car horn plugged with a matchstick and his duty before him—drove hell-bent for the firehouse in an ecstasy of bell and siren. In a minute the ding-ding-ding-ding careened in deafening, happy privilege through every red light in town.

"Big bunch of boys!" Mama laughed. "You can count two Saturdays in good weather when they don't have a fire, and that's during the hunting season!"

They laughed. Then Sarah looked down at Abel, who was still trying to catch the wonderful colors. A madhouse of bells, horns, screaming sirens had gone right past them and he hadn't cried, he hadn't looked, he hadn't turned. Sarah twisted her head sharply away and screamed to the china cats on the whatnot shelf as loud as she could, but Abel's eyes only flickered to the movement and then went back to the sun and its colors.

Mama whispered, "Oh, my dear God!"

Sarah began to cry bitterly, uncontrollably, while her husband and son looked on, confused, embarrassed, unknowing.

The silence drew itself over the seasons and the seasons layered into years. Abel was a good boy; Matthew was a good man.

Later, Rutherford, Lindsay, and Franklin Delano came. They too were silent. Hereditary nerve deafness was rare, the doctors all said. The boys might marry and produce deaf children, but it was not likely. When they started to school, the administrators and teachers told her that the boys would be taught specially to read lips and to speak. They would not be "abnormal," she was told. Nothing would show their handicap, and with training no one need know that they were deaf. But the boys seldom used their lifeless voices to call to their friends; they seldom joined games unless they were forced to join. No one but their mother understood their speech. No teacher could stop all the jumping, turning, gum-chewing schoolboys, or remember herself to face front from the blackboard to the sound-closed boys. The lip-reading exercises never seemed to make plain differences—"man," "pan," "began."

But the boys had work and pride in the farm. The seasons varied their silence with colors—crows flocked in the snowy fields in winter, and tones of golden wheat darkened across acres of summer wind. If the boys couldn't hear the bedsheets flapping on the washline, they could see and feel the autumn day. There were chores and holidays and the wheel of birth and planting, hunting, fishing, and harvest. The boys were familiar in town; nobody ever laughed at them, and when Sarah met neighbors at the store, they praised her sons with exaggerated praise, well meant, saying that no one could tell, no one could really tell unless they knew, about the boys not hearing.

Sarah wanted to cry to these kindly women that the simple orders the boys obeyed by reading her lips were not a miracle. If she could ever hear in their long-practiced robot voices a question that had to do with feelings and not facts, and answer it in words that rose beyond the daily, tangible things done or not done, *that* would be a miracle.

Her neighbors didn't know that they themselves confided to one another from a universe of hopes, a world they wanted half lost in the world that was; how often they spoke pitting inflection against meaning to soften it, harden it, make a joke of it, curse by it, bless by it. They didn't realize how they wrapped the bare words of love in gentle humor or wild insults that the loved ones knew were ways of keeping the secret of love between the speaker and the hearer. Mothers lovingly called their children crow-bait, mouse-meat, devils. They predicted dark ends for them, and the children heard the secrets beneath the words, heard them and smiled and knew, and let the love said-unsaid caress their souls. With her own bitter knowledge Sarah could only thank them for well-meaning and return to silence.

Standing on the back porch now, Sarah heard the wind in the poplars and she sighed. It was getting on to noon. Warm air was beginning to ripple the fields. Matthew would be ready for lunch soon, but she wished she could stand out under the warm sky forever and listen to birds stitching sounds into the endless silence. She found herself thinking about Abel again, and the bride. She wondered what Janice would be like. Abel had gone all the way to Chicago to be trained in drafting. He had met her there, in the school. Sarah was afraid of a girl like that. They had been married quickly, without family or friends or toasts or gifts or questions. It hinted at some kind of secret shame. It frightened her. That kind of girl was independent and she might be scornful of a dowdy mother-in-law. And the house was still a mess.

From down the road, dust was rising. Matthew must have seen it too. He came over the rise and toward the house walking faster than usual. He'd want to slick his hair down and wash up to meet the stranger his son had become. She ran inside and bundled up the unsorted laundry, ran upstairs and pulled a comb through her hair, put on a crooked dab of lipstick, banged her shin, took off her apron and saw a spot on her dress, put the apron on again and shouted a curse to all the disorder she suddenly saw around her.

Now the car was crunching up the thin gravel of the driveway. She heard Matthew downstairs washing up, not realizing that the bride and groom were already at the house. Protect your own, she thought, and ran down to tell him. Together they went to the door and opened it, hoping that at least Abel's familiar face would comfort them.

They didn't recognize him at first, and he didn't see them. He and the tiny bride might have been alone in the world. He was walking around to open the door for her, helping her out, bringing her up the path to the house, and all the time their fingers and hands moved and spun meanings at which they smiled and laughed; they were talking somehow, painting thoughts in the air so fast with their fingers that Sarah couldn't see where one began and the other ended. She stared. The school people had always told her that such finger-talk set the deaf apart. It was abnormal; it made freaks of them. . . . How soon Abel had accepted someone else's strangeness and bad ways. She felt so dizzy she thought she was going to fall, and she was more bitterly jealous than she had ever been before.

The little bride stopped before them appealingly and in her dead, deaf-rote voice, said, "Ah-am pliized to meet 'ou." Sarah put out her hand dumbly and it was taken and the girl's eyes shone. Matthew smiled, and this time the girl spoke and waved her hands in time to her words, and then gave Matthew her hand. So Abel had told that girl about Matthew's deafness. It had never been a secret, but Sarah felt somehow betrayed.

They had lunch, saw the farm, the other boys came home from their summer school and met Janice. Sarah put out cake and tea and showed Abel and Janice up to the room she had made ready for them, and all the time the two of them went on with love-talk in their fingers; the jokes and secrets knitted silently between them, fears told and calmed, hopes spoken and echoed in the silence of a kitchen where twenty-five years of silence had imprisoned her. Always they would stop and pull themselves back to their good manners, speaking or writing polite questions and answers for the family; but in a moment or two, the talk would flag, the urgent hunger would overcome them and they would fight it, resolutely turning their eyes to Sarah's mouth. Then the signs would creep into their fingers, and the joy of talk into their faces, and they would fall before the conquering need of their communion.

Sarah's friend Luita came the next day, in the afternoon. They sat over tea with the kitchen window open for the cool breeze and Sarah was relieved and grateful to hold to a familiar thing now that her life had suddenly become so strange to her. Luita hadn't changed at all, thank God—not the hand that waved her tea cool or the high giggle that broke into generous laughter.

"She's darling!" Luita said after Janice had been introduced, and, thankfully, had left them. Sarah didn't want to talk about her, so she agreed without enthusiasm.

Luita only smiled back.

"Sarah, you'll never pass for pleased with a face like that."

"It's just—just her ways," Sarah said. "She never even wrote to us before the wedding, and now she comes in and—and changes everything. I'll be honest, Luita, I didn't want Abel to marry someone who was deaf. What did we train him for, all those special classes? . . . not to marry another deaf person. And she hangs on him like a wood tick all day. . ." She didn't mention the signs. She couldn't.

Luita said, "It's just somebody new in the house, that's all. She's important to you, but a stranger. Addie Purkhard felt the same way and you know what a lovely girl Velma turned out to be. It just took time. . . . She's going to have a baby, did she tell you?"

"Baby? Who?" Sarah cried, feeling cold and terrified.

"Why, *Velma*. A baby due about a month after my Dolores'."

It had never occurred to Sarah that Janice and Abel could have a baby. She wanted to stop thinking about it and she looked back at Luita whose eyes were glowing with something joyful that had to be said. Luita hadn't been able to see beyond it to the anguish of her friend.

Luita said, "You know, Sarah, things haven't been so good between Sam and me. . . ." She cleared her throat. "You know how stubborn he is. The last few weeks, it's been like a whole new start for us. I came over to tell you about it because I'm so happy, and I had to share it with you."

She looked away shyly, and Sarah pulled herself together and leaned forward, putting her hand on her friend's arm. "I'm so happy for you. What happened?"

"It started about three weeks ago—a night that neither of us could get to sleep. We hadn't been arguing; there was just that awful coldness, as if we'd both been frozen stiff. One of us started talking—just lying there in the dark. I don't even know who started, but pretty soon we were telling each other the most secret things—things we never could have said in the light. He finally told me that Dolores having a baby makes him feel old and scared. He's afraid of it, Sarah, and I never knew it, and it explains why he hates to go over and see them, and why he argues with Ken all the time. Right there beside me he told me so many things I'd forgotten or misunderstood. In the dark it's like thinking out loud—like being alone and yet together at the same. I love him so and I came so close to forgetting it. . . ."

Sarah lay in bed and thought about Luita and Sam sharing their secrets in the dark. Maybe even now they were talking in their flower-papered upstairs room, moving against the engulfing seas of silence as if in little boats, finding each other and touching and then looking out in awe at the vastness all around them where they might have rowed alone and mute forever. She wondered if Janice and Abel fingered those signs in the dark on each other's body. She began to cry. There was that freedom, at least; other wives had to strangle their weeping.

When she was cried out, she lay in bed and counted all the good things she had: children, possessions, acres of land, respect of neighbors, the years of certainty and success. Then she conjured the little bride, and saw her standing in front of Abel's old car as she had at first—with nothing; all her virtues still unproven, all her fears still forming, and her bed in another woman's house. Against the new gold ring on the bride's finger, Sarah threw all the substance of her years to weigh for her. The balance went with the bride. It wasn't fair! The balance went with the bride because she had put that communion in the scales as well, and all the thoughts that must have been given and taken between them. It outweighed Sarah's twenty-five years of muteness; outweighed the house and barn and well-tended land, and the sleeping family keeping their silent thoughts.

The days went by. Sarah tortured herself with elaborate courtesy to Janice and politeness to the accomplice son, but she couldn't guard her own envy from herself and she found fault wherever she looked. Now the silence of her house was throbbing with her anger. Every morning Janice would come and ask to help, but Sarah was too restless to teach her, so Janice would sit for a while waiting and then get up and go outside to look for Abel. Then Sarah would decide to make coleslaw and sit with the chopping bowl in her lap, smashing the chopper against the wood with a vindictive joy that she alone could hear the sounds she was making, that she alone knew how savage they were and how satisfying.

At church she would see the younger boys all clean and handsome, Matthew greeting friends, Janice demure and fragile, and Abel proud and loving, and she would feel a terrible guilt for her unreasonable anger; but back from town afterwards, and after Sunday dinner, she noticed as never before how disheveled the boys looked, how ugly their hollow voices sounded. Had Matthew always been so patient and unruffled? He was like one of his own stock, an animal, a dumb animal.

Janice kept asking to help and Sarah kept saying there wasn't time to teach her. She was amazed when Matthew, who was very fussy about his fruit, suggested to her that Janice might be able to take care of the grapes and, later, work in the orchard.

"I haven't time to teach her!"

"Ah owill teeech Ja-nuss," Abel said, and they left right after dinner in too much of a hurry.

Matthew stopped Sarah when she was clearing the table and asked why she didn't like Janice. Now it was Sarah's turn to be silent, and when Matthew insisted, Sarah finally turned on him. "You don't understand," she shouted. "You don't understand a thing!" And she saw on his face the same look of confusion she had seen that day in Mama's fussy front room when she had suddenly begun to cry and could not stop. She turned away with the plates, but suddenly his hand shot out and he struck them to the floor, and the voice he couldn't hear or control rose to an awful cry, "Ah ahm dehf! Ah ahm dehf!" Then he went out, slamming the door without the satisfaction of its sound.

If a leaf fell or a stalk sprouted in the grape arbor, Janice told it over like a set of prayers. One night at supper, Sarah saw the younger boys framing those dumb-signs of hers, and she took them outside and slapped their hands. "We don't do that!" she shouted at them, and to Janice later she said, "Those . . . signs you make—I know they must have taught you to do that, but out here . . . well, it isn't our way."

Janice looked back at her in a

confusion for which there were no words.

It was no use raging at Janice. Before she had come there had never been anything for Sarah to be angry about. . . . What did they all expect of her? Wasn't it enough that she was left out of a world that heard and laughed without being humiliated by the love-madness they made with their hands? It was like watching them undressing.

The wind cannot be caught. Poplars may sift it, a rising bird can breast it, but it will pass by and no one can stop it. She saw the boys coming home at a dead run now, and they couldn't keep their hands from taking letters, words, and pictures from the fingers of the lovers. If they saw an eagle, caught a fish, or got scolded, they ran to their brother or his wife, and Sarah had to stand in the background and demand to be told.

One day Matthew came up to her and smiled and said, "Look." He put out his two index fingers and hooked the right down on the left, then the left down gently on the right. "Fwren," he said, "Januss say, fwren."

To Sarah there was something obscene about all those gestures, and she said, "I don't like people waving their hands around like monkeys in a zoo!" She said it very clearly so that he couldn't mistake it.

He shook his head violently and gestured as he spoke.

"Mouth eat; mouth kiss, mouth tawk! Fin-ger wohk; fin-ger tawk. E-ah" (and he grabbed his ear, violently), "e-ah dehf. *Mihn,*" (and he rapped his head, violently, as if turning a terrible impatience against himself so as to spare her) "*mihn not* dehf!"

Later she went to the barn after something and she ran into Lindsay and Franklin Delano standing guiltily, and when she caught them in her eye as she turned, she saw their hands framing signs. They didn't come into the house until it was nearly dark. Was their hunger for those signs so great that only darkness could bring them home? They weren't bad boys, the kind who would do a thing just because you told them not to. Did their days have a hunger too, or was it only the spell of the lovers, honey-honeying to shut out a world of moving mouths and silence?

At supper she looked around the table and was reassured. It could have been any farm family sitting there, respectable and quiet. A glance from the father was all that was needed to keep order or summon another helping. Their eyes were lowered, their faces composed. The hands were quiet. She smiled and went to the kitchen to fix the shortcake she had made as a surprise.

When she came back, they did not notice her immediately. They were all busy talking. Janice was telling them something and they had their mouths ridiculously pursed with the word. Janice smiled in assent and each one showed her his sign and she smiled at each one and nodded, and the signers turned to one another in their joy, accepting and begging acceptance. Then they saw Sarah standing there; the hands came down, the faces faded.

She took the dinner plates away and brought in the dessert things, and when she went back to the kitchen for the cake, she began to cry. It was beyond envy now; it was too late for measuring or weighing. She had lost. In the country of the blind, Mama used to say, the one-eyed man is king. Having been a citizen of such a country, she knew better. In the country of the deaf, the hearing man is lonely. Into that country a girl had come who, with a wave of her hand, had given the deaf ears for one another, and had made Sarah the deaf one.

Sarah stood, staring at her cake and feeling for that moment the profundity of the silence which she had once tried to match by stuffing cotton in her ears. Everyone she loved was in the other room, talking, sharing, standing before the awful, impersonal heaven and the unhearing earth with pictures of his thoughts, and she was the deaf one now. It wasn't "any farm family," silent in its strength. It was a yearning family, silent in its hunger, and a demure little bride had shown them all how deep the

hunger was. She had shown Sarah that her youth had been sold into silence. She was too old to change now.

An anger rose in her as she stared at the cake. Why should they be free to move and gesture and look different while she was kept in bondage to their silence? Then she remembered Matthew's mute notes, his pride in Abel's training, his face when he had cried, "I am deaf!" over and over. She had actually fought that terrible yearning, that hunger they all must have had for their own words. If they could all speak somehow, what would the boys tell her?

She knew what she wanted to tell them. That the wind sounds through the poplar trees, and people have a hard time speaking to one another even if they aren't deaf. Luita and Sam had to have a night to hide their faces while they spoke. It suddenly occurred to her that if Matthew made one of those signs with his hands and she could learn that sign, she could put her hands against his in the darkness, and read the meaning—that if she learned those signs she could hear him. . . .

She dried her eyes hurriedly and took in the cake. They saw her and the hands stopped, drooping lifelessly again; the faces waited mutely. Silence. It was a silence she could no longer bear. She looked from face to face. What was behind those eyes she loved? Didn't everyone's world go deeper than chores and bread and sleep?

"I want to talk to you," she said. "I want to talk, to know what you think." She put her hands out before her, offering them.

Six pairs of eyes watched her. Janice said, "Mo-ther."

Eyes snapped away to Janice; thumb was under lip: the Sign.

Sarah followed them. "Wife," she said, showing her ring.

"Wife," Janice echoed, thumb under lip to the clasp of hands.

Sarah said, "I love. . . ."

Janice showed her and she followed hesitantly and then turned to Matthew to give and to be received in that sign.

DISCUSSION

Joanne Greenberg, who also wrote "Hunting Season," is a well-known contemporary writer of short stories and novels. She often uses handicapped persons as her central characters and writes with particular sensitivity to their problems and feelings. Her accuracy of perception brings an awareness to the reader of the many limitations that a handicapped person must silently overcome in order to get along in everyday life. In this story, the author develops the character of Sarah from unmarried girl to a wife and mother. When Sarah marries Matthew, she is concerned about his lack of hearing in case of an emergency. She soon learns that this concern, which she had considered dire, is actually trivial compared to the more significant absence of spoken communication. Although eye contact and body messages between Sarah and Matthew convey love, she misses the bantering and affectionate words used between a husband and wife. With her deaf children she does not share the pleasure of jokes and verbal asides and hear the occasional raucous laughter common in most homes. Because their method of communication is limited to what can be written hastily on a note pad or gestured, the range of what is discussed in the home is limited to the concrete—work, weather, food, and sleep.

Sarah's family lives in a small rural community, which for the handicapped has both some advantages and some disadvantages. The biggest advantage is that the family is totally accepted in the community's social group; the boys are not teased as they might be in a larger city school. Nevertheless, Sarah has not had access to support agencies to help her deal with her feelings when she marries Matthew or when each of her sons is born with hereditary nerve deafness. She is given only one point of view regarding education for her children. The authorities make it very clear to her that her first task is to keep them from seeming "abnormal," and they have little regard for the total development of the boys. She is admonished not to expose the boys to sign language; they would appear to be "people waving their hands around like monkeys in a zoo." The school does not have trained teachers to carry through an aural method of communication that stresses lipreading and using as much voice as possible, and only some intermittent instruction in lip-reading is available to the boys. Sarah's sons do not fare much better in communicating than their father, who was educated a generation before them.

When Janice comes into the home, Sarah realizes how restricted her life has been. She has some natural jealousy toward the young woman who has become the most important object of her son's love and attention. Her greatest jealousy is reserved for the animation of the world of words that Janice brings into her silent home. Matthew and the boys revel in their newly found freedom to unlock a world that was previously limited. Sarah's unspoken hurts and prejudices rise to the surface, and for the first time she turns on her husband's muteness. She still retains the prejudice of the advice not to expose her sons to sign language. This story is unusual because the central issue is not the handicapped individual's adjustment to society, but instead the normal person's ability to adjust to her handicapped family. Miss Greenberg movingly portrays Sarah's painful emergence into a new relationship with her family.

SPRINGBOARDS FOR INQUIRY

1. Go through the story and list Sarah's attitudes toward the deaf. Check those feelings about the deaf that you think are popularly held beliefs.

2. If Sarah lived in a community that had ideal services for the deaf and hard of hearing, which services would she have used?

3. Read arguments for total communication and those for an aural method of communication in any of the textbooks mentioned in this chapter and discuss which method you would choose for your own child if he or she were deaf. Give supporting reasons for your choice.

4. In what ways would you find being deaf a handicap in your everyday life?

CHAPTER EIGHT

The Blind
and the
Partially Sighted

A 1961 survey that asked educators to rank exceptional children according to those they would most prefer to teach and those they most understood revealed that the great majority put the visually handicapped on the rejection end of the spectrum while indicating that they knew very little about them.[1] In a college classroom a few years ago, a professor was delivering his usual opening lecture when a steady tap-tap off to his right became distracting. A reprimanding look was cast at the offender, but the tapping did not cease. Finally, the instructor had to make a public, verbal objection. At the end of the hour the errant student came to the lectern to explain that she was taking notes in braille; the noise had been generated by a braille machine that tapped.

The old, sad cliché regarding blindness is that there is "an *automatic* compensation with increased acuity of the other senses when a person loses sight."[2] What *is* true is that it is possible for *all* human beings to achieve greater sensory discrimination given the proper motivation and circumstances. Children can learn to sharpen any receptive skill, provided they follow a planned skill-training curriculum. Claudell S. Stocker "discovered that most [blind] people came into the class for

[1] Albert T. Murphy, "Attitudes of Educators Toward the Visually Handicapped," *International Journal for the Education of the Blind*, 10 (1961), 103–107.
[2] Claudell S. Stocker, *Listening for the Visually Impaired* (Springfield, Ill.: Charles C. Thomas, Publisher, 1973), p. vii.

the improvement of listening efficiency, with the attitude that they did not need a listening class as they had been listening all their lives."[3]

Despite the fact that only a fraction of 1 percent of the total population is blind, "they attract more attention and have more agencies serving them than any other handicapped group."[4] For a variety of reasons, the blind have been the handicapped group most surrounded by an aura of negative mystique. Some have explained this peculiar public response to a blindness-death parallel,[5] others to a Freudian-based castration anxiety.[6] Still others have analyzed the symbolism of the eyes in fairy tales, mythology, folklore, religion, and proverbial sayings.[7] Indeed, "blindness has often been associated with punishment for sexual knowledge and behavior."[8] On the other hand, unrealistic fantasies impute to the blind superior or supernormal mental, artistic, spiritual, or moral powers.

Those who teach the visually impaired or the blind need to be aware not only of the folklore of blindness but also of the facts. It is interesting to note the evolution of the psychology of the blind. Based upon clinical interviews plus case studies of blind children, Thomas Cutsforth concluded in 1933 that the blind are generally neurotic. Though many of his conclusions are currently unacceptable, he did observe that "while the seeing child is developing in relation to his expanding social world and stimulating objective environment, the blind child also is growing in relation to his environment. However, his is not the same expanding social situation or the same stimulating objective environment."[9] Thus, there is almost an insidious combination of forces—ranging from parental overprotection to educational and social segregation—conspiring to prevent the blind child's maturation. Naturally, there follows an erosion of the blind person's self-concept:[10]

---

[3]Ibid., p. xi.
[4]Michael E. Monbeck, *The Meaning of Blindness* (Bloomington, Ind.: Indiana University Press, 1973), p. 2.
[5]Thomas J. Carroll, *Blindness: What It Is, What It Does, and How to Live With It* (Boston, Mass.: Little, Brown and Company, 1961).
[6]Sydell Braverman, "The Psychological Roots of Attitudes Toward Blindness," in *Attitudes Toward Blindness* (New York: American Foundation for the Blind, 1951).
[7]Gerhard Schauer, "Motivation of Attitudes Towards Blindness," *New Outlook for the Blind*, 45 (1951), 39–42; and Hans Von Schumann, *Traüme der Blinden* (Basel: S. Karger Co., 1959).
[8]Donald D. Kirtley, *The Psychology of Blindness* (Chicago, Ill.: Nelson-Hall, 1975), p. 52.
[9]Thomas Cutsforth, *The Blind in School and Society* (New York: American Foundation for the Blind, 1933), pp. 147–48.
[10]In 1933, the term "self-concept" was not current. The concept of "self" did not achieve currency until 1961. Yet, Cutsforth's remarkable book fully recognized the concept but used the terms "self-regard" and "self-respect" (ibid., p. 125).

> In the clinical investigations into the emotional life of the blind that the writer has conducted over a period of years it has been difficult to find any evidence that blindness itself is productive of emotional disturbances. The congenitally blind, never having known experientially what vision is, suffer no feeling of privation save as it is defined for them in their social relations. It will be a revelation to many persons to learn how very rapidly the blinded who have been habituated to vision may become adjusted emotionally to the physical loss of sight, purely as a sensory activity.[11]

Cutsforth explains that the seeing members of society induce negative self-regarding attitudes in the blind and "are entirely responsible for the emotional disturbances found in the blind as a group."[12] Donald D. Kirtley, quoting Cutsforth's work, writes:

> In Cutsforth's view, the only remedy for the emotional pathology of the blind lies in responsible action on the part of the blind person himself, acting in behalf of his own self-growth. Reforming society will not solve his problems. It . . . is the blind person, not the world around him, who must mature to accept himself as he is and to be able to live in his (and the sighted) world as it is.[13]

Blind children display a number of mannerisms that may be distracting to teachers and others who are unprepared for these behaviors. One, for example, is that blind children rarely show emotions in their faces. It is not that they do not have as wide a range of emotions but rather that they have not seen these emotions on the faces of people and, thus, that they have not learned to mimic them. Reacting facially to situations is a learned behavior and, of course, must be imitated. Berthold Lowenfeld suggests that "if parents and teachers make it a point to remind the blind youngster to show in his face what he feels inside, they will have provided the stimulation which is often the only thing needed to promote better facial responsiveness."[14] The acquisition of gestures also needs to be encouraged and taught to blind children. A second mannerism is that blind children frequently do not turn their heads in

---

[11]Ibid., p. 122.
[12]Ibid., p. 124–25.
[13]Kirtley, The Psychology of Blindness, p. 139. Further reading concerning attitudes toward the blind may be found in Michael Monbeck, The Meaning of Blindness (Bloomington, Ind.: Indiana University Press, 1973); Berthold Lowenfeld, Our Blind Children, 3rd ed. (Springfield, Ill.: Charles C. Thomas, Publisher, 1971); Robert Scott, The Making of Blind Men (New York: Russell Sage Foundation, 1969); and Louis Cholden, A Psychiatrist Works with Blindness (New York: American Foundation for the Blind, 1958).
[14]Berthold Lowenfeld, Our Blind Children (Springfield, Ill.: Charles C. Thomas, Publisher, 1971), pp. 207–208.

the direction of the person to whom they are speaking. The incentive to visually observe the other person is not there, yet this is a skill that needs to be acquired early in the life of the blind child. Third, blind children must learn to broadcast their voices. That is, in the absence of turning their heads towards those with whom they are engaged in personal conversation, they speak into space as if no one was there. These mannerisms may be corrected with some instruction.

Persons who expect to teach the blind ought to be thoroughly familiar with the various definitions of the blind. The most commonly used classification, though perhaps not the most accurate, is the one adopted in 1934 during a meeting of the House of Delegates of the American Medical Association: "A person shall be considered blind whose central visual acuity does not exceed 20/200 in the better eye,[15] with correcting lenses or whose visual acuity, if better than 20/200, has a limit of the central field of vision to such a degree that its widest diameter subtends an angle of no greater than twenty degrees." Further refinement of the definition subdivides visually impaired people as blind, with no sense of vision; and as cecutients, with an impaired sense of vision. Obviously a cecutient "is not receiving proper services if he is treated as if totally blind."[16] The most recent update of the AMA definition is offered by the International Society for the Prevention of Blindness who suggest these categories: partial impairment of vision, social blindness, virtual blindness, total blindness, and unspecified or undetermined blindness. All of these categories are defined by visual acuity in the better eye after correction and by the visual field in the better eye.

What is known about the social and psychological components of blindness forms the basis for fashioning the educative environment of the blind. The blind child is limited in the range and variety of experiences since he or she must apply touch for the purpose of cognition. Obviously touching is not always possible or helpful. One cannot with safety touch a lion at the zoo or get the concept of a mountain by touching a piece of it. Berthold Lowenfeld comments that "though touch has some unique advantages, vision functions as a unifying and structuring sense and in this it cannot be replaced by any or all of the remaining senses."[17] Geraldine Sholl writes, "Deprivation of the sense of sight means a reduction in the life experiences of the individual not only cognitively but also

---

[15]The ability to see only at 20 feet what the normal eye is able to see at 200 feet.

[16]Excerpted from Nicholas Hobbs, *Issues in the Classification of Children, A Sourcebook on Categories, Labels, and Their Consequences*, vol. 1 (San Francisco, Calif.: Jossey-Bass, Inc., Publishers, 1975), pp. 240–42.

[17]Berthold Lowenfeld, ed., *The Visually Handicapped Child in School* (New York: The John Day Company, Inc., 1973), p. 56.

to a certain extent in the sheer enjoyment of life itself."[18] Lowenfeld elaborates upon the magnitude of sensory deprivation of the blind by discussing the nature of the sensory input of hearing and touch (which the reader will recall are *not* automatically heightened because of the loss of sight).[19] Hearing gives the blind person some sense of distance and direction but cannot convey any concrete ideas about an object. No idea of shape or size of a tree is possible if a person cannot see it. Knowledge of spatial qualities necessitates touching. Since tactual perception implies the ability to make direct contact with the object, obviously knowledge of sun, moon, clouds, mountains, skyscrapers, flies, ants and objects in motion (such as those that are boiling or frying) is virtually impossible. Unfortunately, only visual perception permits perception of a situation as a whole. In one area only are the blind at an advantage. Tactual perceptions do not depend upon the presence of light; where the power of sight ends in darkness, the power of touch is not impaired.[20]

Irving Zweibelson and C. Fisher Barg investigated concept development in blind children and concluded that blind children function primarily on a concrete level and use abstract concepts less than their sighted peers.[21] They therefore recommend that blind children be richly supplied with concrete experiences and that a multisensory approach be an integral part of their education. Because the blind are less able to deal with abstractions, they learn to name many things without having any real experience or idea of them. Cutsforth calls this naming without real referents "verbalism or verbal unreality"[22] and writes:

> Perhaps nothing very tragic would happen to a blind child if he should never learn to describe an object by its correct visual adjective, but something very serious has occurred, namely, a blind child has developed the desire to employ a visual adjective in lieu of one which is infinitely more

[18]Geraldine Scholl, "The Education of Children with Visual Impairments," in *Education of Exceptional Children and Youth*, ed. William Cruickshank and G. Orville Johnson (Englewood Cliffs, N.J.: Prentice-Hall, Inc., 1967), p. 302.

[19]Berthold Lowenfeld, "Psychological Problems of Children with Impaired Vision," in *Psychology of Exceptional Children and Youth*, 3rd ed., ed. William Cruickshank (Englewood Cliffs, N.J.: Prentice-Hall, Inc., 1971).

[20]In *How Can I Make What I Cannot See?* (New York: Van Nostrand Reinhold Company, 1974) Shiro Fukurai, a sighted sculptor, tells about an assignment teaching blind children art. His discovery that clay is the perfect medium for helping blind children express themselves resulted in a new world of opportunity for his students. The photographs in the book are remarkable evidence of tactual input. Judith Rubin, "Through Art to Affect: Blind Children Express Their Feelings," *The New Outlook for the Blind*, vol. 69, no. 9 (November 1975), sums up this approach more technically than Fukurai.

[21]Irving Zweibelson and C. Fisher Barg, "Concept Development of Blind Children," *New Outlook for the Blind*, 61 (1967), pp. 218–22.

[22]Cutsforth, *The Blind in School and Society*, pp. 48–70.

meaningful to him. . . . the unwarranted use of meaningless visual terminology demonstrates a strong tendency toward unreality in which valid
relationships are utterly disregarded.[23]

Others have either replicated Cutsforth's early work or expanded it.[24]
Paul R. Dokecki refutes Cutsforth and states that

> the view that a verbalism is meaningless and must lead to loose think-
> ing is not in line with current psycholinguistic theory. . . . The placing of a
> value judgment on a natural phenomenon, as Cutsforth has done in the
> case of verbalism, has probably tended to obscure the issue and seems
> to have led to an uncritical acceptance of his notions; this is reflected in the
> concern that educators of the blind have shown in instructional programs
> geared away from non-sensory based concepts.[25]

We have gone into detail about the Cutsforth-Dokecki argument
because most of the education of the blind has been geared to implementing the basic concepts of Cutsforth. Even Dokecki admits "that
while the verbalism phenomenon (as operationally defined) is a real
one," the word-thing concept of language has "led to an overstatement
of the problems attendant to the verbalism concept."[26]

The five most important patterns of education for the blind were
described by John W. Jones and Ann Collins:

Full-time special class.   A specially staffed and equipped room
   in which blind and partially seeing children receive three-
   fourths or more of their formal instruction.

Cooperative special class.   A specially staffed and equipped
   room in which blind and partially seeing children receive
   less than three-fourths of their formal instruction. The re-
   mainder of their school day is spent in regular classrooms.

Resource room.   A specially staffed and equipped room to
   which blind and partially seeing children who are enrolled
   in regular classrooms come at scheduled intervals or as the
   need arises.

[23]Ibid., p. 69.
[24]See Robert Harley, *Verbalism Among Blind Children* (New York: American Foundation
   for the Blind, 1963); Carson Y. Nolan, "On the Unreality of Words to the Blind,"
   New Outlook for the Blind, 54 (1960), 100–102; and Paul R. Dokecki, "Verbalism
   and the Blind: A Critical Review of the Concept and the Literature," *Exceptional
   Children*, 32 (1966), 525–30.
[25]Dokecki, "Verbalism and the Blind," p. 527.
[26]Ibid., pp. 528–29. A review of the field of general semantics will aid the student in
   following the argument better.

Itinerant teacher.   An organizational pattern in which blind and partially seeing children spend most of their school day in regular classrooms but receive special instruction from itinerant teachers who travel among two or more schools devoting more than half of their time to the instruction of such children.

Teacher-consultant.   An organizational pattern in which special teachers serve as itinerant teachers part of the time but spend 50 percent or more of their time in more general duties, such as consulting with regular school personnel and distributing aids.[27]

Regardless of the particular organizational modality chosen, Berthold Lowenfeld's specific goal for the education of blind children is similar to the goal most educators have for all children: "Education must aim at giving the blind child a knowledge of the realities around him, the confidence to cope with these realities, and the feeling that he is recognized and accepted as an individual in his own right."[28] It is the teacher's actions and attitudes that can make the child's educational experience fulfilling or disappointing. Kenneth A. Hanninen contends that

> whether it is an integrated or segregated classroom, the teacher's attitude will be quickly transmitted. . . . Like the sighted child, the visually handicapped child must be taken from where he is to where he needs to go in his development . . . . In addition to an atmosphere of acceptance and understanding, the blind person needs to be able to adequately function independently in his environment.[29]

Berthold Lowenfeld's principles for teaching blind children seem best to sum up the implications of this discussion: "Beyond the teaching of such tool subjects as braille and other modifications in equipment and mediums, special education of the blind must practice certain educational methods which are based on the psychological effects of blindness."[30] He urges educators to be aware of the following:

[27]John W. Jones and Ann Collins, *Educational Programs for Visually Handicapped Children* (Washington D.C.: United States Government Printing Office, 1966).

[28]Berthold Lowenfeld, "The Child Who Is Blind," *Journal of Exceptional Children,* 19 (December 1952), p. 96.

[29]Kenneth A. Hanninen, *Teaching the Visually Handicapped* (Columbus, Ohio: Charles E. Merrill Publishing Company, 1975).

[30]Berthold Lowenfeld, *Our Blind Children,* 3rd ed. (Springfield, Ill.: Charles C. Thomas, Publisher, 1971), pp. 168–69.

1. *Individualization.*   While all modern educational theory
   speaks of tailoring education to the particular and idiosyn-
   cratic needs of each student, visually handicapped children
   differ from each other as much as or more than children in a
   class for the sighted. While the usual sources of individual
   variability are very much a part of the considerations that
   must be accounted for with blind children, it is urgent that
   the following special methods for the visually impaired also
   be considered:
   a. Since not all children are born blind or are totally blind,
      the degree to which a child is blind makes necessary a
      careful consideration of the utilization of remaining
      senses, the use of visual concepts, and the degree to which
      the impairment interferes with learning. The use of optical
      aids, of strategies for teaching mobility, of retained vision
      are all part of the individual inventory that must be made
      for each child.
   b. Children who become blind before about the age of five do
      not have a workable visual memory. The age at onset of
      blindness determines the scope of the child's social and
      education experiences. If blindness is recent, trauma must
      be evaluated for its relevance to the educational strategies
      planned.
   c. The child's current eye condition may determine the de-
      gree of special care to be exercised in school. For example,
      a child may have to wear special glasses and his program
      of physical activities may need to be modified based upon
      the care necessary for those glasses.
   d. The age of school entrance of blind children may have to
      be adjusted. Lengthy hospitalization sometimes leads to
      retardation in the performance of certain skills.
2. *Concreteness in teaching.*   While blind children react with
   all their senses to environmental stimulation, they can only
   gain actual knowledge of the world through touch. As a
   medium of social contact, hearing is vital to the blind child,[31]
   it "gives clues to the presence, location, or condition of ob-

[31]Claudell Stocker comments that "when an individual is deprived of eyesight, the sense of
hearing becomes his primary contact with his environment. As blind persons
practice skills which are dependent upon the sense of hearing there is usually
some secondary improvement in listening efficiency" (Claudell Stocker, *Listening for the Visually Impaired* [Springfield, Ill.: Charles C. Thomas, Publisher,
1973], p. vii).

jects."[32] A British survey contends that "the deepest and most fundamental needs of blind children are a rich and intimate experience of common things, and a direct acquaintance with the many characters that move across the scenes of daily life, and the activities in which these characters engage."[33] Concreteness in teaching gives the blind child an opportunity to realistically appraise his or her surroundings.

3. *Teaching using unified instruction*. The *wholes* of existence—for example, the grocery store rather than a shelf of canned vegetables, the truck rather than the axle, and the house rather than the fireplace—provide a meaningful gestalt for the child. The unit plan of instruction organizes the experiences of all children and particularly gives blind children a total view of their universe.[34] The acquisition of basic concepts of objects and situations in a planned sequence is provided by a unitary curriculum.[35]

4. *Additional stimulation.*   Sighted children themselves bring into the classroom a variety of experiences and impressions.[36] The teacher of the blind must often provide students with plentiful experiences and opportunities that are ordinarily not available and may seem unsuitable to the blind child.

5. *Self-activity.*   Blind children cannot learn by visual imitation. The problem of behaving appropriately in social situations is immense. Only when blind children are encouraged to do things for themselves can they develop self-reliance. Even at the risk of losing time and patience, self-activity must be fostered by the teacher. The rule of thumb suggested by Lowenfeld is "not too much [assistance] because it may deprive him of the feeling of accomplishment and make him depend on others—and not too little because failure may discourage him and he may lose interest."[37]

[32]Lowenfeld, *Our Blind Children*, 3rd ed., p. 159.
[33]Edward Arnold, *The Education of the Blind* (London: Edward Arnold & Co., 1963), pp. 45–47. As quoted in Lowenfeld, *Our Blind Children*, 3rd ed., p. 160.
[34]See Wanda Robertson, *An Evaluation for Social Education of the Culture Unit Method* (New York: Teachers College Press, 1950).
[35]The interest center as a method of instruction may be very helpful here.
[36]This is also true of blind children. The intent of this discussion of special methods of educating the blind child is to emphasize the role of the teacher as a stimulator for the restricted experiences and impressions of blind children.
[37]Lowenfeld, *Our Blind Children*, 3rd ed., p. 167.

The success or failure of education for the blind depends on the teacher.[38] There are, as has been indicated, the special methodologies based upon knowledge of the visually impaired. It should be quite obvious that except for special considerations about the extent and nature of the child's blindness, most of Lowenfeld's insights are applicable to normal students as well: "They must be helped to develop the same feelings about themselves, the same attitudes towards others, and the same familiarity with their environment as is desirable for all children."[39]

[38]See, for example, Elliott Landau, Sherrie Epstein, and Ann Stone, *The Teaching Experience* (Englewood Cliffs, N.J.: Prentice-Hall, Inc., 1976).
[39]Lowenfeld, *Our Blind Children*, 3rd ed., p. 168.

The Fourth World

by Daphne Athas

On the curving highway which rose out of the town, an interstate bus stopped to let a passenger out. This was a young woman about twenty-two years old, whose short, waved, black hair strayed over a serious face. She descended first, then leaned forward to receive a large suitcase which was handed out to her. Across the top of the case were stamped the initials, A.C., in heavy black.

This stood for Actia Clewes. She was glad to see it at this point, for it established her identity in a strange place. She was like a young carrier pigeon started out on its first flight. She nodded a smile. She murmured "Thank you." She stepped back grimacing at the heaviness of the case. She looked at the wheels of the bus as they slipped backward. She put her hand to her hair as the bus grumbled into first gear and rushed off thrusting a wind back at her. And then she stretched her eyes to the broom grass horizon and the cedar trees, looking for something.

She picked up her bag with an extravagant determination and began walking quickly down the road. She brushed off the crumbs of a morning sandwich which clung to the collar of her new navy suit.

"What will it be like? What will become of me? What if I can't stand what they are—the way they look? I have never seen any but raddled old beggars on the street. What if they are depressing?"

In the distance she saw two women coming toward her.

They were both slovenly, in faded blue dresses.

"Can you tell me where is the road that leads off to Canopus Institution?" Actia asked them.

At once she saw their eyes signal to each other. And they stared at her with curiosity naked and fierce, as if she were not watching them.

"Good heavens, they think I'm blind!"

• • •

Gobi Morgan was gangling and lean with wide, thin shoulders. He was about sixteen or seventeen, with a wide, slivered, grinning, sensitive mouth. His eyes were misshapen as two snail shells, and wild.

He formed a battalion of boys. Hawking, shuffling and giggling, they presented themselves to Actia Clewes.

"I am Gobi Morgan. I am glad to meet you," he announced.

"I'm glad to meet you too . . ."

"We wanted to meet you before we get you in a classroom as a teacher where we can't talk so much . . ."

"Shall we do it? Shall we do it?" prodded two boys in back.

"We wanted to show you something . . ." said another boy.

"I am stone blind," said Gobi Morgan proudly, with a smile.

"We wanted to show you something about stone-blind people," said Lennie Barker.

"You want to see it?"

"Come in here."

They cornered Actia. They led her into a cubicle. They shut the door. It was pitch black. Someone giggled.

"The light!" said Lennie Barker. "Are you ready?"

"Go on," said Gobi.

He had the tone of announcing an atomic experiment. There were excited drawings of breath in the darkness.

"Remember. I am stone blind," Gobi said in a solemn voice. "I can see absolutely nothing."

"It takes talent to do what he is about to do," repeated Lennie in an eerie voice.

"Begin," commanded Gobi.

There was a sharp, frenetic clicking. Lennie Barker flicked the light off and on, off and on. Light stabbed. Darkness swallowed the light. Light cut.

The clicking stopped.

"It's on," said Gobi's voice, full of pride.

There came another series of clicks with the world spinning off and on.

"It's off."

Again.

"It's on."

"It's on."

"It's off."

"It's on."

"How can you tell?" whispered Actia.

"Do you really want to know?"

"Is it a trick?" she asked.

"I smell it." Gobi's voice was eerie too.

"You can't smell light!"

"That's just the thing," Gobi whispered. "You can't smell light. But you can smell darkness."

"I don't believe it," said Actia with a wisp of a smile in her voice. "Then how does darkness smell?"

"Well, the only thing I can tell you is . . . you've noticed how different colored people smell from white? Darkness smells like that!"

"How can you see the sky if there is no end to the sky?" the blind children asked.

"How can you see faraway in a picture when it is really flat?"

"Why can't you see the back of an orange?"

There was a note of precocious superiority in these questions to Actia Clewes. "Who are you," they seemed to say disdainfully, "to say you can see, and hand us this illegitimate and irrational picture of the world?"

"Why are people little when they are far away and big when they are near to?"

"How come if you look at water you see yourself?"

"I dare you to explain what a mirror is."

A ball whacked against the brick wall outside. A child's voice said: "The sun is too shining. Come and feel it for yourself."

The sound beckoned Actia. She started up with her eyes wide open.

But at that moment something happened.

The door opened. Tiny hands and fingernails crawled up and down the lintel. A musty odor prevailed, composed of sour-sweet sweat. Squeaks issued from the mouths of the small children.

They threw a dirty stocking in her room and disappeared.

She got up in her bare feet and ran at them. She picked up the dirty stocking and threw it out after them into the corridor. The smell of the stocking was their smell. They did not know she had thrown the stocking out, but in a minute one of them stepped on it, plunked down beside it on the corridor floor, fingered it, and laughed loudly.

She laughed to watch them.

A paradox was revealed. She was not an anthropologist come to explore the habits of a strange species. She was a stranger captured in a coop of noisy, meddlesome familiars.

They descended into her room. They surrounded her. They were the kindergarten children, all four and five years old. They clobbered up on the bed onto her. They sat themselves on her lap. They felt of her—her hair, her nose, her eyes, her collar-bones, her breast, her stomach, her legs, her feet.

"Hair!" they screamed. They twined their fingers in her hair.

"You have pretty hair."

"You have curly hair."

"Nose. Look at this nose."

A covey of hands plucked at her nose.

"What's this?"

"My locket," answered Actia.

"Locket," they whispered.

"It's blue. Blue locket!" A girl with a mophead of hair laid her head on Actia's breast and jingled the blue locket in the sun against her milky eyes.

"I know blue," she said, laughing to herself.

"Blue locket. Blue locket!" the others repeated, laughing.

With all the hands surrounding her and clasping her, she felt inarticulate, a stranger even to herself. One little girl found the nipple of her breast and foraged for it rudely as if she were her own new-born baby. Actia blushed all alone to herself. The rest had hold of her collar, her belt buckle, the skirts of her dress, her hems, her shoes.

A clap of hands and a shout from Miss Vythiard, the albino matron, brought them tumbling and scared to the floor.

"You are not to behave like that with strangers!" Miss Vythiard shouted.

The upper school girls captured her. Fifteen- and sixteen-year-olds, they were dressed in wash-cotton dresses, and their hair was cut in institution bobs. Smiling, nodding, like virtuosi they drew her into their circle. They clustered about her, flattering, cajoling, teasing her, like a celebrity.

"What kind of perfume are you wearing?"

"Are you wearing high heels?"

"Do you always wear high heels?"

"Have you ever seen any blinks before us?"

"What do you think of us?"

"Have you ever been in an institution before?"

"Don't ask her all those questions. How can she answer all that at once? She'll think we have awful manners!"

"You don't think we have awful manners, do you? Eee-hee!"

Two girls took her arm.

"We have decided to be your hostesses."

"Before the teachers take over the job . . ."

"Before you get like the rest of them."

"Before you get to be a Dr. August-indoctrinated Stoic."

Rhea Thomas began to mimic the nasal voice of Dr. August: "The first project on the first day of school year will be to shear off the inertia of the blind accumulated during the summer ———"

"From sitting on their front porches in a rocking chair . . ." someone added.

They all laughed.

"Don't think that we are just a bunch of eccentrics . . ."

"We have decided to give you the low-down on the blind from us, ourselves. This is a privilege, because we usually shut up before tourists and just sit and read braille or do geography, or eat and let people ooh and aah over us."

• • •

As the days passed Actia's feeling for the class ripened to pride. The eight students sat before her, following where she led, polite, matter-of-fact, eager, answering her questions, writing in braille the equations she dictated to them, asking her explanations, and fearing her examinations. She was their authority. They were her possessions.

They became like a garden. Each day they nodded before her their unseeing eye-blossoms.

First was the milk-white variety. Helen Anderson. Her coated, frosty milk-glass bulbs were useless, and the groping large arms seemed suddenly full of sensibility and aspirations, like heavy stalks of lilies waving in the wind.

Lennie Barker had no eyes. They were like closed bean pods, forever in sleep. Yet, like young pods, he was of a lively plant. He skinned around desks. He made a rat-a-tat-tat of his slate and stylus. And he was always laughing with a dancing mouth. He was like a fast-growing, clever-climbing shoot, waving and making music around the bean pole.

Gobi had twirling eyes, like star-flowers. The pupils would soar, straining to the top of the arc, and hold excited there in the thrall of some idea. When the idea came the pupils stamped a wild careening dance. His flower was the treacherous flower, because his eyes moved in a way not to see but to signal. The secrets of his bosom became primeval and potent and frightening in the dance of his eyes. There were days when he was hushed and obscure. Then his pupils hung silent and black in the sky of his eyes.

Rhea had glass eyes. These were the most deceptive of all. For under her mop of molasses hair swarming over the graven face, her eyes were as clear and translucent as young buds in dew. Images even reflected on them, the hung lights of gray days. And so it was odd to see her fumbling along, superior and slow, feeling for the entering wall of the room. She unreeled as she progressed. Her fingers were quick and thin. And her face was mobile.

"My garden," thought Actia. She had the watering, weeding, planting and care. It was the first garden she had ever had, and it was human. She walked delighted and unseen, surveying. To and fro with the book in her hand, they could feel her, as flowers feel the elements.

They could not see her gestures. Sometimes she would sit on her desk raising her hand, explaining a procedure. Sometimes she bit her pencil. Sometimes she stared gravely. Sometimes she twirled a wisp of hair in her hand.

Gobi wondered if Rhea was scared. Suddenly he heard her coming down the hall. But she did not speak to anyone. So he knew that she was on the fifteenth string . . . a harmonic of action. Everything was dispelled except the joke. He ducked quickly into the classroom and sat down.

Actia was poring over her green book. She heard the students entering and sitting down, but she did not look up. She had a new process to explain.

The class was in a state of hysterical anticipation, so they were taut and quiet as unbeat drums.

Rhea entered.

Actia thought: "I must hurry with this notation or I will not be ready when they all get here. Why didn't I do it before?"

Every waiting car except Actia's understood the slow definite steps as Rhea followed the wall. She walked straight across the back of the room, then glided in a swoop to her desk.

Bang went her books on the desk.

Actia looked up but noticed nothing.

Rhea cleared her throat.

Rhea's gall strung the class tight almost to breaking. It was an invisible line. They were paralyzed in silence.

Gobi's throat pressed against his eardrums. He wanted to laugh. But he held.

"All right, class," said Actia with no ceremony, following her forefinger across Problem No. 3. "Copy this down. 3x — 5 multiplied by 2x." The figures of X's and Y's skimmed her eyes.

She raised her head to look at them, thinking of the new concept of squares which she was now to explain.

Something was wrong in the garden.

Before she was aware of it she saw Rhea's head upflung, proud like a queen's. Instead of eyes, there were pegged in her eye sockets two beerbottle caps with double X's.

The effect was horrifying. Two crazy red X's in two yellow eyes.

Actia flung upward like a whippet. "Rhea!" she yelped.

The eyelids blinked over the bottle caps. Rhea spread her lips coldly and swallowed.

Actia saw Gobi's head move sideways like an animal, and a slow grin leaked on his lips. One look at the rest of the class and she knew that they had plotted it together.

Furious with anger she shouted. "Gobi!"

Then she caught sight of Rhea's mouth held tight against her teeth, probably to keep from laughing, and that brave gesture under the flaming X's was so incongruous that it struck a shaft to her heart.

"Gobi, come to my desk, please. Go over the problems one to twenty that you did last night. Out loud. You are going to be the teacher for the next fifteen minutes."

Her voice was loud and nettled.

Gobi stood up. The grin was gone from his face. His lip trembled.

"Rhea." Actia hurried up the aisle and her voice got softer and more firm. "You come with me."

In the teachers' sitting room she made Rhea sit on the ice-blue sofa. She closed the door.

"Rhea, why have you done this?"

Rhea was not moved. She did not think it so howlingly funny now that it had gone wrong. She had expected, at the worst, public admonishment. But being brought to the teachers' room was a felony of a higher order. Meet anger with anger, threats with conciliation, pity with superiority, she thought, waiting with cat-like silence.

"Did you think it was funny?" pursued Actia, whirling around in front of her. It drove her frantic, that ironic placidity out of which stared those two malevolent X's, the algebraic mock of blindness.

Rhea hated woman-to-woman talks when the other woman was a teacher. "Shall I take them out?" she asked sarcastically. "I don't have my eyes with me, but I don't guess that matters. I can go without them till noon."

That ace worked.

Actia sat down on the sofa and learned forward toward her. "You don't have a right to make fun of yourself!"

"She's not angry at all," thought Rhea. She said experimentally, "There's no law that says I can't put anything I want in my eyes." She worked the bottle caps out of her eyes and held them in the palm of her hand as other girls hold earrings. She still wanted to laugh but she knew she must not.

Actia watched the white, defenseless eyelids close down against Rhea's cheek. She had the fierce, thunderstruck awe of a mother who will not believe, even thought it has been suddenly revealed, that behind its own child's innocence lies something horribly incomprehensible.

"You don't want to look like that!" she began with gentle insistence.

"Pity is coming on," thought Rhea. "She is trying to worm her way through the back door into my affections." She jiggled the bottle caps like a rattle.

"It made you into something that wasn't you."

"Bah!" thought Rhea. "How does she know what I am!"

"Blindness isn't something to be made fun of."

From her pinnacle of blindness Rhea began to feel admiration and sorrow for Actia. "How she goes on!" she thought, listening to the winding, tender, persuasive tones.

Actia, now forgetting her own frustration at whether or not Rhea was taking in anything she said, mounted on the crest of her earnest and loving outrage.

"Why, Rhea, you are such a pretty girl! You are only beholden to yourself to look the pretty girl you are!"

This remark penetrated like a quivering arrow. Somewhere in Rhea's mind echoed a memory. The memory was of vision. The red, white and blue of the flag flashed. Having the memory, Rhea found that Actia had turned the tables on her. She suddenly became Actia with Rhea's old memory of vision. But now she was looking at a new Rhea, a grown-up Rhea, a girl Rhea, a figure Rhea who reflected in mirrors and sighted eyes. Pretty? A bob-scratched, grubby, blurred,

fan-tailed urchin of a child was the only remnant of herself in the mirror. She remembered she had tried the propensities of her vision. She had only looked to see if she could see her tongue stuck out, and she had to get so close that her tongue licked the mirror. It was cold-tasting, of lime and glass-polish alcohol.

How dared she! How dared she turn a joke into an excavation, amazing her with vision or awing her with love?

In a pulsation her lips trembled. She tried to hide her face, which a minute before she had tried to flaunt with the bottle caps. The bottle caps in her hand, forgotten, escaped and fell rolling on the floor.

"What have I said?" Actia thought.

She bent forward to help Rhea's jerky blind searching. The arms outstretched collided.

Suddenly Rhea grabbed Actia around the neck and held on in an embrace of affection and fury.

DISCUSSION

For most people blindness evokes particularly negative and frightening feelings. Even Actia Clewes, who has chosen to work with the blind, is concerned that immersing herself in their world may be too depressing. She has never had any experience with the blind or with blind children in school. Like many people entering the field of education, Actia's knowledge about teaching has been limited to what she has learned in college classrooms and from books. Nevertheless, she does amazingly well in her new post.

Rather than finding the students at Canopus Institution depressing, Actia learns that these children who cannot see have a rich inner life. They are intelligent, are curious, and ask astute questions of their sighted teacher. She is drawn to their warmth and exuberance. Unlike retarded children or children who have been handicapped through illness, Actia's students seem particularly verbal about the extent and reason for their blindness. She quickly learns that they are wary of the presumption of "experts" who think they know more about the blind than the blind themselves. They reserve particular disdain for those who pity them.

Soon after Actia's arrival, she is the object of intense scrutiny by the students, who use many different cues to learn about people in their midst. They use smell, sound, and touch to round out their impressions of people. Their impulses are outgoing and friendly. They want to know all about Actia because they want to like her and make her one of them. Nevertheless, the incident between Actia and Rhea demonstrates that blindness is difficult for the sighted to comprehend and that Actia is an "outsider" among her blind students.

The children at Canopus are intensely conscious of their minority status, and like any minority group, they develop their own sense of humor. Laughing at themselves helps to build their sense of belonging and to relieve their self-consciousness and concern for being different. They are aware that many people have stereotyped ideas about the blind as a group, and beneath their humor is a certain amount of cynicism, sensitivity, and defensiveness.

Living together in an institution for the blind has psychological advantages and disadvantages for the students. On the positive side is the camaraderie, which is felt when living with others who are just like oneself. One of the disadvantages is the heightened defensiveness that is bound to grow out of a segregated environment. Another disadvantage is the adjustment students must make when they leave the institution after spending their growing up years in a protected and exclusive environment. In many communities in the United States, blind children attend local schools where they receive special instruction in braille. This trend toward the least restrictive environment is in line with the new federal legislation for special education that will be in effect in the next decade. Residential schools for the blind such as Canopus Institution are only for those children whose families cannot meet the special needs of the blind child, for diagnosis of the blind, multiply handicapped child, or for those living in outlying communities where instruction in learning braille is not available in a local school.

SPRINGBOARDS FOR INQUIRY

1. Is there a state school for the blind in your state? What services does it provide?

2. Why are there so many stereotyped and false impressions about the blind?

3. How would you have handled the last incident in this excerpt from *The Fourth World*?

4. What personal characteristics do you think a person should have in order to work with or to teach the blind?

5. Many parents have written about their experiences with a handicapped child. Choose one such book and discuss the parents' reactions and contributions to their child's adjustment to his or her handicap.

CHAPTER NINE

The Behaviorally Disordered and the Emotionally Disturbed

Larry is a healthy ten year old in fifth grade, from a middle-class background. His verbal IQ is 115 and his performance IQ is 110 which means his intellectual functioning is in the high average range. His reading is at a low third grade level. In class he uses foul words, calls out whenever he pleases, makes cutting remarks about other children and is generally disruptive. He cannot get along at recess and is benched frequently. He is easily angered and often calls the teacher "unfair." Several times he has left school grounds and run home after a fight with another child.

When the children are seated before you in your newly mainstreamed classroom, your problem as a teacher will be to provide educational experiences for Larry and for Susan who, you were told, has minimal neurological impairment, and for Marie who comes to you as a "normal" fifth grader. Because of Larry's history, you may expect that his performance will be erratic. At times he functions fairly well in the classroom and at other times he may lead the class into frenzied activities. Your attention is frequently needed for his acting out behavior and for his inability to read at grade level. As each day concludes visions of Larry keep popping into your mind, and they are of his misbehaving and not learning. Eli Bower writes the following about his first teaching experience:[1]

[1]Eli M. Bower, "Education of Exceptional Learners," *The American Journal of Orthopsychiatry*, vol. 39, no. 5 (October 1969), 855–56.

My first serious exposure to the world of work came as a teacher of emotionally disturbed children. About the only thing I had going for me at the time was youth, ignorance, and a determination to survive . . . .. Nothing in my experience and education had prepared me for this. I sought help from my learned colleagues in education and mental health, from great books, from my puzzling students. I ran eagerly to case conferences with all cerebral and sensory neurons quivering and ready. . . . Every once in a while there was a psychic click that led me to try something new in the classroom. After two years, however, I began to sense that the gap between knowing a person's state of mind and knowing how to help him learn in school were difficult "knowings" to bridge. I also began to sense that emotionally disturbed children were, like other children, action-oriented, competence-seeking animals interested in learning and in learning how to learn. Why not start from this side of the bridge and ask the clinicians to zero in their skills on educational as well as therapy goals?

Frank Hewett describes the emotionally disturbed child as "a socialization failure . . . his behavior . . . is maladaptive and deviates from what is expected for his age, sex, and status . . . maladaptive behavior interferes with learning."[2] After analyzing five hundred cases of maladjusted children, Lester E. Hewett and Richard L. Jenkins defined three types of behavior disorders:

1. *The unsocialized aggressive child* defies all authority; is hostile to authority figures: is cruel, malicious and assaultive; and has no attachments to anyone or any group.
2. *The socialized delinquent* is all of the above except that he is able to relate to a peer group. He or she had early childhood security at home but was later rejected.
3. *The overinhibited child* is shy, timid, withdrawn, sensitive, submissive, overdependent, and easily depressed.[3]

Herbert C. Quay, William C. Morse, and Richard L. Cutler, building upon Hewett and Jenkins, redefine and relabel their categories and investigate the "behavioral characteristics" of 441 children in public school classes for the emotionally disturbed.[4] On a forty-three-item

[2]Frank Hewett, *The Emotionally Disturbed Child in the Classroom* (Boston, Mass.: Allyn & Bacon, Inc., 1968), pp. 3–4.

[3]Lester E. Hewett and Richard L. Jenkins, *Fundamental Patterns of Maladjustment: The Dynamics of Their Origin* (Springfield, Ill.: State of Illinois, 1945), pp. 34–57. Examples of each type of child are given in the study.

[4]Herbert C. Quay, William C. Morse, and Richard L. Cutler, "Personality Patterns of Pupils in Special Classes for the Emotionally Disturbed," *Exceptional Children*, vol. 32, no. 5 (January 1966), 297.

checklist of problem behaviors completed by sixty teachers, the new labels clustered around three types of behaviors:

1. *Conduct disorders* are characterized by unsocialized aggression (compare with Hewett and Jenkins), defiance, disobedience, impertinence, uncooperativeness, irritability, boisterousness, showing off, bullying, temper tantrums, hyperactivity, restlessness, and negativism.[5]
2. *Children with personality problems* are hypersensitive, shy, self-conscious, easily flustered, fearful and anxious, have inferiority feelings, and lack self-confidence.
3. *Inadequate-immature* children are inattentive, sluggish uninterested in school, lazy, preoccupied, daydreamers, drowsy, and reticent.

As Mary A. White and June Clarry indicate, behavioral disorders in children who are in schools are detected and defined most often on the basis of their learning behaviors.[6] Eli M. Bower, Eli Z. Rubin and his colleagues, and Paul S. Graubard confirm the fact that children labeled as behaviorally disordered are often behind their peers both in grade and level of achievement.[7] Graubard believes that "appropriate curricular content can be a major vehicle for working with behaviorally disordered youth. The number of responses in a child's behavioral repertoire can be widened considerably through the medium of curriculum."[8]

---

[5]Cloyd R. Partridge has taken a new tack in treating the conduct-disordered child whom he calls "comfortable, confident, aggressive kids." He calls these children victims of immature character development. His therapy is essentially based upon working with parents and modifying behavior so that patients "respect the basic realities of community living and the rights of other individuals." A more lengthy discussion may be found in Partridge's article, "Immature Character Development: A New Look at Etiology and Remediation of Character Disorders in Children," *Journal of Clinical Child Psychology*, vol. 5, no. 1 (Spring 1976), 45–47.

[6]Mary A. White and June Clarry, eds., *School Disorder, Intelligence, and Social Class* (New York: Teachers College Press, 1966).

An especially good discussion of the diagnosis and treatment of behavioral disorders in children exclusive of educational strategies may be found in Harry and Ruth Bakwin, *Behavior Disorders in Children*, 4th ed. (Philadelphia, Pa.: W. B. Saunders Company, 1972), part v.

[7]Eli M. Bower, *Comparison of the Characteristics of Identified Emotionally Disturbed Children with Other Children in Classes* (Sacramento, Calif.: Bulletin of the California State Department of Education, vol. 27, no. 6, 1958). Eli Z. Rubin, Clyde B. Simpson, and Marcus C. Betwell, *Emotionally Handicapped Children and the Elementary School* (Detroit, Mich.: Wayne State University Press, 1966). Paul S. Graubard, "The Relationship Between Academic Achievement and Behavior Dimensions," *Exceptional Children*, vol. 37, no. 10 (Summer 1971).

[8]As quoted in Lloyd M. Dunn, *Exceptional Children in the Schools*, 2nd ed. (New York: Holt, Rinehart and Winston, Inc., 1973), p. 271.

What are the characteristics of emotionally disturbed children as learners? It would appear that any attempt to modify curriculum should be based upon implementing a program consistent with what is known of the learning characteristics of these children. Peter Knoblock notes three issues that must be understood before designing learning experiences for emotionally disturbed children:

1. Most analyses, clinical and experimental, refer to the discrepancy between the potential of the disturbed child and his actual performance.
2. Learning disabilities are a relatively new category of exceptionality. The category creates a problem in classifying children into mutually exclusive categories that in reality overlap considerably.
3. There is a tendency to overlook very bright and creative disturbed children.[9]

It would be wise for the student of special education to keep these issues in mind as the variety of educational strategies currently in use are discussed. In addition to the Knoblock characteristics, the 1971 research data of Lyndal M. Bulloch and Richard J. Whelan that describe the skills or competencies rated very important by forty-seven teachers of emotionally disturbed children should be continually used in any assessment of the educational strategies that follow (see table 9–1).[10] This study is based on earlier research by Romaine P. Mackie, William Kvaraceus, and Harold William. Of the eighty-eight competencies identified by Mackie and his colleagues, only twelve were still in use nearly fifteen years later. In table 9–1, for items ranked very important (rank importance 1–6), there is a great deal of agreement in the far right column where the teachers rated their own proficiency for each of the eighty-eight items. Particular attention should be paid to the second item—"A knowledge or understanding of the education and psychology of various types of exceptional children." Thus, teachers on the job profess to believe that second only to "providing experiences in which pupils can be successful" (rank importance 1 and rank proficiency 2) is an understanding of the education and psychology of exceptionality.

[9]Peter Knoblock, "Psychological Considerations of Emotionally Disturbed Children," in *Psychology of Exceptional Children and Youth*, 3rd ed., ed. William M. Cruickshank (Englewood Cliffs, N.J.: Prentice-Hall, 1976), pp. 581–82.
[10]Lyndal M. Bulloch and Richard J. Whelan, "Competencies Needed by Teachers of the Emotionally Disturbed and Socially Maladjusted: A Comparison," *Exceptional Children*, vol. 37, no. 7 (March 1971), 487. The authors of the research give credit to Romaine P. Mackie, William Kvaraceus, and Harold William's pioneer study, *Teachers of Children Who Are Socially and Emotionally Handicapped* (Washington, D.C.: United States Government Printing Office, 1957).

Table 9–1

Competencies Rated as Very Important by Teachers of the Emotionally Disturbed in Selected School Districts

Rank importance	Very important items	Rank proficiency
1	A knowledge or understanding of the advantages of providing experiences in which pupils can be successful	2
2	A knowledge or understanding of the education and psychology of various types of exceptional children	59
3	The ability to tolerate antisocial behavior particularly when it is directed toward authority	1
4	A knowledge or understanding of basic human physical and psychological needs	3
5	A knowledge or understanding of techniques adaptable to classroom situations for relieving tensions and promoting good mental health	4
6	A knowledge or understanding of the advantages of flexibility of school programs and schedules to permit individual adjustment and development	5
7	The ability to establish "limits" of social control (neither overprotective nor overrestrictive)	8
8	The ability to develop self-imposed social control within the pupils	22
9	The ability to establish and maintain good working relationships with other professional workers, such as social workers and psychological personnel	6
10	The ability to teach remedial reading	25
11	The ability to avoid identical, stereotyped demands of maladjusted pupils	20
12	A knowledge or understanding of curriculum and methods of teaching the normal pupil	7

Source: Lyndal M. Bulloch and Richard J. Whelan, "Competencies Needed by Teachers of the Emotionally Disturbed and Socially Maladjusted: A Comparison," *Exceptional Children,* vol. 37, no. 7 (March 1971).

Frank Hewett classifies educational strategies for emotionally disturbed children under four headings:[11]

1. The Psychodynamic-Interpersonal Strategy
   Goals. The primary goal is to understand why the child is be-

[11]Frank Hewett, *The Emotionally Disturbed Child in the Classroom*, pp. 9–43. We have taken the liberty of using Hewett's categorizations and of then paraphrasing.

having as he or she is in school. The goal is achieved through interpretation of behavior in a psychodynamic context (a rich mixture of the Freuds, Erickson, Bettelheim, Wineman, Redl, and others) with special emphasis upon the child's relationship to his total environment.[12]

Methodology. This approach is essentially child-centered, aiming to understand maladaptive behavior while providing a school atmosphere that is supportive and permissive and that aims continually to help the child gain insight into himself. Critics such as Edward Pinckney and Cathey Pinckney have literally termed psychoanalysis a hoax.[13] Rebuttals are numerous, but this quotation from Norman Cameron seems to sum up the rebuttals of the psychodynamacists:

> One who neglects these furious fantasies and mental ghosts and shadows, will never gain a deep therapeutically helpful understanding of the true mechanisms that underlie mental life. From the psychodynamic point of view . . . the behavioristic approach to psychopathology . . . is not a study of the real mind of man but it is rather a point of view that assumes that man is, in fact, not a living human being but an inanimate computer.[14]

2. The Sensory-Neurological Strategy

Goals. The primary goal is to discover the child's sensory and neurologically based deficits.

Methodology. The classroom becomes a place of great order and routine. The teacher is directed in each step of the program. Development of preacademic perceptual motor skills has to be achieved through explicit goal setting and constant repetition and by mastering of one level before pro-

---

[12]In other contexts, this is called the ecological approach and is exemplified by Hobbs's Project Re-Ed (Nicholas Hobbs, "Helping Disturbed Children: Psychological and Ecological Strategies," in *Educating Emotionally Disturbed Children*, ed. Henry Dupont (New York: Holt, Rinehart and Winston, Inc., 1969). Compare with Susan Swap, "Disturbing Classroom Behaviors: A Developmental and Ecological View," *Exceptional Children*, vol. 41, no. 3 (November 1974), 163–72; and Sybil Kritchevsky, Elizabeth Prescott, and Lee Walling, *Planning Environments for Young Children: Physical Space* (Washington, D.C.: Association for the Education of Young Children, 1969).

[13]Edward Pinckney and Cathey Pinckney, *The Fallacy of Freud and Psychoanalysis* (Englewood Cliffs, N.J.: Prentice-Hall Inc., 1965).

[14]Norman Cameron, *Personality Development and Psychopathology: A Dynamic Approach* (Boston, Mass.: Houghton Mifflin Company, 1963). Lloyd H. Silverman, "Psychoanalytic Theory: The Reports of My Death Are Greatly Exaggerated," *American Psychologist*, vol. 31, no. 9 (September 1976), 621–37, is a more recent supportive view of the psychoanalytic model. Maurice Freehill, *Disturbed and Troubled Children* (New York: John Wiley & Sons, Inc., 1973), presents a number of cases treated by a mixture of therapeutic modalities.

ceeding to the next. In general, there is little concern with inferred psychological meaning of a child's behavior. One of the current problems with the approach is the strong tendency to use labels such as "brain damage," "cerebral dysfunction," and "dyslexia." A recent report to the United States Secretary of Health, Education and Welfare said this about labels:

> Categories and labels are powerful instruments for social regulation and control, and they often are employed for obscure, covert, or hurtful purposes: to degrade people, to deny them access to opportunity, to exclude "undesirables" whose presence in society in some way offends, disturbs familiar custom, or demands extraordinary effort.[15]

3. The Behavior Modification Strategy

Goals.   The basic goal is the identification of maladaptive behaviors that interfere with learning and assisting the child in developing more adaptive behavior. Each child is a candidate for learning something regardless of his or her degree of psychopathology or other problems.

Methodology.   The child is presented with tasks he or she needs to do (a child-centered approach would place more of the choice of tasks in the hands of the child, not the therapist), is ready to do, and can be successful doing. The tasks are accomplished gradually, and positive consequences follow the achievement of each task. Rewards are considered positive consequences, and they are withheld until a child performs.[16] What is essential to the behavior modification strategy is its systematic application.

Hewett has added a fourth strategy that he terms "developmental." It is "a generalist approach which has direct relevance to all exceptional children."[17] Hewett has designed a developmental sequence of educational goals (see figure 9–1). He hypothesizes that in order for successful learning to occur, the child must pay attention, respond, follow directions, freely and accurately explore the environment, and function appropriately in relations to others. It includes mastery of self-care and intellectual skills and the achievement of self-

[15]Nicholas Hobbs, *The Future of Children: Categories, Labels and Their Consequence* (Nashville, Tenn.: Center for the Study of Families and Children, 1975).

[16]A stimulating discussion of these rewards may be found in Frederic Levine and Geraldine Fasnacht, "Token Rewards May Lead to Token Learning," *American Psychologist* (November 1974), 816–20.

[17]Hewett, *The Emotionally Disturbed Child in the Classroom*, p. 41.

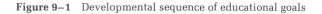

Figure 9–1   Developmental sequence of educational goals

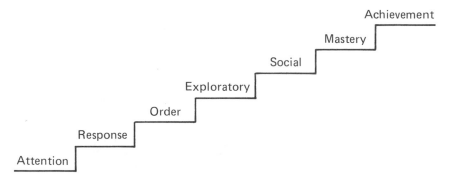

motivation. It is Hewett's contention that "if a teacher can provide three ingredients in a learning program for each child, there is not emotionally disturbed child . . . who cannot be taught something."[18] Hewett has developed these three ingredients into what is termed "the learning triangle."[19] If the teacher can select a task that the child is ready for and that is consistent with the educational goals most relevant to his or her problem, provide the child with a meaningful reward for his or her efforts, and maintain the degree of control necessary to insure efficient learning, the learning process is under way. Figure 9–2 illustrates the learning triangle for the child. Note that the child is at the center. Figure 9–3 uses the learning triangle to show the teacher how central a position he or she occupies. (Figures 9–2 and 9–3 on page 184.)

Children with emotional (behavioral) problems often arrive in school never having achieved the ability to pay attention, to respond to learning, to order their behavior, and so on. As they are exposed to the stresses of the typical school's demands, they encounter failure and drop out. It may well be that they have literally been pushed out. Children may really fail because of teacher failure. Hewett believes that "to succeed in teaching any child, the teacher must be highly oriented to success and firmly believe that despite a lack of readiness to be in school, every child is ready to learn 'something' and if he learns 'nothing' the fault lies in the teaching program."[20]

[18]Ibid., p. 61.
[19]Ibid., pp. 60–76.
[20]Ibid., p. 61.

Figure 9–2   The learning triangle (child)

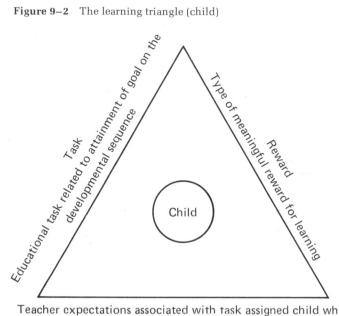

Teacher expectations associated with task assigned child which
determine conditions under which reward will be provided
Structure

Figure 9–3   The learning triangle (teacher)

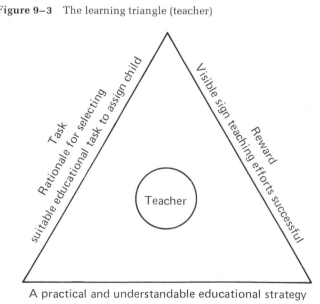

A practical and understandable educational strategy
Structure

The Life You Save

by William Melvin Kelley

"You mean his brother really tried to burn him alive?" Peter leaned forward onto the table, and smiled involuntarily at the horror of it.

The director nodded; he too could not help smiling. "Right. Carlyle, the older brother, told the mother he was just initiating Mance into a club. But she didn't buy it. She told the father, but he wouldn't believe it, not about his oldest boy, his namesake. He doesn't even know what kind of place we got here. He thinks it's just a regular day camp. He'd probably pull the kid out if he found out—disgrace and all that stuff."

Peter sat back. "Wow!" He shook out a cigarette and lit it.

The director tore the cellophane from a cigar. "So any-

way, that's what you got. At eleven, this Mance Bedlow's seen it all. I can only tell you one thing: don't hit him, don't even try to punish him, or any of them. They've been smacked enough to last them a lifetime. That's why they're here. If you hit them, you'll lose them, sure." He pulled himself forward, lit the cigar, and continued through dense smoke. "I'll give you all this stuff." He tapped Mance Bedlow's folder with a thick brown finger. "Okay?"

"Okay." Peter sighed, put out his cigarette and left the director's office. He went down the hall to the room, where, in an hour, he would greet his eight eleven-year-olds. They were all so-called emotionally disturbed children. Some of them had already flirted with minor crime. Peter would be their counselor for the next eight weeks.

The settlement house had recently moved from a small, old building to the ground floor of one of the buildings in a new low-rent housing project; the walls of the room were bleak, bare, pale-green cinder blocks. In the room, there were only two tables and ten folding chairs. Peter sat in one of the chairs, lit a cigarette, and waited for his boys to come, a bit nervous now with the thought that in a short while he would have the responsibility of helping to guide, or even the opportunity to change the lives of eight small human beings. When he realized what was running through his mind, he laughed at his earnestness. The feeling was honest, but to put it into words made it seem conceited and pompous. He would have to watch such attitudes. If his boys sensed them, they would never trust him.

The boys entered one by one, in shapeless, beltless dungarees, in torn and faded T-shirts. Each carried, in a brown paper bag, his lunch. Their mothers had pomaded and brushed their heads fervently, flattening the tiny beads of black hair. As they came in, Peter introduced himself, and each in turn, mumbled a name. Finally, eight had arrived. But there was no Mance Bedlow.

"I guess one of us isn't here." Peter, seated now at the head of one of the tables, scanned their dark faces. "Anybody here know Mance Bedlow?"

The boys glanced at one another. One of them, who had introduced himself as Randolph Wayne, said he did.

"Have you seen him, Randolph?"

"I seed him on the way over here, Mister Dunford. He say he ain't making it. He say this a wasted gig." There was an impish look on the boy's dark-brown face, as if he held the same view. His eyes were dark, and twinkled.

"Okay. You fellows wait here." Peter got up. "I'll go check on him." He left the room and headed for the director's office. Halfway down the hall he realized there was no Randolph Wayne on the list the director had given him.

"What's the problem, Peter?" The director was reading his mail.

Peter remained in the doorway. "I have the right number of kids, but no Mance Bedlow."

"Oh?" The director put down a letter he had just opened. "Who's the extra?"

"A kid named Randolph Wayne."

The director sighed. "They do that sometimes. They see their buddies on the way here and just tag along." He got up.

They walked back down the hall and stopped at the door. The director looked in at the boys. "Which is the Wayne boy?"

The boys turned to the door now, some smiling politely.

Peter indicated Randolph Wayne.

The director shook his head and chuckled. "That is Mance Bedlow."

The room filled with high squealing and cackling, the boys talking to each other: "Man, you see that cat go for that shit?"

"Yeah. Man, he dumb!"

Mance Bedlow sat at the table, basking in his triumph, staring at Peter, interested to see what he might do. Peter felt his embarrassed anger bubbling, and knowing he could not afford to let the boys see it, left the door, took two steps, and leaned against the wall, trying to control himself.

The director put a hand on Peter's shoulder. "Don't let it get you. That's the way they live."

Peter nodded.

The director went back to his office.

Peter fixed a smile on his face, and entered the room. "That's a point for you, Mance." He looked into hard brown eyes, understanding now what the director had told him before. Mance Bedlow's eyes were not at all those of an eleven-year-old. Peter realized suddenly that at eleven, he would not have survived in Mance Bedlow's world, even though he had always lived in Harlem. Peter's father was a doctor and earned a good living; Peter had been sent to private schools.

Mance returned his stare. Finally Peter looked at another boy. "Well, let's paint a little bit."

The boys were not enthusiastic. They waited quietly as Peter brought out huge sheets of paper, brushes, and jars of paint, and passed them around. Finally one of them, George, light-skinned and shaved bald, asked what Peter wanted them to paint.

"What do you guys want to paint?" Peter was sitting again, and looked around the table. The boys were surprised. The director had told Peter that most of the time boys like these were told exactly what to do. Their choice was to obey or rebel. Obedience brought little reward or admiration; rebellion brought harsh punishment. "You can paint anything you want. But if you can't think of anything, paint a picture of your family." He suggested that purposely, knowing the settlement house psychologist might learn something from the paintings.

Automatically, the boys painted their families. Peter walked around behind them. As he approached, they would usually tighten their bony shoulders. He encouraged them all and from time to time received smiles.

Mance Bedlow's picture was entirely in brown. There were three figures, the two biggest on one side of the page, the smallest on the other side. Peter asked Mance to name them. The two big ones were his father and brother. He was the small one.

"Where's your mother?"

"She in the kitchen cooking their dinner." He looked up at Peter. "Mister Dunford, what color should I paint the sun?"

"Any color you want; it's your picture." Peter smiled and went on to George, who smiled at him timidly.

Behind him, Peter heard scuffling. "Cut that shit out, boy."

Peter turned around to find Mance glaring at the boy on the other side of him. Then he picked up his own picture and began ripping it into tiny pieces. Peter decided not to stop him.

When he was through destroying his picture, Mance turned to Peter. "This place is shit!"

Peter smiled.

"And you're a cock-sucker!"

Still Peter smiled, although now it was an effort.

"I'm going home!" Standing up, he knocked over his chair, then raced around the table away from Peter, and scrambled out the door. Peter stood his ground. The boy would come back.

Five minutes later, Mance had not re-appeared. Peter, who had started the boys painting again, told them he would return in a few moments and went down to the front door and looked out.

The settlement house was in one of twenty buildings in the red-brick project. Black asphalt paths connected the buildings, which were separated by chained-off plots of grass. Wooden benches lined the paths.

Mance sat watching the door of the settlement house. When he saw Peter at the door window, he stood up.

Peter opened the door. "Why don't you come back inside?"

"I'm going home!"

Peter stepped through the door. "What do you want to do that for?"

"I'm going home!" His fists were clenched; he was yelling.

Peter came part way down the front stairs, speaking softly. "Come on, Mance, don't . . . "

He had gotten too close and the boy was running. Peter trotted after him, closing the space between them. He did not want to catch and drag him back, knowing it would be better to convince the boy to return of his own free will. They ran past a brown woman wheeling a baby carriage, shouting at a toddler clinging to her skirts, past a seated old man leaning his white-whiskered chin on his cane, past a group of young girls chanting and skipping rope. Finally, Mance neared the curb, the outer boundary of the project, and without looking, darted out into the street, avoiding cars, the drivers startled behind their windshields, stopping only when he had reached the other side.

Peter waited until the cars passed, then started across. "Why don't you tell me what's wrong?"

Mance watched Peter drawing closer to him until they were only five steps apart, then began to run again, along the sidewalks now, in front of the brownstone houses' high stairs, occupied by Negro men and women sitting in undershirts and housecoats. They ran around groups of conversing brown people, through mobs of playing children. Peter could see Mance was tiring now, his thin legs growing heavy and wobbly.

Peter slowed to a walk. Mance looked over his shoulder, and began to walk himself. "Why don't you tell me what's wrong?" Peter was shouting; several people turned around. He felt foolish.

"I don't like painting pictures!" They were still walking, a distance now of two cars between them.

"We aren't going to paint pictures all day."

Mance stopped. "What was we going to do?"

They stood shouting at each other. "I don't know—we were going to the park and play some ball."

"Who wants to do that?"

Peter wondered if Mance would sit down if he did, and moved back to some empty steps behind him. "We're taking trips downtown and on the Staten Island ferry, and to the car show." He saw Mance Bedlow's face flicker with interest, but did not know exactly what had interested him. He guessed. "You like cars?"

"When you got a car nobody can mess with you." Mance inched closer. He was standing in the gutter directly in front of Peter. "One of these days I'll hit the number and buy me a Cadillac and won't nobody mess with me." He was staring at the middle of the sidewalk.

Peter wanted to keep this conversation going and grabbed at a question. "What color car will you get?"

"I'm getting me a black one, with air conditioning and a radio." He was in the middle of the sidewalk now. "Some niggers run out and get white Cadillacs; they get dirty and look jive. But I'm getting me a black one, and even when it dirty it'll still look good." He paused for an instant. "I'll get in the car and nobody'll mess with me and I'll go away."

Peter was tempted to ask why Mance wanted to go away, but he suspected the boy would balk. "Why did you want to go home?"

"I told you—I don't want to paint no pictures."

"Well, you don't have to. You can do something else when the other guys are painting."

"What?" His chin was lifted high.

"I don't know. You decide." Peter got up, planning something new. Mance backed up. "Look, I'd like you to come back. You don't have to, of course, but I do, because I'm taking the other guys to the park." Peter descended the steps. Mance had retreated to the gutter. "Why don't you come along? We'll have a good time." Peter knew he was overacting but he did not think Mance would see it. "Well, so long. I hope you come back." He started up the street.

He walked slowly, not turning around and came to a store, the window of which was slanted so he could see behind himself. At a distance of three cars, Mance was following him. Peter smiled to himself, a little proud. Perhaps he had broken through.

Peter soon found it was not that easy. Mance ran out two times that afternoon, racing in a different direction each time. Contrary to the declaration—"I'm going home!"—he never seemed to be heading toward any particular place. He simply ran until he got tired, or until Peter could engage him in conversation. Between flights he talked to no one. He would seem as engrossed as the other boys, then suddenly, he would bolt.

At the end of the day, alone now, Peter had a chance to read Mance Bedlow's report. Two things particularly interested him. The first was that Mance had a recurring nightmare: He would be standing with his parents on a grassy mound. He would be quite happy. A wolf would appear then, and, snapping at his legs, would drive him off the mound, away from his parents. He would try to outsmart the wolf by running around to the other side of the mound to sneak to the top again. But the wolf would always get there before him and keep him away.

The second thing was that Mance lived in the Bronx. Yet, though the settlement house was in Manhattan, when he ran away, he never went anywhere near the subway.

Next day, Peter had the boys paint animals. Predictably, Mance painted a wolf standing on top of a mound of grass. Peter stood watching. "What's that?" He tried to give the question no weight.

"That's my wolf." Mance seemed indignant. "Didn't they tell you about my wolf? They all know about it—all the people here."

Peter was startled by the answer, but went on as he had planned. "They didn't tell me about him."

"Hell, they should-a. He's important. I got this wolf, see? I dream about him most every night and . . ." He stopped short. "You're jiving me. You know all about my wolf."

Peter shook his head. "No. No, I don't know a thing about it."

Mance tilted his head, studying Peter. "Then," he started slowly, "you are one stupid bastard and I ain't wasting my time telling you." He stood up, rather slowly this time. "I'm going home." He did not even bother to run; he ambled.

Peter stood fighting anger, waited until he had calmed himself before he followed, catching up to the boy in a small playground at the other end of the project. He was still a bit angry, but remembered all the director had told him, and all he had learned from the report. He told himself again that a counselor was supposed to be a good example for boys like Mance. He fixed a gentle look on his face, but before he could say anything, Mance was coming toward him. "You go to college?"

"Yes, I do." Peter sat down and was surprised when the boy sat beside him, quite close.

"What they teach you there?" The boy was genuinely interested. Peter wished he knew what turn his mind had taken.

"I guess the same things you learn, only harder." Mance Bedlow's interest in his personal affairs was a good sign.

"You ever get into any fights there?" Mance was inspecting Peter's hands.

"No, I don't." Peter had the unsettling feeling his answers were all wrong.

"What happens when somebody robs your stuff?"

"Nobody does." In front of them, two small boys were pretending to be airplanes.

Mance scowled. "Don't nobody hate you at college?"

"I hope not." Peter chuckled. "I don't think so."

"Must be a jive place." He

stood up. "I guess you want me to go back, huh?"

"Yes, I do." Peter did not know what to make of all this.

"Okay. I'll save you a speech. Come on." Mance started toward the settlement house, Peter following obediently.

Mance did not run away again. But as the weeks went by, Peter realized this was not a sign of progress. Mance got along no better with the rest of the boys. He got into his share of fights. But despite these brief signs of involvement, Peter knew Mance was lonely and unhappy. It seemed that he knew he had to attend the day camp, and had decided to endure it, but no more. Even Peter's success with the other boys did not balance the disappointment of having failed with Mance Bedlow.

Peter did not know if it was this failure, or simply the demands the entire group made on him, but he began to get more tense, more tired, and more frustrated. When he arrived home at night, he would skip dinner with his parents, go to his room, and sleep. He could not rid himself of his tight feelings and could not show them to the boys, and so after six weeks of hiding them, each day was harder to get through. He was fighting anger all the time.

In the afternoons, if they had not gone on a trip, Peter would take his boys to the project's large playground, which was used not only by the settlement house, but by all of the children, boys, and young men in the neighborhood. One hot, humid day, the air conditioner had burned out and the room had steamed, forcing sweat down the dark faces of his boys, staining their shirts. Peter took them to the playground an hour early; Mance as usual tagged behind.

Peter organized seven of the boys into a game of basketball, leaving Mance to wander the playground alone. Then he sat down to watch, mopping himself with an already damp and wilted handkerchief.

The game would have been laughable if Peter had felt like laughing. The boys' shots either did not reach the backboard or went over it. Instead of dribbling, they ran, and when one had the ball, the others, no matter what team, descended on him like a mob. Even so, they seemed to be having a good time.

Peter did not see the older boys until it was too late. They were standing at the far end of the court, watching and laughing. They wore tight dark pants, button-down shirts in browns and wine-red, and thin brimmed hats.

George, his bald head glistening with sweat, threw the wild pass. It bounced down the court and was caught by one of the older boys, who began to drib-

ble it neatly, between his legs. George ran down the court after it, yelling: "Hey, man! Hey! Give me that ball!"

The older boy, thin and dark, ignored him, continued to bounce the ball, low and hard, behind his back.

"Hey, man, give me the ball!" George stood ten feet away, watching, and after asking for the ball once more, charged the boy, who laughing, passed the ball to one of his friends.

George did not change direction. He was swinging his fists wildly, his blows falling on the boy's thighs and stomach. Peter was up now, running down the court, telling George to stop. Just as Peter reached them, the older boy stopped laughing, stepped back, and punched George square in the face, knocking him to the ground, where he burst into fuming tears.

Peter, whose only aim until then had been to retrieve the ball and to stop George, found himself flying at the boy, a loud rushing, like heavy rain, filling his ears, his fists clenched. He caught the boy by surprise with a punch on the ear, and when the boy turned, shocked, followed through with two punches to the stomach and one to the eye. The boy stumbled, and backed up, holding his eye. "Hey, man, what you do that for?"

Peter was screaming. "What did you hit that kid for?"

"Awh, man, I was only playing." The boy was still backing up. His friends stood behind him, timidly, not looking at him.

"Well, you play some place else or I'll break your ass for you!" Peter marched forward and took the ball from the boy who was holding it. Then suddenly he realized what he had done. He spun around and found his boys in a group, staring at him, their mouths open. To one side of them, his hands in his pockets, a scowl on his face, stood Mance Bedlow.

Avoiding their gaze, Peter helped George up and hurried his boys back to the settlement house, where he let them go home immediately though it was a half hour early. He sat alone in the room, smoking, thinking how he would repair the damage he had done. All summer, he had tried to build an image they could see and perhaps copy; he had tried to show them there were people in the world who were completely different from their aggressive, brutal fathers and brothers. In ten seconds, he had destroyed six weeks' work, and now he could not discover a way to salvage himself in their eyes.

As he was just about to push open the front door, he saw Mance sitting on one of the benches in front of the settlement house. He was still scowling.

Peter did not want to speak to him; he pushed open the door quickly and waved: "Good night, Mance." He walked as fast as he could.

Behind him, he heard running footsteps. "You learn to fight like that in college?"

"No!" He stopped now, and spun on his heels, expecting to find the boy taunting him. The boy's face was blank. Peter changed his tone. "No, I didn't. Look, Mance, it's not good to settle things by ———"

Mance cut him off. "Where'd you learn to fight?"

Peter sighed. "I don't know—I guess my father taught me." He started to walk again.

Mance tagged along at his elbow. "What do he do?"

"My father? He's a doctor."

"And he really taught you how to fight?" Mance did not seem to believe him.

"That's right." They were out of the project now, almost to the corner where Peter waited for his bus. He hoped one would come soon.

"You mean, doctors really get in fights?"

He looked up the block for the bus. "Sometimes. I guess sometimes everybody gets into a fight."

"Just like me."

Something in the boy's tone forced Peter to look at him. Mance was staring at him. "When I was a kid I wanted to be a doctor."

Peter was about to speak,

when behind him, he heard the gasping of a bus door. He turned around uncertain whether to get on. This was too good to let slip.

"He leaving without you. You better get on."

Peter did as the boy directed. After he had paid his fare and found a seat, and the bus had begun to move, he looked out of the window, back to the bus stop and saw Mance Bedlow, standing on tiptoes, his hand just at ear level, waving him a timid, tentative good-by.

DISCUSSION

A summer day camp for emotionally disturbed children is one of the best albeit trying settings for a counselor to learn about these children. The advantage of the setting is that it eliminates the necessity to impose academic tasks on children who usually have repeatedly failed in school. The most difficult aspect of a day camp entirely devoted to children with emotional problems is that there are few healthy behavioral models. It is also difficult to impose structure in a camp setting when the purpose of the camp is recreational; yet most of these children cannot operate without well-defined limits.

The opening days of the camp season are when the children are most intense in their testing of the adults. Peter soon learns that his eleven-year-olds are far more resourceful in controlling the situation than he is. Using foul language and running away are two of the more usual behaviors used by the disturbed child in a group setting. Usually the most disturbed children are the ones who act out in bizarre ways. Beneath the façade of arrogance, toughness, or craziness, however, are frightened children who need protection from their ill-considered actions. There are no definite rules about how to handle these kinds of confrontations. Redesigning the physical environment may prevent children from running away. Establishing rules and enforcing the consequences for breaking them is another method to establish limits. Peter follows his instincts and runs after Mance each time he runs away, probably communicating to Mance that he really cares about him. Mance enjoys the situation because he is getting attention from Peter, even if it is in a negative way. Peter has difficulty in keeping a sense of balance in working with Mance. He realizes that he should not take confrontations with Mance as personal affronts, but Peter has invested a great deal of his pride in winning Mance's friendship and respect.

Young counselors working with children often become personally involved with their more troubled students. A counselor-student involvement may help a child to form a dependable relationship with other adults. On the other hand, circumstances in the child's life may be beyond the control of the most well-meaning person. Progress in building a positive relationship is not always immediately observable. Good influences may show results a year or more following the experience. One of the most trying aspects of working with the emotionally disturbed is that it is so difficult to quantify what is taking place. Behaviorists who do research in this area attempt to target a particular behavior that is observable and measurable. In the relationship between Peter and Mance, a research worker might attempt to show that there was a decrease in Mance's running away behavior.

Peter has set his goals for the summer very high and needs concrete evidence of his success. Peter is overly hard on himself and does not deal with the anger that Mance provokes in him. He is fortunate that the amount of energy he devotes to Mance does not reduce his effectiveness with the other children in the group. Frequently people who work in the helping professions need an opportunity to vent their own feelings of frustration regarding their work. Many agencies use staff conferences for this purpose.

At the end of the story Peter steps out of his role as model and permits himself a gut level reaction to an older boy who victimizes George. Much to Peter's surprise, this action is a turning point in his relationship with Mance. Seeing Peter display real anger and get into a fist fight makes Peter seem more human to Mance and consequently someone with whom he can identify. The fact that Peter, a college boy and the son of a doctor, can react by fighting makes Mance feel that he has a chance to take his place alongside worthy people like Peter and his father.

SPRINGBOARDS FOR INQUIRY

1. Predict what will happen to Peter and Mance's relationship following the last incident in the story.

2. Ideally what kinds of therapeutic interventions would a boy like Mance require?

3. Construct a hypothetical case of a ten-year-old emotionally disturbed girl or boy. Give details of the home background, school history, and current behavioral problems at home and in school.

4. Research the residential schools, day treatment centers, and outreach programs available in your community for behaviorally disturbed minors. What does each offer?

Something Missing

by John L'Heureux

After the fire in the school, reporters tried to find out all they could about the Goldfarbs. Information about the son, Isaac, was repeatedly self-contradictory, and about Avram they learned nothing at all. He had come either from Hungary or Holland and was currently employed by a music publishing firm. That was all anybody knew. They were a quiet suburban family like any other. There was no story in them.

Avram Goldfarb was a child prodigy of seven, a pianist, when a drunken Nazi broke his hands. The soldier had been sent to round up the whole family, but the boy played Schubert so beautifully that he took only the father and mother and left the boy behind, having first taken care to smash his small hands with a rifle butt. At nine Avram had murdered a man who had threatened to reveal his hiding place, and at ten he escaped to Holland where he grew up, married a German girl, and taught music. He was determined his son would be the pianist he himself could have been; when his wife became pregnant, therefore, they emigrated to America where, everyone knew, opportunities abound. Thus Isaac Joseph Goldfarb was born in Bridgeport, Connecticut.

Isaac was a child of extraordinary beauty. His large luminous eyes seemed always filled with tears, and his hair was a mass of glossy black curls. "What a beautiful baby! What is her

name?" women would some-
times ask, and Karen Goldfarb
would smile with pleasure. She
had wanted a daughter. When he
was three, he hacked a path down
the center of his hair with his
mother's scissors because the boy
next door had called him a girl.
After that Karen took him regularly to the barber shop.

As he grew, Isaac displayed a
keen intelligence and great
depths of emotion. Not only did
he throw tantrums, he knew
when not to throw them; he could
delay his fury for hours until the
time was right. "Temperament in
an artist is good," his father said,
and at once set him to the piano.
Isaac's hands were long and
white, with an impressive open
spread, and in very short time
they flowed across the keys with a
life and control of their own. The
boy's technical mastery was
amazingly in advance of his years
or his training, and his father
held great hopes for him. With
time the boy's technique became
nearly flawless. Still, the father
said, something was missing.
Had he been more honest, he
would have admitted that the
missing something was genius;
but his life depended on that not
being so, and he spent much of
his day trying to infuse his own
genius into his angry, despairing
son. Neither understood who the
other was.

Isaac was persecuted by the
other children at school. At first
they hated him because he was
beautiful and was cooed at and
tickled by the teachers. Later they
hated him because he was unlike
them; he wore short pants and
knee stockings; while they
played baseball, he practiced
piano; he seemed to think he was
somehow better than they. He
was a sissy. Finally they hated
him out of habit. He didn't belong. They knew it and he knew
it. Before he was twelve, he had
been condemned forever.

And so it came as a relief to
Isaac when, after that first disas-
trous year at high school, his
father moved the family from
Bridgeport to a small town outside Boston where he had been
offered a job with a music publishing firm.

That summer was the hap-
piest time of Isaac's life. Everything was beginning new. His
father, busy with his new job, did
not have time to hound him about
his practice, about the something
missing. His mother had given up
hoping for a daughter and had
stopped thinking of Isaac as a
substitute. He was alone, and he
spent long hours walking in the
woods, sketching the pine trees
by the reservoir, imagining a future in which there would be
nothing to fear. The less he practiced piano, the more his sketching improved. He began to think
he might give up music for painting. And then he discovered his
voice. It was a thin, sweet sound
that seemed to come from somewhere outside of him; a tone not

of complaint but of intense sorrow, the legacy of thousands of years of exile. All that summer he sang in the woods, convinced that in the fall everything would be different.

But in late August his face began to break out. By the time school began in September, his face and neck swarmed with ripe pustules, three and four running into one another to form a sickening purple mass between his nose and his lip. Karen could not bear to look at him, her beautiful son, disgusting. Avram scarcely noticed, aware as he was only of the boy's absence of soul, his brilliant articulating fingers on the keyboard telling always of something missing.

The first day of school was everything Isaac had feared. He had succeeded in registering as Joseph Goldfarb and had been careful not to speak unless spoken to, not to walk in that way people always made fun of, not to gesture with his beautiful hands. Despite his face, he would succeed as a man. In fact, his face might be a help; no one would notice now the long curled lashes or the limpid eyes. They nudged one another whenever he spoke, but that might be only because he was new and they had all been together for a long time. And at lunch he walked alone behind animated groups of three and four, but after all he was new and must give the others a chance to get used to him. Yes. It was be-

cause he was new. He wouldn't force himself on anyone this time, wouldn't drive them away with his . . . whatever it was. He would eventually have friends and be like the rest of them. No one knew him here.

After lunch Isaac reported to the locker room for physical education class. He had trouble finding 2-A, not realizing that 2-A was a euphemism for the cellar, and so he came late.

The locker room was a cavernous cement affair that reeked of disinfectant. Jutting from the wall were six long benches, and built above the benches were racks for clothes and equipment. To the left was a wire cage filled with baskets, each marked with the owner's number, containing sneakers, socks, supporters, shorts, and whatever more elaborate equipment the boy might have—knee pads or ankle stiffeners or straps for eyeglasses. There was a window in the cage, and the coach, a short beefy man whose huge chest and stomach muscles had long since gone to fat, stood behind it handing out the baskets to their owners. To the right was a short flight of stairs leading to another cement room, this one smaller, equipped only with spigots on one wall and a huge rubber tray of disinfectant on the other.

Entering the locker room, Isaac stood dumfounded. Most of the boys had on gym shorts by this time and were noisily comparing biceps or punching one another or pretending to. A few stood there naked, putting on athletic socks or supporters. Never having seen anyone naked before, he could not believe they all stripped bare this way in front of one another. He blushed and looked around him, frightened.

"Hey, you!" Buck Carey, the coach, stood behind the wire grill. "You're supposed to be on time, you know. You ever hear of being on time?"

The noisy chatter fell off.

"I'm sorry. I didn't know where . . . " Isaac could hear his voice and knew it was too high. He stopped. The coach, studying him in evident disgust, said nothing. "I'm sorry. What do I do?" He hoped he would be sent away.

"What do you do?" He looked around and addressed the boys. "He wants to know what he does." They laughed as they were expected to. "You strip. First you strip."

Painfully Isaac began to remove his clothes. The blood had rushed to his head, and he was so dizzy he thought he would fall over. No one said anything; he knew everyone was looking at him. Finally he stood before them naked.

"Now what?" the coach asked him.

"Now what?" Isaac repeated.

"Now you put on your jock and your shorts. Unless you want to go out on the field like that." Everyone laughed.

"I don't have any. I didn't know."

"What are you? A freshman or something?"

"I . . . no . . . I'm new. I'm a sophomore, but this is my first year. At this school, I mean." If only he could cover himself, but that would be worse. They'd make comments.

"Next time bring your equipment. Today you can use common stock. Understand?"

"Yes, sir."

"Yes, Coach," he corrected.

"Yes, Coach."

"All right now. Name?" He scanned the class list; he knew every name but one.

"Joseph Goldfarb. Joe." He swallowed. He glanced around for reassurance, but the boys avoided his eyes.

"Nope. There's no Joseph Goldfarb here. There's an Isaac Goldfarb. You sure you're not Isaac?"

"Well, Isaac is my middle name. The name I go by is . . ."

Ed LaCroix, quarterback and captain of the football team, made a show of looking at Isaac's privates and announced loudly, "Yeah, he's Isaac all right, Coach."

Isaac's explanation was lost in the tense, uproarious laughter. Dimly he understood what Ed LaCroix knew well from association with the coach: only Isaac's humiliation would stop his badgering. It had to end that way. It always did.

Before school let out everyone knew the hilarious story about the new boy's encounter with Buck Carey.

Two weeks passed during which Isaac was ignored altogether. He had thought this was what he wanted, but he found isolation more suffocating than insult; it was as if they were telling him he didn't exist. His skin became worse, glossy red bumps puffing up his lips and blotting his forehead, until at last the terror of facing school each day kept him constantly on the brink of tears.

Avram Goldfarb, ignoring the threat of tears, went on urging the boy to deepen his playing. "You have no soul," he would scream, "look at me, look at me; you have no soul." And shaking him violently by the shoulders, he would stare deep into the boy's eyes where he saw nothing, nothing at all. He did not guess and would not have understood his son's terror of school. Karen suspected but said nothing; she was disappointed in her son, who was not manly and authoritative like his father. In school Isaac would sketch caricatures of his teachers and his fellow students, but usually of himself—his hooked nose and his long, skinny body easily lending themselves to caricature —and at home he would walk in the woods singing in his pure, sad voice. He was totally alone.

There were two people who had some inkling of what went on in Isaac's mind: Buck Carey, who felt an unreasoning hatred whenever he saw the boy; and Ed LaCroix, who felt guilty for what he had done. Both quietly resolved to do something about their feelings. It was Miss Connolly who gave them their opportunity.

Despite the locker room story, or perhaps because of it, the teachers continued to call the boy Joseph. They never knew what to make of him. He turned away from the few kindnesses offered him, and yet he seemed so lonely. And certainly there was no denying that he was terrible to look at, Miss Connolly thought. He was bright and sensitive. Somebody should help him. His essays, grammatically sound and well-structured, were always the best in the class; they had what all the others lacked, a completely unfettered imagination, perhaps too unfettered, and it was on the pretext of talking about this—his imagination—that she kept him after school. Their conversation, halting and stumbling as it was, uncovered to Miss Connolly a depth of suffering and violence that frightened her. Nonetheless she carried through with her original intention and told Isaac, before dismissing him, that perhaps he found his facial condition embarrassing and perhaps he could see a skin doctor. She felt it might help, she said, smiling with genuine kindness. Tears leaped to his eyes; it was a long time since anyone had smiled that way at him. When he left, Miss Connolly reported to Mr. Gorham, the student counselor, that she was worried about the boy. Mr. Gorham promised he would look into it, but busy as he was with four hundred student profiles, each to be made out in triplicate, he did not get around to Isaac until it was too late.

Two more weeks passed, and Isaac stole the money from his mother and went to a skin doctor, who gave him a bottle of pink fluid which, when dry, covered his face with an opaque film. He used this each night, and then one day worked up courage enough to wear it to school. It caused a sensation.

"Joe Goldfarb is wearing makeup!"

"Josie, you mean."

"Ike the kike forgot his lipstick."

In the girl's room nobody talked of anything else, and in the boys' room each tried to make his comment on Isaac the funniest and the most obscene. Buck Carey—since there was no phys ed that day—had to wait until football practice to share his remarks with the boys he knew he could trust.

Isaac's makeup was the talk of the school, and so he was not surprised at the end of the day to discover on the main bulletin board one of his own caricatures of himself; someone had drawn a skirt on it. He was surprised, however, when Ed LaCroix pushed through the giggling crowd and without a word tore the picture down. The next day Ed's steady girl, a sophomore, smiled at Isaac and did not turn away.

Linda Davis had smiled at him and meant it. All during the day Isaac turned this over in his mind. Perhaps it was still possible. Perhaps he could still have friends and be like all the others. Perhaps. Please, God, yes, he found himself saying, though he did not believe in God and had never prayed. Please, yes.

When phys ed period came, he skipped it. Filled with excitement at the possibility of a new life, he could not face the hard eyes and ugly tongue of Buck Carey, and so when the bell rang he slipped down the side stairs to the glee club room. It was another cement cavern, rendered nearly soundproof by the boiler that stood between it and the locker room. Nobody ever came here except the glee club and the band, so Isaac knew he would be safe. He sang to himself for a while, thinking of Linda, and then he played a Schubert sonata, but softly, very softly.

Buck Carey, having saved choice comments for Isaac, was not pleased to find he was absent.

"You, LaCroix," he said. "Go check the office and see if your friend has been excused. And then check study hall and the auditorium, see. And bring him back here in ten minutes." He had heard about LaCroix taking down the picture.

Ed LaCroix shifted his weight from foot to foot. "My friend?"

There was an unspoken understanding between them regarding how much liberty one could take with the other. Ed after all was a very good quarterback.

"Goldfarb, I mean. Go check the office, would you?" His tone was different now.

"Yes, I'll go."

He took a shortcut through the boiler room and, passing the glee club door, he thought he heard music. He pushed open the peephole as Isaac began the sonata. Ed LaCroix, pleased for some reason he himself did not understand, listened for five minutes and then returned to the locker room.

"He's been excused. He hurt his foot or something."

"Foot. *My* foot. I'll get that fairy yet."

The next morning Isaac found on his desk a note telling him to report to the principal's office. Mr. Millar studied him for a moment as if he were something under a microscope—he had heard unpleasant reports about this difficult, high-strung young man—and then coldly summarized. "Coach Carey will see you after school in the locker room. If you are not there, Mr. Goldfarb, you will be suspended from this school. Is that clear?" And he dismissed him.

When he returned to his desk he did not notice Linda's smile. A feeling of doom hung over him all during the morning, and at lunch period, unable to eat anything, he walked by the river, letting his eye follow the curve of branches where they bent to the water, pretending to himself that the other world of cruelty did not exist. "I'll survive him," he told himself. "I'll survive them all."

The afternoon was clear and windy, with just enough nip in the air to be perfect football weather. Buck Carey sent his team, jogging in their bulky uniforms, out to the field for calisthenics while he lingered behind with Isaac. The boy's pimpled face disgusted him.

"Okay, Ikey. You decided to show up today, did you? Huh? Decide to show up?"

Isaac stared at the cement floor. Three hours from now all this will be over, he thought.

"I'm talking to you!" He grabbed the boy's skinny shoulder and pressed his thumb painfully into the joint. "Nothing to say, huh? Nothing to say to the coach?" He brought his face close to Isaac's, and his voice was intense. "Well, listen to me, boy. I'm gonna run your ass right off. Now get out on that field."

Isaac joined the uniformed football team. No one acknowledged him, and he was grateful for that; humiliation became somehow easier as it became less personal. He felt now almost like an anonymous viewer at his own execution.

And then Ed LaCroix approached him.

"Listen, you want a ride home afterward? I'll give you a ride home. I'm going to meet Linda in 24, so if you get out first, go to 24. And don't let Carey get you down."

Before Isaac could even acknowledge his offer, Ed LaCroix disappeared into the crowd of milling athletes.

"Okay, men, Everybody in position. Come on. Come on. You, Goldfart, I want you in the front row over on the side." The coach seemed in good humor this afternoon. "We're only going coed for this afternoon, men, so don't get worried."

He paused for the ripple of laughter that came, though begrudgingly.

"Okay then, let's go, let's go. Jog in place, ONE two, ONE two, IN place, IN place. ONE two. Keep up with them, Goldfart."

For over an hour he barked commands, his attention so fixed on Isaac's situps and pushups and deep knee bends that he was oblivious to his bored and tired team. He was astonished that the skinny, sickly-looking boy did not collapse. He began to hope he wouldn't. Suddenly he saw himself as something more than a high school football coach; he was a savior. The little kike actually had guts enough to survive a calisthenics workout with some

very tough guys. With a strong hand to guide him and toughen him up, he might yet become a man. A Buck Carey creation. Buck, married eight years, had no children of his own.

"Practice time! LaCroix, you take them through the offensive plays. Okay men, two teams. Break it up. And don't go easy on anybody, Ed."

The team broke and reassembled in two huddles as Buck Carey ambled over to Isaac, who was bent in a crouch, one arm clutched around his stomach.

"Well, you think you're pretty smart, don't you? Don't you? Hey, I'm talking to you!"

"No, sir. Not pretty smart." Isaac was still gasping for breath.

"No, Coach."

"No, Coach."

"Okay now, stand up here with me and look at those guys. That's what a real man is." He turned and watched Ed LaCroix spiral the ball with deadly accuracy into the arms of Jimmy Kelly, the end, who stumbled on his own feet and dropped it. "Come on, you punks, get on that ball. What the hell's the matter with you? Back up your man," he shouted. But to Isaac he said, "See that pass? That was more than thirty yards, right on target. That's what a real man can do."

Isaac by now had stopped panting and stood, triumphant almost, beside the coach. He had done something, he thought, had been given a physical test and passed it. He felt for a moment different toward the coach; he felt the way he did when he was first learning piano technique and his father would nod his head slowly in approval of his progress. I did it, he said to himself. I survived them all.

They watched in silence until Buck Carey was sure the boy had his breath back.

"Okay now, wiseguy. Try a few laps around the field."

Isaac started off at a brisk trot.

"Not on the grass; on the cinder track, you horse's ass. And don't go so fast or you'll never make it."

Watching Isaac slow to the natural stride and rhythm of a trackman, Buck Carey nodded his head in approval. Yes, I'll make that fairy into a man if it kills him, he thought.

Practice was short that day, and everybody was in high spirits returning to the locker room. "Nice going," someone said to Isaac. It was Jimmy Kelly and he didn't stop, just sort of whispered it to the side as he jogged by but at least he said it. Isaac was glad.

The noise in the locker room was tremendous. They sang in the showers and two of them were boxing; through the splashing and the tangle of legs and arms, it was impossible to see who.

"Knock it off, Ryan!" the coach shouted. It was usually Ryan who caused trouble anyway.

For the first time Isaac was not terrified by the locker room. He recognized in an obscure way that the rough talk and the shoving and the noise were a way of affirming a male companionship he had never experienced before. It had something to do with having struggled together, with having tested their bodies together and pushed them as far as they would go, with being naked together. He was at once conscious of his exhaustion and of an exhilaration at being a man among other men, naked and accepted.

He felt a hand move on his shoulder. It was not like the shoves and bumps inevitable in the packed shower room. It was gentle. He turned large, frightened eyes up to Ed LaCroixs wide grin as the quarterback tightened his grip on Isaac's shoulder, shook him a little, and said, "Nice going, man. You done real good."

Isaac tried to answer and could not. He tried to smile, but his face was frozen. He was aware only of the hand upon his shoulder and the wide grin with its small white teeth and the blond hair curling on Ed LaCroix's chest. He felt dizzy and looked down, brushing the hand from his shoulder. But it was too late. He had begun to stiffen the way he did in bed nights when he touched himself; and Ed LaCroix had seen.

Stepping out of the shower and into the footbath, Isaac

foresaw everything. The coach would stare at him, there, and tell him to stay after the others left. He would be sent to the principal or the student counselor. Everyone in school would know. He could not face it. He had faced enough.

As Isaac stepped from the footbath, the coach stared at him, there, and held out a towel. "You'd better stick around after the others leave, Goldfarb." Isaac dried himself quickly, crouching so that no one would notice, but by now everyone had noticed, and the loud horseplay had fallen off.

When the others had left, Buck Carey called Isaac to his window in the wire cage. "Look, Goldfarb, I'm gonna have to report this to the student counselor. It looks like you need some special help. Meantime I think you'd better just forget about phys ed for a while. I don't want anybody getting in trouble around here, if you get me."

Isaac nodded. He knew it would get to the student counselor. It was his fate.

Slowly he climed the three flights of stairs to Room 24. Linda was not there, nor was Ed La-Croix. He hadn't expected they would be. Who would wait around for a queer?

Isaac had never been in Room 24, though he knew it was the senior homeroom. On an impulse now he went from desk to desk, checking papers and books, until he found Ed LaCroix's. He sat down. The seat was low for him, but he stretched his legs out on both sides of the chair in front and slouched in that professional way the football players had. Then methodically he went through the contents of the desk, tearing pages out of books, breaking the pencils that were not already broken, stabbing the ruined books with Ed's compass. After a while he took the compass and carved on the desk top, *I hate you.*

Isaac did not go home at once. He went instead to the glee club room where, having foreseen that this too would happen, he sat silent for a moment at the piano.

There were some music sheets on the rack; someone had transcribed a Bach cantata, scoring it for piano accompaniment. It was to be the glee club's Thanksgiving concert. Having struggled endless hours with the Art of Fugue, Isaac knew Bach, but his father did not like the cantatas, and so he had never played them. Sitting down to No. 57, "Selig ist der Mann," Isaac felt he was recognizing a piece he had learned ages ago. He played the cantata through, softly, tentatively, letting the music inform his hands. There were no words, just the music; but the four arias spoke through Isaac's fingers of exile and the desire for death, death's sweetness and its joy, delivery from the martyred body. He played the piece again and again until he knew it in his fingers and in his soul, and then he went home.

Karen was angry that he was late for dinner, Avram that he had missed his practice. Isaac, his voice brittle with exhaustion and determination, was stolid under their scolding. It was as if he were already disembodied.

"Do you want to hear me play?" he asked. "Do you want to hear what you have been waiting to hear?"

"Yes, play, always play," his father said, expecting no miracle. It was too late for the soul to appear.

When Isaac finished the cantata, he turned to them and saying only, "Now you know," he walked from the room. He went to the cellar and, lugging the heavy can of kerosene, walked back to the school.

He did not know, though he suspected, that his father was sitting before the piano weeping with joy and fulfillment. "My son," he said over and over. "Karen, my son. After all these years. After all my sacrifices, he plays. At last he plays. The something missing is there. My son."

His son entered the school by the door he had left ajar. He knew it would be ajar; he had foreseen it. He climbed to the third floor, resting on the landings, changing the can of kerosene from hand to hand.

In Room 24 he splashed the kerosene methodically in a large circle, gradually narrowing the compass until he stood with the empty can at Ed LaCroix's desk. He put the can down and rested once more. After a moment he took the compass and gouged away *I hate you* and carved his name, *Isaac,* deep into the top of the desk. Now that it was nearly over he was tired. He sat there staring straight ahead for a long time.

DISCUSSION

Although the newspaper reporters covering the suicide and fire at the local high school found the Goldfarbs to be "a suburban family like any other," the reader knows that Isaac is not a boy like any other. Isaac has lived with unusual stress for achievement and has a long history of unsatisfactory relationships with his peers. In fact, Isaac fits the descriptions of the youthful suicide victim. Researchers have increased their efforts in the last few years to explain the 100 percent increase in suicide among teen-agers.[21] Studies have identified predisposing factors such as excessive family pressure as well as young person's feelings of being

---

[21]R. Seiden, *Suicide in Youth* (Washington, D.C.: United States Government Printing Office, P.H.S. Publication No. 1971, 1969).

unloved and unlovable. Many young people who commit suicide have parents who want their child to succeed in order to compensate for their own feelings of failure, inadequacy, and insecurity. Avram Goldfarb, a victim of Nazi cruelty, is unswerving in his ambition for Isaac to achieve the level of musicianship he had wished for himself, and Isaac's feelings are ignored.

In school Isaac is too dissimilar in appearance and interests to find an accepting peer group. He copes with monumental rejection through his sketching, caricaturing, intellectual pursuits, and musical abilities, which are sources of pleasure and comfort. A compassionate attitude toward social isolates takes more inner tranquility than most adolescent students have. Ed LaCroix and Linda, who are capable and popular students, reach out to Isaac, but he does not have the social skill to know how to accept their offer of friendship. Isaac's emotional disturbance does not go unnoticed in school. His English teacher is aware of the seriousness of his despair, yet she is unable, by virtue of her work load and lack of training, to counsel a boy as severely disturbed as Isaac. Her request for the counselor's help goes unheeded. Unfortunately, this situation is the norm rather than the exception in many schools. Often counselors find that the necessity to meet with students regarding their programs and their classes leaves them little time to meet with individuals with behavioral problems. In some schools, there is a serious lack of communication between the counseling department, the teachers, and the administrators. In many large high schools, the nurse is also involved in matters of mental health of individual students. Nevertheless, she too is limited in the amount of time she can spend counseling. Often she makes referrals, but unless a student is behaving in an aggressively antisocial manner, he or she may not come to the attention of the school psychologist or counselor for several months or even a semester. School psychologists and counselors at the elementary school level, however, are sometimes more available to spend their time with students who are having problems with social adjustments or feelings of low self-esteem and insecurity.

Most readers should not be surprised that someone as insensitive and cruel as Buck Carey can continue to teach in the schools. There is an unspoken understanding in most schools that teachers do not interfere with colleagues' methods of classroom control or individual discipline. At the high school level, there is often stringent separation among departments. Students are usually too intimidated to speak out against a teacher like Buck Carey.

The incident that precipitates Isaac's suicide is unfortunate but not surprising in view of Buck Carey's pathological emphasis on "being a real man." The author intimates that the coach has some concern about his own virility, a concern that may explain his rigid "locker room" thinking about maleness. Buck Carey also has a basic lack of knowledge regarding male physiology. The autonomic nervous system that regulates an erection is so complex that it may be stimulated by a wide variety of emotions, all of which are not necessarily related to sexual feelings. A variety of feeling such as fear, excitement, and pleasure may, in any situation, cause an erection. Buck Carey considers this incident of sufficient deviance to refer Isaac to the school counselor, even though Isaac's more serious depression and isolation were not considered important by the coach. Isaac, like most young boys, is not knowledgeable about the diverse causes of an erection, and he is appalled by the possibility that he might be "queer." His devastation is complete. Isaac's first feelings of self-hatred are projected on to Ed LaCroix, and Isaac methodically goes through Ed's desk destroying his property. Isaac emerges from this initial agonized reaction and decides to take his own life. He no longer feels the pain of his situation and goes through the real and symbolic actions he must perform before death as if disassociated from his own personality.

The reader is left with many questions. Was Isaac in a psychotic state during the period in which he carried out his self-destruction? Did the locker room incident precipitate an otherwise unlikely suicide, or was Isaac sufficiently emotionally disturbed and vulnerable that any traumatic incident would have triggered his course of action? Was suicide the impulsive act of a distraught adolescent? Was Buck Carey's cruelty largely responsible for Isaac's decision, or was Avram Goldfarb's impossible demands on his son the underlying cause of Isaac's suicide?

SPRINGBOARDS FOR INQUIRY

1. Ideally, how could the school counselor have intervened to help Isaac?

2. Would you have predicted that Isaac would have chosen suicide? Explain your answer.

3. Have you known a student who you felt was in need of counseling for an emotional problem? What behavioral indications did you note that made you consider this student emotionally upset?

4. Visit a suicide prevention center in your area, and list the services they provide and the brochures and pamphlets they distribute.

5. Some behaviors of the emotionally disturbed person are self-destructive, while other behaviors are directed outward toward other people. Make a list of the inner-directed symptoms of emotional disturbance and another of the outer-directed symptoms of emotional disturbance.

CHAPTER TEN

The Severely Emotionally Disturbed and the Autistic

Psychotic (defined as suffering from childhood schizophrenia) and autistic children were once thought to be of no particular concern to the school because they were usually classified as mentally retarded and were frequently institutionalized. Today, medicine and education have intervened in the educational and social adjustment of these children. There seem to be two major differences between infantile autism and childhood schizophrenia: one, the age of onset of symptoms; and two, the delayed and deviant language development of autistic children.[1] Lawrence Bartok and Michael Rutter define autism as "a disorder evident before thirty months of age in which there [is] a profound and general failure to develop normal social relationships together with delayed and deviant language development and the presence of ritualistic or compulsive phenomena."[2] When infantile autism was first described,

---

[1]It is interesting to note that in a recent article by James Gallagher and Ronald Wiegerink ("Educational Strategies for the Autistic Child," *Journal of Autism and Childhood Schizophrenia*, vol. 6, no. 1 [March 1976], 15–26), they report that in the Soviet Union they saw a youngster identified as schizophrenic whom they would label as autistic. International as well as national agreement on classification is still in a state of turmoil. Efforts to resolve the matters are reported in Nicholas Hobbs, ed., *Issues in the Classification of Children: A Sourcebook on Labels, Categories, and Their Consequences*, vol. 1 (San Francisco, Calif.: Jossey-Bass, Inc., Publishers, 1975), chapter 10.

[2]Lawrence Bartok and Michael Rutter, "Differences Between Mentally Retarded and Normally Intelligent Autistic Children," *Journal of Autism and Childhood Schizophrenia*, vol. 6, no. 2 (June 1976), 109.

it was thought to be a variant of schizophrenia because in both cases the child exhibits severely disturbed relationships with people:

> There is an important difference. In schizophrenia, the individual develops normally at first. It is only with the onset of illness that he [loses] touch with reality. The autistic child . . . shows abnormalities of development from early infancy.[3]

Leo Kanner was the first clinician to describe infantile autism in 1943.[4] He characterized autistic children as being withdrawn and having an obsessive desire for the preservation of sameness, a skillful and even affectionate relation to objects, a thoughtful and intelligent personal appearance, and either mutism or noncommunicative speech. Inasmuch as time of onset is the most significant difference between the two pathologies, for the purposes of this volume we treat infantile autism and childhood schizophrenia as if they were identical.

Arthur D. Sorosky and his colleagues describe typical behaviors associated with autistic children (see table 10–1).[5] The pathologic behaviors unique to autistic children are diverse, falling under seven different general headings.

Of particular importance to those who may teach autistic or schizophrenic children over five years old is the research on imitation (or lack of it) among young autistic children. Imitation of both verbal and nonverbal activities of parents stimulates the communicative and adaptive learning that is so vital to the socialization of the child. In fact, Bernard Rimland and Virginia I. Douglas and Frances A. Sanders regard failure to imitate another person before the age of three as an item that differentiates autistic from retarded children.[6] If it is true that autistic

[3]Michael Rutter, "The Development of Infantile Autism," in *Annual Progress in Child Psychiatry and Child Development,* ed. Stella Chess and Alexander Thomas (New York: Brunner/Mazel, Inc., 1975), p. 331.

[4]For those students interested in a longitudinal approach to the study of infantile autism it is essential to begin with Leo Kanner's, "Autistic Disturbances of Affective Contact," *Nervous Child,* 2 (1943), 217–50. The article by Michael Rutter is an excellent summary of relevant research on infantile autism. The student wishing to proceed further might well consult the *Journal of Autism and Childhood Schizophrenia.*

[5]Arthur D. Sorosky et al., "Systematic Observations of Autistic Behavior," *Archives of General Psychiatry,* vol. 18, no. 4 (April 1968), 439.

[6]Bernard Rimland, *Infantile Autism: The Syndrome and Its Implications for a Neural Theory of Behavior* (New York: Appleton-Century-Crofts, 1964); and Virginia I. Douglas and Frances A. Sanders, "A Pilot Study of Rimland's Diagnostic Check List with Autistic and Mentally Retarded Children," *Journal of Child Psychology and Psychiatry,* 9 (1968), 105–109.

Table 10–1
Behaviors Observed in Autistic Children

Pathologic behaviors unique to autistic children

Motor Behaviors
  Total Body Movements
  Whirling
  Circling
  Darting motions
  Running or walking on toes
  Bizarre gaits

  Hand Movements
  Flapping
  Flicking
  Spinning objects
  Oscillating

  Inhibitory Movements
  Arrest reactions
  Posturing

Perceptual Behaviors
  Visual Behaviors
  Regarding
  Staring
  Visual scrutiny
  Voluntary strabismus

  Auditory Behaviors
  Attending to self-induced sounds
  Covering, flicking, and banging on ears

  Olfactory Behaviors
  Sniffing and smelling objects

  Tactile Behaviors
  Tactile scrutiny

Pathologic behaviors common to autistic and other children

Rhythmic Behaviors
  Body rocking
  Repetitive jumping (bouncing)
  Head rolling
  Head banging
Miscellaneous Behaviors
  Repetitive banging on body with hands
  Repetitive banging on surroundings with hands
  Preoccupation with excretory products
  Tantrums

Normal behaviors common to autistic and other children

Crying
Verbal sounds
Miscellaneous oral behaviors (licking, sucking, biting, and so on)

Source: Arthur D. Sorosky et al., "Systematic Observations of Autistic Behavior," *Archives of General Psychiatry,* vol. 18, no. 4 (April 1968), 439.

children may imitate only after the age of five, then educational strategies at that time may be more important than ever.[7] Marian K. De Myer and her colleagues found "that autistic and schizophrenic children use objects spontaneously better than they imitate the actions of others."[8] In their work with retarded and autistic or schizophrenic children, they found that there was a difference in these two groups in their relationships to people: "Subnormal children looked at us when we spoke to them, smiled in response to our smiles and waved at us when we waved. The parents did not speak of them as 'lost in their own worlds' even though they had a variety of emotional and interpersonal problems."[9]

Before proceeding to a discussion of the educational treatment for autistic or schizophrenic children, Michael Rutter's summary of the research on these children as of 1974 is useful:

> In conclusion, research findings have amply confirmed the validity of Kanner's delineation of the syndrome of infantile autism. As knowledge on the characteristics and course of the disorder gradually increased, it became clearer what were the clinical observations which demanded an explanation. Views that autism might be a variant of schizophrenia or mental retardation or that autism was a psychogenic disorder gave way as the evidence mounted that autistic children had a specific cognitive deficit. The existence of this deficit has now been demonstrated beyond dispute, although its exact limits have still to be established. An impairment in linguistic functions is central but which cognitive skills are affected to give rise to the linguistic impairment has still to be determined. It is generally supposed that the deficit gives rise to the other symptoms of autism. This remains a plausible hypothesis supported by the very limited studies so far carried out into the mechanisms underlying the syndrome. However, critical tests of the hypothesis have still to be made. The biological basis of the cognitive defect remains unknown and it has still to be established whether autism is a single disease entity, a syndrome of biological impairment, or a collection of symptoms which may be due to a heterogeneous group of influences both biological and psychosocial.
>
> Although much has yet to be learned about the syndrome of infantile autism, understanding of the nature of the disorder has advanced rapidly

---

[7]Rimland and Wing (John K. Wing, ed., *Early Childhood Autism* [London: Pergamon, 1966]; also Lorna Wing, *Autistic Children* [New York: Brunner/Mazel, Inc., 1972]) maintain that some autistic children after the age of five became less withdrawn and less autistic.

[8]Marian K. De Myer et al., "Imitation in Autistic, Early Schizophrenic, and Non-Psychotic Subnormal Children," *Journal of Autism and Childhood Schizophrenia*, vol. 2, no. 3 (1972), p. 279.

[9]Ibid., p. 282.

over the last dozen years. This increase in understanding has had important implications for treatment.[10]

The first educational treatment for autistic or schizophrenic children (and one that is still used) is the one-on-one psychodynamic approach in which psychotherapy is used to change the behavior of the patient. Bruno Bettelheim, working in an institutional setting, utilized this type of treatment.[11] Bettelheim stressed the mother as the primary pathology, particularly the lack of affection from the mother. To make up for this, he created at the University of Chicago's Orthogenic School a permissive regimen of warmth, loving acceptance, and compliance with his personal demands. Michael Rutter suggests that it is more productive to "focus on the measures needed to aid more normal social and linguistic development in spite of the cognitive defects, and in the steps required to avoid the development of secondary handicaps."[12] O. Ivar Lovaas at the University of California, Los Angeles, concentrates on developing patterns of speech by withholding food until a child utters certain sounds and finally learns to imitate adults.[13]

Helen Clancy and Glen McBride take strong exception to Bettelheim's treatment and "believe that permissiveness is actually harmful to the autistic child. . . . Accordingly we reject permissiveness and would argue for forceful demands by parents, to intrude and reinforce

[10]Rutter, "The Development of Infantile Autism," in *Annual Progress in Child Psychiatry and Child Development*, p. 349.

[11]In this respect, Eric Schopler's caustic review of Bettelheim's *A Home for the Heart* (New York: Alfred A. Knopf, Inc., 1974) may be instructive. Schopler's statement seems to us to epitomize the disdain currently in vogue for those who treat autism or schizophrenia by anything other than operant methods: "In summary, the professional reader who expects to learn about autistic and schizophrenic children, how to make a differential diagnosis . . . and formulate hypotheses of etiology and early family influences, will find little knowledge in this book, but, on the contrary, much that is misleading (Eric Schopler, 'The Art and Science of Bruno Bettelheim,' *Journal of Autism and Childhood Schizophrenia*, vol. 6, no. 2 [1976], 193)." In a March 1976 article, however, David Helm concludes, "I have drawn freely from the work of both psychodynamic and behavior modification practitioners. I have found their distinctive emphases—interpersonal relatedness and directed behavioral change—not contradictory, but complementary. . . . There is evidence of an increasing convergence in the methods of intervention adopted by workers of differing theoretical persuasion (David Helm, 'Psychodynamic and Behavior Modification Approaches to the Treatment of Infantile Autism ,' *Journal of Autism and Childhood Schizophrenia*, vol. 6, no. 1 [March 1976], 27—41)."

[12]Rutter, "The Development of Infantile Autism," in *Annual Progress in Child Psychiatry and Child Development*, p. 348.

[13]O. Ivar Lovaas, "Breaking Through to the Autistic Child," *Medical World News* (October 28, 1966), pp. 85—92.

negatively both cut-off behavior and temper tantrums."[14] They report on a two-pronged approach to the problem of the primary socialization of the child (the child in the context of his family) and next the acquisition of behaviors normally developed through the use of language. Of the fifty-three male children they treated, they report varying degrees of success. Their first attention in the reeducation of the autistic child is promoting the mother-child bond. Thus, they start with the feeding problem because "of its importance for establishing a bond between child and mother."[15] The child is starved so that when the mother does feed him, her behavior is viewed by the child as a catalyst to the affiliative behavior between the two. Their regimen for promoting speech and language is not adequately described, but the inference is that once the feeding program is inaugurated and successful (usually within one week) language usage increases.[16]

The work of James Gallagher and Ronald Wiegerink summarizes the research related to the nonlearning behavioral characteristics of the autistic child.[17] Based upon these findings, some concrete suggestions for educational strategies seem to follow:

RESEARCH FINDINGS	EDUCATIONAL STRATEGIES
1. Basic defect in autistic children is a short-term memory defect[18] and the failure to register experience in cognitive tasks and interpersonal relation-	1. Tasks should be arranged so that there is a minimal elapsed time between whatever is taught and the "demand" for recall and and should proceed slowly

---

[14]Helen Clancy and Glen McBride, "The Autistic Process and Its Treatment," *Journal of Child Psychology and Psychiatry and Allied Disciplines*, vol. 10, no. 4 (December 1969), 242.

[15]Ibid., p. 238.

[16]Mother and child are hospitalized, the therapist introduces new foods camouflaged by preferred foods, and in one week the mother takes over. Using water play and rough and tumble games is the beginning of the development of language interaction between mother and child *after* the feeding routine has been established.

[17]Gallagher and Wiegerink, "Educational Strategies for the Autistic Child."

[18]Karl Pribram, "Autism: A Deficiency in Context-Dependent Processes?" *Proceedings of the National Society for Autistic Children* (Rockville, Md.: United States Public Health Service, United States Department of Health, Education and Welfare, 1970); Alexander Luria, *Higher Cortical Functions in Man* (New York: Basic Books, Inc., Publishers, 1966); Carolyn Bryson, "Systematic Identification of Perceptual Disabilities in Autistic Children," *Perceptual and Motor Skills*, 31 (1970), 239–46; and Carolyn Bryson, "Short Term Memory and Cross-Model Information Processing in Autistic Children," *Journal of Learning Disabilities*, 5 (1972), pp. 25–35.

RESEARCH FINDINGS

ships. Major learning is through contiguity (visual linking of two experiences that occur at the same time). Visual short-term memory and auditory-visual information processing are two clearly identifiable deficiencies.

EDUCATIONAL STRATEGIES

from very simple to more complex. Any auditory stimulus (note the use of the singular in "stimulus," implying the efficacy of only one stimulus at a time) must be presented simultaneously with a visual stimulus, not before or after. Simultaneous linking of the auditory and the visual is important with a very slow extension of the interval between each.

2. Autistic children prefer visual over auditory stimuli.[19] Autistic children learn through manipulation[20] and position cues, that is, there is a strong motor component to their perceptual processes. The motility (the persistent rocking, hand flapping, head banging, ear flickering, and whirling) of autistic children is independent of environmental influence. Autistic motility patterns may be the way autistic

2. Learning must not be primarily verbal. Lectures, demonstrations, recordings, and so on should be minimal with direct contact experiences being the primary learning modality. Motility patterns of the child should not prevent the teacher from continuing with visual experiences for these children. Structured programs with immediate feedback components produce moderate results.

[19]Edward Ornitz, "The Modulation of Sensory Input and Motor Output in Autistic Children," in *Psychopathology and Child Development,* ed. Eric Schopler and Robert Reichler (London: Plenum Press, 1976), pp. 115–33; Edward Ornitz et al., "Environmental Modification of Autistic Behavior," *Archives of General Psychiatry,* 22 (June 1970), 560–65; Marian K. De Myer et al., "Prognosis in Autism : A Follow-up Study," *Journal of Autism and Childhood Schizophrenia,* 2 (1972), 359–77; and Marian K. De Myer, "The Nature of Neuropsychological Disability in Autistic Children," in *Psychopathology and Child Development,* Schopler and Reichler, pp. 93–114.

[20]Beate Hermelin and Neil O'Conner, *Psychological Experiments with Autistic Children* (Oxford: Pergamon Press, 1970, 1976).

RESEARCH FINDINGS	EDUCATIONAL STRATEGIES
children make sense of the sensations of their environment.	
3. Verbal skills of all kinds are severely retarded (especially in very low IQ autistic children). Abstraction skills are generally low in all autistic children. Most autistic children retain their pattern of learning dysfunction and generally low IQ scores. Despite poor prognosis, about 8 percent of autistic children can make some progress.	3. Nonverbal experiences of short duration have some effect. Using abstract terms, for example, Was that a *way* to behave? or I thought I could *trust* you, are ineffectual. Assume the possibility of educability and teach accordingly.
4. When autistic children are taught,[21] they improve in responsiveness, speaking, and reading.	4. The structured, organized, and logical (rather than permissive) classroom environment can produce significant educational progress.
5. Reducing the auditory input for autistic children helps them code and store auditory signals.[22]	5. Attendance to auditory input may be facilitated by shutting out random auditory input. If instructions need to be given, equipping the children with earmuff-type protectors will cut out "other" sounds.

Gallagher and Wiegerink conclude the following:

1. Autistic children are educable.
2. Their unique learning characteristics are due to basic cognitive deficits in information processing.

---

[21]Lawrence Bartok and Michael Rutter, "Educational Treatment of Autistic Children," in *Infantile Autism: Concepts, Characteristics and Treatment*, ed. Michael Rutter (London: Churchill Livingstone, 1971).

[22]Joan Fassler and N. Dale Bryant, *Task Performance, Attention and Classroom Behavior of Seriously Disturbed, Communication Impaired, Autistic-Type Children Under Conditions of Reduced Auditory Input* (New York: Teacher's College, Columbia University, 1970).

3. Such deficits can be compensated for, in part, by carefully structured educational programs with specified developmental learning sequences and enhanced reinforcing stimuli.

4. Structured education programs should begin early in life, with the parent or parent surrogate as the primary teacher.

5. Educational programs for these children are feasible, and in the long run, less costly than institutional care.

6. The provision of appropriate educational programs for these children is not a manifestation of public generosity but rather a reflection that these children, too, have a clear right to an appropriate education.[23]

[23]Gallagher and Wiegerink, "Educational Strategies for the Autistic Child," p. 26.

Wednesday's Child

by Joyce Carol Oates

Around the high handsome roof of the house birds flew in the first hours of daylight, calling out, so that their small shadows fell against the bedroom curtains harmless as flowers thrown by anonymous admirers. Squirrels ran along the gutters. At some distance the horns of river freighters sounded, melancholy and exciting. Today he was not going to work; today he woke slowly, with a sense of luxury, aware of these sounds and their lovely softness, thinking that sound itself seemed a kind of touch.

His wife lay sleeping beside him. She was a dark-haired woman of thirty-five, attractive, exhausted even in sleep, wounded by small impatient lines in her forehead; he did not quite believe in those lines. He always expected them to be gone. Even in sleep his wife seemed to him thoughtful, thinking, sensitive to his feeling of luxury—so she lay perfectly still, not waking. She would not join him in it.

Several shadows fell against the curtains—the weightless shadows of birds. He watched. Everything was still. This house, thirty years old, had stood firm and wonderfully solid among its more contemporary neighbors, a high brick colonial home with white shutters, quite perfect. It was not his idea of a final home. It was his idea of a home for himself and his wife and daughter in this decade, just as this famous suburb was his idea of a way of preparing for a distant, delightful, aristocratic life in another part of

Reprinted from *Marriages and Infidelities and Other Stories* by Joyce Carol Oates by permission of the publisher, Vanguard Press, Inc. Copyright © 1968, 1969, 1970, 1971, 1972 by Joyce Carol Oates.

the country. He was an architect and worked for an excellent firm. Only thirty-seven, he was successful in the eyes of his parents and even in the eyes of his friends, who were themselves scampering like squirrels with their tiny shrewd toenails pulling them, pulling them up, always up, their cheeks rosy with the exhilaration of success. He was one of them. He was not his parents' son any longer; his father had been a high-school teacher, a good, deferential, exploited man.

So he woke on Wednesday morning, very early. The day would be a long one. His wife was evidently not going to wake, but lay frowning and severe in sleep, as if giving up to him the burden of this day. Already he could hear his daughter. Coming out of her room . . . in the hall . . . now on her way downstairs. He listened closely. He could hear, or could imagine, her pulling the piano bench away from the piano, down in the living room. Yes, she must be there. The bench was white—a white grand piano, very beautiful—and she sat at it, seriously, frowning like her mother, staring down at the keys. White and black keys. Even the cracks arrested her attention. He lay in bed on the second floor of his house, imagining his daughter almost directly below him, sitting at the piano. He heard the first note. His face went rigid.

He got dressed quickly. He put on a tie his mother had given

him, a very conservative tie, dark green. His secret was a dark, serious, grimly green soul—he liked to hide it behind smiles, enthusiasm for football, hearty compliments to his wife. . . . She had turned over in bed, she was still asleep or pretending to sleep. The other day she had told him she would not remain herself much longer. "I can't live like this much longer," she had said. It was not a threat or a warning, only a curious, exploratory remark. They had come in late from a dinner party, from a marvelous evening, and she had told him suddenly that she was failing, giving up, being conquered, defeated . . . all she had accomplished as a mother was failure. Failure.

Why should she wake up to see him off?

Downstairs he saw with a slight shock Brenda at the piano, seated just as he had imagined her. She was running her fingers gently over the keyboard. The sound was gentle, soft. It would not shatter any crystal; there was no power behind it. Down at the far end of the living room the wide French windows were seared with light, the filmy curtains glowing. He appreciated that; he appreciated beauty. The living room had been decorated in white and gold. His daughter's face was pale, not quite white, and her legs pale, limp, motionless. She had put her little white socks on perfectly. She wore a yellow dress, perfectly ironed by the laundry that did her father's shirts so meticulously, and her hair was a fine, dull gold, very neat. Everything matched. He appreciated that.

She was playing the "Moonlight Sonata" with a numb, feverish, heavy rhythm, leaning too hard on the more emphatic passages, too breathy and rushed with the delicate ones. She played like a sixteen-year old girl who had taken lessons dutifully for years, mediocre and competent, with a firm failure of imagination underlying every note. Brenda was only six and had never had any music lessons, did not even listen in any evident way to music, and yet she could play for hours with this mysterious subcompetence—why? He stood staring at her. She was oblivious to him. Why, if his daughter must be insane, why not brilliantly insane? Why not a genius?

Instead, she was extraordinary but not astonishing. She might be written up in someone's textbook someday, but the case history would not be important; there wasn't enough to her. "Good morning, honey," he said. He came to her and put his arms gently around her. She stopped playing the piano but did not seem to notice him. Instead, as if paralyzed by a thought that had nothing to do with him, she sat rigid, intense, staring at her fingers on the keyboard.

"You're all ready, are you? Scrubbed and clean and ready for the trip?"

She did not appear to have heard him. She did hear him, of course, every word, and some words hardly audible—they had discovered that when she was hardly a year old, her uncanny animal-like omnipotence. She heard what was breathed into his ear by his wife, up in their secret bed, she heard the secret date of her next appointment with the Dreaded Doctor, she knew instinctively when an innocent drive would take her to the dentist, she knew everything. . . . Today, Wednesday, was not a fearful day. She was not afraid of school. She gave no indication of liking it, or of anticipating it, but she was not afraid and she would not go limp, forcing them to carry her out to the car.

"I'll have some coffee, then we'll leave. Mommy's staying home today and I'm taking you. I thought we'd have a nice drive to school, then come back through the park. . . . I took the whole day off today. I hope the sun stays out."

He was aware of the paragraphs of his speech. Talking to his silent, frowning daughter, a child of six with an ageless look, he understood how silence mocks words; her blocks of silence, like terrible monstrous blocks of stone, fell heavily on either side of his words. What he said was never quite accurate. He was speaking to a child when, perhaps, he should have been speaking to an adult. Brenda's intelligence had never been measured. She might be ten years old, or eighteen, or two. It was a mystery, an abyss. As soon as he entered the kitchen he heard her begin to play where she had left off, the "Moonlight Sonata" in that sun-filled living room. . . .

He made instant coffee. His hands had begun to tremble. The harmonic green and brown of the kitchen did not soothe him, he could not sit down. When he came home from the office each day he always came out to the kitchen to talk to his wife, and he talked energetically about his work. His wife always appeared to listen with sympathy. His paragraphs of words, tossed against her appreciative silence, were attempts to keep her quiet; he realized that now. She made dinner and listened to him, flattering him with her complete attention. He hinted of trouble at work, maybe a union threatening to strike, or the federal government again raising mortgage interest . . . tricks to keep his wife from talking about Brenda. He realized that now.

When he returned to the living room Brenda slid dutifully off the bench. She never resisted physically; her body was not really her own. She was quite small for her age, with knobby white knees. He loved her knees. Her hair was thin and straight, cut off to show her delicate ears. Her face was a pretty face, though too thin, unnaturally pale; her eyes were a light green. Seeing her was always a shock; you expected to see a dull, squat child, a kind of dwarf. Not at all. Everyone, especially the two sets of grandparents, remarked on her beauty. "She's so pretty! It will all work itself out!" both grandmothers said constantly. They were anxious to share in her mythical progress and contributed toward the tuition charged by the private, expensive school she went to, though Arthur resented this. He made enough money to send his own child to school. But the grandparents wanted to get as close as possible, nudging their beautiful prodigy into life, breathing the mysterious breath of normal life into her. Why, why was she not normal, when it was so obviously easier to be normal than to be Brenda? Perfectly stupid children were normal, ugly children were normal, and this golden-haired little lady, with her perfect face and ears and limbs, was somehow not . . . not "normal." It was an abyss, the fact of her.

Drawing slightly away from him, with a woman's coolness, she put on her own coat. He knelt to check her, to see if the buttons were lined up correctly. Of course. It had been years since she'd buttoned them wrong. "All set? Great! We're on our way!" Arthur said heartily. She did not look at him. She never met his eye, that was part of her strangeness—she would not look anyone in the eye, as if some secret shame or hatred forced her away, like the invisible force of like magnets.

And so . . . they were on their way. No backing out. His wife had driven Brenda to school ever since Brenda had begun, and today he was driving her, a generous act. Minutes flew by. It was a surprise how quickly time had passed, getting him up out of bed and on his way, drawing him to the ride. The minutes had passed as if flying toward an execution. . . . He had tried to think of this day as a gift, a day off from work, but it had been nothing but pretense. He was afraid of the long trip and afraid of his daughter.

Between his wife and himself was the fact of their daughter. They had created her together, somehow they had brought her into the world. It was a mystery that jarred the soul; better not to think of it. His wife had accused him more than once of blaming her for the child. "You hate me unconsciously. You can't control it," she had said. Her wisdom was sour and impregnable. "You hate failure," she said. Didn't he hate, in his cheerful secretive way, his own father because his own father was something of a failure?

"Jesus Christ, what are you saying?" he had shouted. He denied everything.

The school was experimental and chancy, very expensive. Was it really quite professional? The several doctors they'd taken Brenda to were not enthusiastic; they expressed their opinion of the school with a neutral shrug of the shoulders. Why not try? And so, desperate, they had driven fifty miles to talk with the director, a long-nosed, urgent female with grimy fingernails and great excitement, and she had agreed to take Brenda on. "But we make no promises. Everything is exploratory," she had said. "Nothing is given a form, no theories are allowed to be hardened into dogma, no theories are rejected without trial, no emotions are stifled. . . . " Why not try? After several months Brenda showed no signs of improvement, and no signs of degeneration. If she showed any "signs" at all, they were private and indecipherable. But Wednesday had become the center of the week. He and his wife looked to Wednesday, that magic day, as a kind of Sabbath; on that day he drove to work with a sense of anticipation, and his wife drove Brenda fifty miles to school and fifty miles back again, hoping. This was the usual procedure. Then, when he came home, he would always ask, "How do you think it went today?" and she would always reply, "The director is still hopeful . . . I think it's going well . . . yes, I think it's going well."

In the car Brenda seated herself as far from him as possible. No use to urge her to move over. She was not stubborn, not exactly. It was rather as if no one inhabited her body, as if her spirit had abandoned it. "A great day for a ride!" he said. He chatted with her, or toward her. His voice sounded nervous. He disliked silence because of its emptiness, the possibility of anything happening inside it—no warning, no form to it. He was amorous of forms, solid forms. He distrusted shapelessness. In his daydreams he had always wanted to force action into a shape, to freeze explosions into art, into the forms in which beauty is made bearable. He lived in one of those forms. The style of his living was one of them. Why not? The work he did was professional in every way, geared to a market, imagination within certain limiting forms. He was not a genius, he would not revolutionize architecture. Like his daughter, he was extraordinary but not astonishing.

Brenda took a piece of spaghetti out of her coat pocket. It was uncooked, broken in half. She began to chew on it. Except for random, unlikely things— fish sticks, bits of cardboard, cucumber, grapes with seeds— she ate nothing but uncooked spaghetti. She bit pieces off slowly, solemnly, chewing them

with precision. Her green eyes were very serious. Every day she stuffed her pockets with pieces of spaghetti, broken in pieces. Bits of spaghetti were all over the house. His wife vacuumed every day, with great patience. It wasn't that Brenda seemed to like spaghetti, or that she had any concept of "liking" food at all. Perhaps she could not taste it. But she would not eat anything else. Arthur had long ago stopped snatching it away from her. He had stopped pleading with her. For what had seemed a decade she had sat at the table with them, listless and stoney-eyed, refusing to eat. She did not quite *refuse*— nothing so emphatic. But she would not eat. She had no obvious conception of "eating." What she did was nibble slowly at pieces of spaghetti, all day long, or chew cardboard and shape it into little balls, or suck at grapes and very carefully extract the seeds. She walked around the house or out in the back yard as if in a trance, slow, precise, unhurried, spiritless. Demurely she turned aside when someone approached her. She went dead. The only life she showed was her piano playing, which was monotonous and predictable, the same pieces over and over again for months. . . . Her silence was immense as a mountain neither Arthur nor his wife could climb. And when the silence came to an end—when Brenda cried, which was infrequent—

they heard to their horror the sobs of a six-year-old child, breathy and helpless. But how to help her? She could not be embraced, even by a distraught parent. A bump on the head, a bleeding scratch, would not soften her. The jolly mindlessness of Christmas would not give any grandparent the right to hug her. No nonsense. No touching. When his wife took Brenda for her monthly checkup, at which time the doctor gave her vitamin shots, she always asked the doctor how Brenda was "doing"; and the doctor always said, with a special serious smile to show how sorry he was about all this, "She's surprisingly healthy, considering her diet. You should be thankful."

It was a long drive. Arthur began to think longingly of his office—an older associate of his whom he admired and imitated, the naïveté of a secretary he could almost have loved, in another dimension. Elevators, high buildings. Occasional long lunches. He thought of his office, of his working space. He liked to work. He liked problems. They came to him in the shape of lines with three dimensions. It was remarkable how they were then transferred into shapes that were solid, into buildings. He was working on a shopping plaza. A shopping "mall." With love he dreamed of the proper shapes of banks, the proper shapes of supermarkets, of

hardware stores—seductive as music! Their lines had to be gentle, seductive, attractive as the face of his secretary, who was only twenty-three. He wanted to love them. Certainly he had enough love in him . . . love for his work, for his wife, his secretary, his parents, his friends, his daughter. . . . Why did he feel so exhausted though it was early morning?

He entered the expressway in silence. Brenda was awake but silent. It was worse than being truly alone, for a swerving of the car would knock her around; if he slammed on the brakes she would fly forward and crack her skull. A limp weight. No true shape to her, because she was so empty. What was she thinking? He glanced sideways at her, smiling in case she noticed him. He and his wife believed that their daughter was thinking constantly. Her silence was not peaceful. It seemed to them nervous, jumpy, alert, but alert to invisible shapes. Something unseen would move in the corner of her eye and she would shiver, almost imperceptibly. What did she see? What did she think? Idiot children who giggle and squirm happily in their mothers' embraces make more sense, being only defective of intelligence. It would be possible to love them.

"Look at the cows!" he said, pointing. "Do you see the cows?" No response. No cows.

"Look at the big truck up ahead . . . all those new cars on it. . . ." He felt the need to talk. He wanted to keep a sense of terror at some distance; her silence, her terrifying silence! He stared at the carrier with its double row of shining cars, cars of all colors, very handsome. He was preparing to pass the truck. What if, at the crucial moment, the truck wobbled and the cars came loose? They seemed precariously fastened to the carrier. He imagined metal shearing through metal, slicing off the top of his skull. The steering wheel would cut him in two. And his daughter would be crushed in an instant, pressed into her essential silence. The end.

"Like to hear some music, Brenda?" He turned on the radio. Strange, how he felt the need to talk to her in spurts, as if offering her a choice of remarks. Like his wife, he somehow thought that a magic moment would arrive and Brenda would wake up, a fairy princess awakened by the right incantation. . . . If only she would let them kiss her, perhaps the perfect kiss would awaken her. But she did not hear the words, did not hear the love and yearning behind them, would not suffer the kiss, nothing. She did not need them. She was a delicate weight in the corner of his eye, not a threat, not really a burden because she wanted nothing— unlike other children, she wanted nothing. And so there was nothing to give her.

She ate uncooked spaghetti for the rest of the drive.

The school was housed in a one-story building, previously a small-parts shop. On the walk he noticed a bit of drool about Brenda's mouth—should he wipe it off? He wanted to wipe it off, not because he was anxious for her to look neat for school but because he was her father and had the right to touch her.

"Do you have a handkerchief, honey?"

This was too mild. She sensed his weakness. She wiped her own mouth with her hand, blankly and efficiently. A college-age girl with a suntanned face took Brenda from him, all pop-eyed charm and enthusiasm. He watched Brenda walk away. It pained him to see how easily she left him, how unconnected they were. There was nothing between them. She did not glance back, did not notice that he was remaining behind. Nothing.

He drove around for a while, feeling sorry for himself, then stopped to have some coffee. Then he walked around the university, browsing in bookstores, wondering if he could remain sane—he had several hours to get through. What did his wife do on these holy Wednesdays? At noon he went to a good restaurant for lunch. Two cocktails first, then a steak sandwich. Women shoppers surrounded him. He admired their leisure, their rings, their gloves; women who had the air of being successes. They seemed happy. Once at a party he had noticed his wife in deep conversation with a stranger, and something in his wife's strained, rapt face had frightened him. When he asked her about it later she had said, "With him I felt anonymous, I could have begun everything again. He doesn't know about me. About Brenda." Like those bizarre unshaped pieces of sculpture that are placed around new buildings to suggest their important ties with the future, he and his wife had lost their ability to maintain a permanent shape; they were always being distorted. Too many false smiles, false enthusiasm and fear covered over. . . . The very passage of days had tugged at their faces and bodies, aging them. They were no longer able to touch each other and to recognize a human form. But he had seen her touch that man's arm, unconsciously, wanting from him the gift of a sane perspective, an anonymous freedom, that Arthur could no longer give her.

He wandered into another bookstore. In a mirror he caught sight of himself and was surprised, though pleasantly—so much worry and yet he was a fairly young man, still handsome, with light hair and light, friendly eyes, a good face. The necktie looked good. He wandered along

the aisles, looking at textbooks. These manuals for beginning lives, for starting out fresh. . . . Engineering texts, medical texts. French dictionaries. A crunching sound at the back of the store put him in mind of his daughter eating. Spaghetti being bitten, snapped, crunched, chewed . . . an eternity of spaghetti. . . . He wandered to another part of the store and picked up a paperback book, *Forbidden Classics.* An Egyptian woman, heavily made up, beckoned to him from the cover. He picked up another book, *Bizarre Customs of the World;* on this cover a child beckoned to him, dressed in an outlandish outfit of feathers and furs. . . . He leafed through the book, paused at a few pages, then let the book fall. Garbage. He was insulted. A sense of disorder threatened. Better for him to leave.

He strolled through the campus but its buildings had no interest for him. They were dead, they were tombs. The sidewalks were newer, wide, functional. The university's landscaping was impressive. Students sat on the grass, reading. A girl caught his attention—she wore soiled white slacks, sat with her legs apart, her head flung back so that the sun might shine flatly onto her face. Her long brown hair hung down behind her. She was immobile, alone. Distracted, he nearly collided with someone. He stared at the girl and wondered why she frowned so, why her face was lined though she could not have been more than twenty—what strange intensity was in her?

He walked in another direction. There were too many young girls, all in a hurry. Their faces were impatient. Their hair swung around their eyes impatiently, irritably. His blood seemed to return to his heart alert and jumpy, as if infected by their intensity, by the mystery of their secret selves. He felt panic. A metallic taste rose to his mouth, as if staining his mouth. He felt that something was coming loose in him, something dangerous.

What did his wife do on these long hateful days?

He went to the periodical room of the university's undergraduate library. He leafed through magazines. World affairs; nothing of interest. Domestic affairs: no, nothing. What about medicine, what new miracles? What about architecture? He could not concentrate. He tried to daydream about his work, his problems, about the proper shapes of banks and stores. . . . Nothing. He thought of his salary, his impressive salary, and tried to feel satisfaction; but nothing. His brain was dazzled as if with sparks. Suddenly he saw the girl on the grass, in a blaze of light, her white slacks glowing. An anonymous girl. Beginning again with an anonymous girl. The girl shivered in his brain, wanting more from the sun than the sun could give her.

He wanted to leave the library and find her, but he did not move. He remained with the magazines on his lap. He waited. After a while, when he thought it was safe, he went to a campus bar and had a drink. Two drinks. Around him were music, noise; young people who were not youthful. People jostled his chair all the time, as if seeking him out, contemptuous of his age. A slight fever had begun in his veins. Around him the boys and girls hung over one another, arguing, stabbing the air with their fingers, scraping their chairs angrily on the floor. "I am not defensive!" a girl cried. Now and then a girl passed by him who was striking as a poster—lovely face, lovely eyes. Why didn't she glance at Arthur? It was as if she sensed the failure of his genes, the quiet catastrophe of his chromosomes. He heard beneath the noise in the bar a terrible silence, violent as the withheld violence of great boulders.

When he picked Brenda up he felt a sense of levity rising in him, as if he had survived an ordeal. "How was it today, honey? What is that you've got—a paper flower?" He took it from her buttonhole, the buttonhole indifferent as her face. Yes, a paper flower. A red rose. "It's great. Did you make it yourself, honey?" He put it in his own buttonhole, as if his daughter had made it for him. She did not glance up. In the car she sat as far from him as possible, while he chattered wildly, feeling his grin slip out of control. Around him boulders precarious on mountainsides were beginning their long fall, soundlessly.

"We'll stop in the park for a few minutes. You should get out in the sun." He tried to sound festive. Parks meant fun; children knew that. The park was large, mostly trees, with a few swings and tennis courts. It was nearly empty. He walked alongside her on one of the paths, not touching her, the two of them together but wonderfully independent. "Look at the birds. Blue jays," he said. He wanted to take her hand but feared her rejection. Only by force could anyone take her hand. She took a stick of spaghetti out of her pocket and bit into it, munching slowly and solemnly. "Look at the squirrels, aren't they cute? There's a chipmunk," he said. He felt that he was in charge of all these animals and that he must point them out to his daughter, as if he had to inform her of their names. What terror, not to know the names of animals, of objects, of the world! What if his daughter woke someday to a world of total blankness, terror? He was responsible for her. He had created her.

"Stay nearby, honey. Stay on the path," he said. He was suddenly exhausted; he sat on a bench. Brenda walked along the path in her precise, spiritless baby steps, munching spaghetti.

She seemed not to have noticed that he was sitting, weary. He put his hands to his head and heard the notes of the "Moonlight Sonata." Brenda walked on slowly, not looking around. She could walk like this for hours in the back yard of their house, circling the yard in a certain space of time. A safe child, predictable. She might have been walking on a ledge, high above a street. She might have been stepping through poisonous foam on a shore. . . . The shadows of leaves moved about her and on her, silently. Birds flew overhead. She saw nothing. Arthur thought suddenly of his father sitting on the steps of the back porch of their old house, his head in his hands, weeping. Why had his father wept?

It seemed suddenly important for him to know why his father had wept, and why Brenda so rarely wept.

And then something happened—afterward Arthur was never able to remember it clearly. Brenda was on the path not far from him, no one was in sight, the park was ordinary and unsurprising, and yet out of nowhere a man appeared, running. He was middle-aged. In spite of the mild September day he wore an overcoat that flapped around his knees; his face was very red; his hair was gray and spiky; he ran bent over, stooped as if about to snatch up something from the ground. Arthur was watching Brenda and then, in the next instant, this outlandish running figure appeared, colliding with her, knocking her down. The man began to scream. He seized Brenda's arm and shook her, screaming down into her face in a high, waspish, womanish voice, screaming words Arthur could not make out. "What are you doing—what are you doing?" Arthur cried. He ran to Brenda and the man jumped back. His mouth worked. He was crouching, foolishly alert, his face very red—he began to back up slowly, cunningly. Arthur picked Brenda up. "Are you all right? Are you hurt?" He stared into her face and saw the same face, unchanged. He wondered if he was going out of his mind. Now, as if released, the man in the overcoat turned and began walking quickly away. He was headed back into the woods. "You'd better get out of here before I call the police!" Arthur yelled. His voice was shrill. He was terribly agitated, he could not control the sickening fear in his body.

The man was nearly gone. He was escaping. Arthur's heart pounded, he looked down at Brenda and back up, at the woods, and suddenly decided to run after the man. "You, hey wait! You'd better wait!" he yelled. He left Brenda behind and ran after the man. "Come back here, you dirty bastard, dirty filthy pervert bastard!" The man crashed into something. He stumbled in a thicket. Arthur caught up with him and could hear his panicked breathing. The back of the man's neck was dirty and reddened, blushing fiercely. He turned away from the thicket and tried to run in another direction, but his knees seemed broken. He was sobbing. Panicked, defeated, stumbling, he turned suddenly toward Arthur as if to push past him—Arthur swung his fist around and struck the man on the side of the neck. One hard blow. The man cried out sharply, nearly fell. Arthur struck him again. "Dirty bastard! Filth!" Arthur cried. His third blow knocked the man down, and then he found himself standing over him, kicking him—his heel into the jawbone, into the nose, crunching the nose, splattering blood onto the grass, onto his shoe. He could actually feel the nose break! Something gave way, he felt even the vibrations of the man's screams, his stifled screams. Arthur bent over him, pounding with his fists. *I'll kill you, I'll tear you into pieces!* The man rolled over wildly onto his stomach, hiding his face in his hands. Arthur kicked viciously at his back. He kicked the back of his head. "I'm going to call the police—throw you in jail—you can rot—you dirty pervert, dirty bastard ———" Arthur kicked at the body until he could not recall what he was doing; the paper rose fell out of his buttonhole and onto the man's back, and onto the ground. "You'd better get the hell out of here because I'm going to call the police. You'd better not be here when I come back," he said, backing away.

And he had forgotten . . . about Brenda. . . . What was wrong with him? He ran back to her and there she was, safe. Only her leg was a little dirty. A small scratch, small dots of blood. Nothing serious! Greatly relieved, panting with relief, Arthur bent to dab at her knee with a Kleenex. She stepped away. "There, there, it's just a tiny scratch . . ." he said. He was very hot, sweating. He could feel sweat everywhere on his body. Hardly able to bear the pounding of his heart, he made another attempt to blot the blood, but Brenda side-stepped him. He looked sharply up at her and saw her look away from him. Just in that instant she had been looking at him . . . and then she looked away, at once. Their eyes had almost met.

He took her back to the car. They were safe, nothing had happened. Safe. No one had seen. His clothes were rumpled, his breathing hoarse, but still they were safe. He was alarmed at the pounding of his heart. Excitement still rose in him in waves, overwhelming his heart. . . . Wait, he should wait for a few minutes. Sit quietly. The two of them sat in the front seat of the car, in silence. Arthur wiped his face. He looked over at his daughter and saw that her coat was perfectly buttoned, her hair was not even mussed, her face was once again composed and secret. His panting alarmed him. Did she notice? Of course she noticed, she noticed everything, understood everything and yet would never inform on him; what gratitude he felt for her silence!

After a few minutes he felt well enough to drive. He was a little nauseous with excitement. A little lightheaded. He turned on the radio, heard static and loud music, then turned it off again, not knowing what he was doing. He headed for the expressway and saw with burning eyes the signs pointing toward home; everything had been composed in a perfect design, no one could get lost. It was impossible to get lost in this country. Beside him, in the far corner of the seat, his daughter took out a small piece of spaghetti and began to chew on it. They were safe. He glanced at her now and then as if to check her—had that man really collided with her? Knocked her down and shaken her, screamed into her face? Or had he imagined it all—no man, no smashed nose, no blood? There was blood on his shoes. Good. He drove home at a leisurely pace, being in no hurry. Brenda said nothing.

DISCUSSION

Joyce Carol Oates is an author who has won many literary awards for her short stories and novels. In a compelling style she penetrates the inner feelings of people who are under particular emotional stress. In this story she writes with astonishing accuracy concerning the behavior of an autistic child and the reactions of her parents. The story is particularly helpful in pointing out the many unknowns that parents and professionals face concerning various aspects of autism. Children like Brenda who are completely normal in appearance yet so emotionally unresponsive are particularly disturbing and puzzling children. Brenda's chilling silence and lack of rapport are in stark contrast to the behavior usually expected of a beautiful, well-formed child. Her parents' weariness and silent desperation when all of their communications to Brenda are met with no response are understandable.

Autistic children often repeat a particular behavior that is self-stimulating and seemingly purposeless, such as repeatedly turning lights on and off. Brenda constantly chews raw spaghetti, and in Brenda's case this compulsive behavior is her main source of nourishment. The unnatural quality of Brenda's diet is repelling: the dry crunch of spaghetti contrasts with Brenda's silence, and the thought of her swallowing the hard bland material is unpleasant.

Leo Kanner's theory of autism emphasizes the child's lack of ego development.[24] This theory propounds that the parents are generally remote and unavailable to their child because they are more involved in intellectual pursuits than in childrearing. Oates seems to emphasize this aspect of Brenda's existence. Arthur and his wife are "beautiful" people. They have decorated their perfect home in impeccable taste. The author draws a vivid picture of the ghostlike Brenda who exists in this home but does not live there with the noise and clutter that is generally associated with early childhood.

Brenda has many of the qualities associated with autistic children. Oates speaks of Brenda's tense alertness; Brenda seems to know what is happening around her, despite her lack of participation. She does not react normally to pain or discomfort. Brenda, like some autistic and retarded children, has an isolated ability; she played the piano at an early age with no formal training, suggesting a very special talent for music. Consistent with her other behavior, however, Brenda's piano playing is mechanical, without spirit or depth.

[24]Kanner, "Autistic Disturbances of Affective Contact."

Like any responsible parent, Arthur fears for Brenda's future and is concerned over her helplessness. He suspects his own genetic defectiveness for having produced an abnormal child. Even a child with more obvious and serious mental or physical impairment is more lovable than Brenda. Arthur's need to interact with Brenda is consuming. Nevertheless, venting his frustration and disappointment upon the drunk in the park is senseless and can bring only temporary relief.

Brenda's parents are tremendously isolated. Brenda's school meets just once a week, and there is no attempt to involve the parents. The aides at the school remove Brenda from her father in such a detached manner that Arthur reexperiences particularly poignant feelings of frustrated helplessness. The director of the school emphasizes that she cannot promise results. Her methods are as vague as her prognosis for Brenda.

Some states are now including special education classes specifically for autistic children. These classes usually have a high ratio of adults to children. So little is known about treating autism that special training for teachers is still in its earliest stages. Generally most programs have a heavy emphasis on language training and behavioral training. Autism is no longer seen as primarily a personality disturbance. The deficient acquisition of language is viewed as a central factor in the syndrome. Parents are encouraged to use at home those methods that have proven successful in the classroom.

SPRINGBOARDS FOR INQUIRY

1. List the behaviors that would lead the pediatrician to suspect autism in a five-year-old.

2. If you were Brenda's parent, what measures would you take to help your child?

3. What personality characteristics do you think a teacher of autistic children should have?

4. What are the facilities in your area for autistic children at the elementary and high school levels and beyond?

5. List some state and nationwide organizations concerned with autistic children.

6. Discuss how art, music, or dance therapy has been used in work with the severely emotionally disturbed.

CHAPTER ELEVEN

The Exceptional Child in the Family

A wise teacher of developmentally disabled children observed that when dealing with exceptional children it is best to consider their parents as part of the solution rather than to view them as part of the problem. This observation is both pragmatic and true because handicapped children are very dependent on their parents, sometimes even through adulthood. The parents, of course, need help to make decisions involving medical care, education, recreation, and vocational training. If the parents are resilient, conscientious, and optimistic, the handicapped child benefits from their attitude.

A 1974 symposium on "The Human Side of Exceptionality" involved various professionals who deal with handicapped childen.[1] A pediatric neurologist, a child psychologist, a school psychologist, a director of services for handicapped children, a nurse, and a social worker discussed moral, ethical, and practical issues relating to the handicapped child in the family. Some of the more difficult problems they discussed included the question of who should tell the parents about their baby's condition. Should it be a pediatrician who is brought into the case while the mother and child are still in the hospital? Should it be a social worker who is specially trained to give comfort and support along with

---

[1]Lester Mann, ed., *The Human Side of Exceptionality* (Philadelphia, Pa.: JSE Press, 1974).

the medical facts? When should parents be told about their child's disability? When the doctors recognize a problem exists (perhaps at birth), or later when the family is at home and better able to cope with the information? Who should deal with the question, Why me? asked by most parents when they hear of the existence of a handicap in their child? Who can best help parents deal with the long-range concern about what will happen to their handicapped child after they have died?

It is important for professionals who work with handicapped children and their families to be realistic about the emotional and physical strain on these families. Eugene McDonald discusses the serious disagreements between husband and wife that are likely to grow out of problems related to the exceptional child.[2] Fathers may feel they have lost the attention of their wives when so much time is devoted to the handicapped child. Mothers often complain that the father is not helpful enough in caring for the handicapped child. There also may be disagreement over the assessment of the extent of the child's handicap. Brooding suspicions that the other mate is in some way responsible for the handicapping condition is another strain on the stability of the marital relationship engendered by the birth of a handicapped child. Fear of producing another handicapped child may estrange both parties in the marriage. Therefore, the parents of exceptional children often need special counseling not only to learn how to help their children but also to learn how to cope with the natural disappointment that accompanies their birth. Counselors for parents of exceptional children have found it helpful to outline and discuss with them the stages of the coping process that most parents undergo as they deal with their complex feelings.

George Hexter, a psychiatrist who has worked extensively with parents of mentally retarded children, has diagrammed the coping reactions that seem valid for parents of children with any disability, whether mental or physical (see figure 10–1).[3]

Hexter describes the first stage as shock, which may last from a few days to several months. During this initial phase, parents are numbed by the information about their child and experience feelings of detachment as they go through the motions of everyday life. Denial follows the period of initial shock, and parents often shop for another diagnosis. Parents harbor feelings that the condition will not persist or that the doctor really does not know what he or she is talking about. In this period, par-

---

[2]Eugene T. McDonald, *Understanding Those Feelings* (Pittsburgh, Pa.: Stanwix House, Inc., 1962).

[3]George Hexter, "Mental Retardation," in *Handbook of Community Mental Health Practice*, ed. Richard Lamb, Don Heath, Joseph J. Downing (San Francisco, Calif.: Jossey-Bass, Inc., Publishers, 1969).

Figure 10–1 Coping reactions for parents of an exceptional child

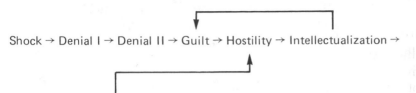

Shock → Denial I → Denial II → Guilt → Hostility → Intellectualization →

Involvement → Resolution

ents experience fear, disappointment, and disbelief. Later feelings of guilt take over. This phase may be marked by the parents' private quest to seek reasons why this happened to them. Parents may engage in obsessive thinking and fantasizing about their own imagined transgressions that could have accounted for their present tragedy. Along with guilt feelings, parents experience feelings of shame, and they worry about what their relatives and friends think. Soon feelings of hostility, a direct outgrowth of the guilt feelings, begin to manifest themselves. Anger may at first be directed toward one's spouse or other children in the family. Sometimes aggressive energies are directed toward agencies and individuals that do not seem to be able to meet the family's needs, such as the hospital, schools, doctors, or therapists. During this phase, the parents may at the same time become oversolicitous and overprotective of the handicapped child. In the next phases energies are put to more constructive use as the parents join groups to help children and families with similar problems. Hexter's diagram suggests an ebb and flow of energy sometimes directed inward as in the denial phase but later directed outward in positive constructive ways as in the involvement stage. This schema does not imply that every parent must go through every stage. Parents bring to the coping process individual personalities and family backgrounds as well as current emotional and constitutional strengths. The diagram can help professionals to recognize that coping is a long and painful process. At times parents may slip back from one stage into another. Some of the most common reversals in the major trends are noted in the diagram. Professionals may find in dealing with families of an exceptional child that at times all their attempts to be helpful are rejected or even found faulty. During these periods, parents may be erroneously labeled "hostile," "rejecting," or "overprotective" when, in fact, they may be in a painful phase and in need of more help rather than isolation by frustrated professionals.

Leo Buscaglia, author of a particularly perceptive book devoted to the challenge of counseling the disabled and their parents, makes it clear that guilt and hostility are appropriate feelings for parents faced with the realization that their child is permanently disabled.[4] The inordinate demands for their time, patience, and physical endurance can make parents feel trapped and tied down and awaken disturbing feelings of hate and rejection toward themselves and the disabled child. Buscaglia states that these feelings are not an indication of being weak, inadequate, or ignorant, but "an affirmation of being human." He recognizes that parents and siblings may have to work for many years understanding these feelings. At the same time, Buscaglia stresses that the following five rights belong to the family of the disabled:

1. The right to knowledge regarding their child's disability.
2. The right of reevaluation of their child and of a lucid explanation of findings.
3. The right to know about educational opportunities, rehabilitation sources, and community resources.
4. The right to some hope and reassurance as they meet the challenge of raising a child with special needs.
5. The right to actualize their personal rights as growing, unique individuals apart from their children.

Sol Gordon offers practical guidance to handicapped persons and their families.[5] He and his associates discuss practical aspects of life for the handicapped teenager and adult, including how to get a job and what one needs to know about sex and marriage. He acknowledges the concerns siblings may have regarding their own interaction and that of their friends with their disabled sister or brother. He suggests that siblings can be helpful to others outside of the family by explaining the nature of their sister's or brother's handicap without making excuses or asking for pity. When a handicapped child makes excessive demands on time, however, the normal sibling may feel resentment, and he or she may then need help in accepting the negative feelings rather than being overwhelmed by them.

In the past decade there has been widespread recognition of the need to involve parents in the training and education of their handicapped children.[6] Parents are no longer viewed simply as the recipients of information at a parent conference but are encouraged and trained to modify behavior and help in the educational process. Edith Levitt and

[4]Leo Buscaglia, The Disabled and Their Parents: A Counseling Challenge (Thorofare, N.J.: Charles B. Slack, Inc., 1975).
[5]Sol Gordon, ed., Living Fully (New York: The John Day Company, Inc., 1975).
[6]J. Eugene Clements and Ronnie N. Alexander, "Parent Training: Bringing It All Back Home," Focus on Exceptional Children, vol. 7, no. 5 (Denver, Colorado: Love Publishing Co., October 1975), 1–12.

Shirley Cohen review the parent education approaches used in different settings.[7] In some schools mothers act as teacher aides to help them assume a more active teaching role with their own child.[8] In some instances educators instruct parents through workshops, films, and demonstrations in the use of particular materials and in methods that might be effective. Another approach to improve parent-child (usually mother-child) interaction is a home-based program.[9] Home visits by a social worker are begun early in the child's life to help promote a positive attitude on the part of the mother toward her handicapped child.

Parent involvement has culminated in the founding and support of such organizations as the National Association for Retarded Children and United Cerebral Palsy Association for Neurologically Handicapped Children. These organizations have led the way in pressuring state legislatures to fund special education programs, sheltered workshops, and other vocational and recreational opportunities for handicapped children. Each organization usually holds regional monthly meetings providing an opportunity for parents to share ideas, to hear talks by knowledgeable professionals, and to contribute and respond to their organization publication. Indeed, these publications are usually well-written and current, making them valuable sources of information for teachers, school psychologists, and other health workers.

In addition to these supportive organizations, parents of handicapped children have several other resources available to them. One resource worth mentioning is a journal entitled *The Exceptional Parent*, founded in 1971 to improve communication among parents of children with a wide variety of special needs.[10] Perhaps the most valuable resource for parents is the United States Department of Health, Education and Welfare, which sponsors the National Information Center for the Handicapped called *Closer Look*.[11] *Closer Look* responds promptly to requests for information. The packet they send out contains (1) a pamphlet, *Practical Advice to Parents*; (2) a list of regional and local organizations closely related to the handicap specified by the inquirer; and (3) a list of special education personnel in the state who may be contacted for information about services. As a first step in seeking help regarding a

---

[7]Edith Levitt and Shirley Cohen, "Educating Parents of Children with Special Needs," *Young Children* (May 1976), pp. 263–72.

[8]L. Headley and H. Leler, "A Nursery School for Cerebral Palsied Children," *Children* (1971), pp. 17–21.

[9]Selma Fraiberg, Marguerite Smith, and Edna Adelson, "An Educational Program for Blind Infants," *Journal of Special Education*, 3 (1969), 121–39.

[10]*The Exceptional Parent*, P.O. Box 101, Back Bay Annex, Boston, Mass. 02117.

[11]*Closer Look Report*, National Information Center for the Handicapped, Box 1492, Washington, D.C. 20013.

diagnostic center, preschool program, and so on, *Closer Look* advises parents to contact their local school system.[12]

It is important to realize that in many homes the handicapped child inspires confidence and good feelings in those around him. Resources for the handicapped are improving, although not adequate in many areas. Recently great strides have been made by the handicapped themselves in their demands for equal treatment. With the increasing number of street ramps for wheelchairs, access platforms on buses, and special parking spaces reserved for the handicapped, the handicapped person can attain greater degrees of freedom. The heightened visibility of disabled persons and their new militancy for equal advantages in education and job opportunity provide more hope for the disabled and their families.

[12]Educators need to be aware that parents of handicapped children are often advised to seek help from their local schools. Therefore, it behooves school personnel to be knowledgeable of current programs, resources, and options open to the handicapped.

The Scarlet Ibis

by James Hurst

It was in the clove of seasons, summer was dead but autumn had not yet been born, that the ibis lit in the bleeding tree. The flower garden was stained with rotting brown magnolia petals and ironweeds grew rank amid the purple phlox. The five o'clocks by the chimney still marked time, but the oriole nest in the elm was untenanted and rocked back and forth like an empty cradle. The last graveyard flowers were blooming, and their smell drifted across the cotton field and through every room of our house, speaking softly the names of our dead.

It's strange that all this is still so clear to me, now that that summer has long since fled and time has had its way. A grindstone stands where the bleeding tree stood, just outside the kitchen door, and now if an oriole sings in the elm, its song seems to die up in the leaves, a silvery dust. The flower garden is prim, the house a gleaming white, and the pale fence across the yard stands straight and spruce. But sometimes (like right now), as I sit in the cool, green-draped parlor, the grindstone begins to turn, and time with all its changes is ground away—and I remember Doodle.

Doodle was just about the craziest brother a boy ever had. Of course, he wasn't a crazy crazy like old Miss Leedie, who was in love with President Wilson and wrote him a letter every day, but was a nice crazy, like someone you meet in your dreams. He was born when I was six and was, from the outset, a disappointment. He seemed all head, with a tiny body which was red and shriveled like an old man's. Everybody thought he was going to die—everybody except Aunt Nicey, who had delivered him. She said he would live because he was born in a caul and cauls were made from Jesus' nightgown. Daddy had Mr. Heath, the carpenter, build a little mahogany coffin for him. But he didn't die, and when he was three months old Mama and Daddy decided they might as well name him. They named him William Armstrong, which was like tying a big tail on a small kite. Such a name sounds good only on a tombstone.

I thought myself pretty smart at many things, like holding my breath, running, jumping, or climbing the vines in Old Woman Swamp, and I wanted more than anything else someone to race to Horsehead Landing, someone to box with, and someone to perch with in the top fork of the great pine behind the barn, where across the fields and swamps you could see the sea. I wanted a brother. But Mama, crying, told me that even if William Armstrong lived, he would never do these things with me. He might not, she sobbed, even be "all there." He might, as long as he lived, lie on the rubber sheet in the center of the bed in the front bedroom where the white marquisette curtains billowed out in the afternoon sea breeze, rustling like palmetto fronds.

It was bad enough having an invalid brother, but having one who possibly was not all there was unbearable, so I began to make plans to kill him by smothering him with a pillow. However, one afternoon as I watched him, my head poked between the iron posts of the foot of the bed, he looked straight at me and grinned. I skipped through the rooms, down the echoing halls, shouting, "Mama, he smiled. He's all there! He's all there!" and he was.

When he was two, if you laid him on his stomach, he began to try to move himself, straining terribly. The doctor said that with his weak heart this strain would probably kill him, but it didn't. Trembling, he'd push himself up, turning first red, then a soft purple, and finally collapse back onto the bed like an old worn-out doll. I can still see Mama watching him, her hand pressed tight across her mouth, her eyes wide and unblinking. But he learned to crawl (it was his third winter), and we brought him out of the front bedroom, putting him on the rug before the fireplace. For the first time he became one of us.

As long as he lay all the time in bed, we called him William Armstrong, even though it was formal and sounded as if we were referring to one of our ancestors, but with his creeping around on the deerskin rug and beginning to talk, something had to be done about his name. It was I who re-named him. When he crawled, he crawled backwards, as if he were in reverse and couldn't change gears. If you called him, he'd turn around as if he were going in the other direction, then he'd back right up to you to be picked up. Crawling backward made him look like a doodlebug, so I began to call him Doodle, and in time even Mama and Daddy thought it was a better name than William Armstrong. Only Aunt Nicey dis-agreed. She said caul babies should be treated with special re-spect since they might turn out to be saints. Renaming my brother was perhaps the kindest thing I ever did for him, because nobody expects much from someone called Doodle.

Although Doodle learned to crawl, he showed no signs of walking, but he wasn't idle. He talked so much that we all quit listening to what he said. It was about this time that Daddy built him a go-cart and I had to pull him around. At first I just paraded him up and down the piazza, but then he started crying to be taken out into the yard and it ended up by my having to lug him wher-ever I went. If I so much as picked up my cap, he'd start crying to go with me and Mama would call from wherever she was, "Take Doodle with you."

He was a burden in many ways. The doctor had said that he mustn't get too excited, too hot, too cold, or too tired and that he must always be treated gently. A long list of don'ts went with him, all of which I ignored once we got out of the house. To discourage his coming with me, I'd run with him across the ends of the cotton rows and careen him around cor-ners on two wheels. Sometimes I accidentally turned him over, but he never told Mama. His skin was very sensitive, and he had to wear a big straw hat whenever he went out. When the going got rough and he had to cling to the sides of the go-cart, the hat slipped all the way down over his ears. He was a sight. Finally, I could see I was licked. Doodle was my brother and he was going to cling to me forever, no matter what I did, so I dragged him across the burning cotton field to share with him the only beauty I knew, Old Woman Swamp. I pulled the go-cart through the saw-tooth fern, down into the green dimness where the palmetto fronds whispered by the stream. I lifted him out and set him down in the soft rubber grass beside a tall pine. His eyes were round with wonder as he gazed about him, and his little hands began to stroke the rubber grass. Then he began to cry.

"For heaven's sake, what's the matter?" I asked, annoyed.

"It's so pretty," he said. "So pretty, pretty, pretty."

After that day Doodle and I often went down into Old Woman Swamp. I would gather wildflowers, wild violets, honeysuckle, yellow jasmine, snakeflowers, and water lilies, and with wire grass we'd weave them into necklaces and crowns. We'd bedeck ourselves with our handiwork and loll about thus beautified, beyond the touch of the everyday world. Then when the slanted rays of the sun burned orange in the tops of the pines, we'd drop our jewels into the stream and watch them float away toward the sea.

There is within me (and with sadness I have watched it in others) a knot of cruelty borne by the stream of love, much as our blood sometimes bears the seed of our destruction, and at times I was mean to Doodle. One day I took him up to the barn loft and showed him his casket, telling him how we all had believed he would die. It was covered with a film of Paris green sprinkled to kill the rats, and screech owls had built a nest inside it.

Doodle studied the mahogany box for a long time, then said, "It's not mine."

"It is," I said. "And before I'll help you down from the loft, you're going to have to touch it."

"I won't touch it," he said sullenly.

"Then I'll leave you here by yourself," I threatened, and made as if I were going down.

Doodle was frightened of being left. "Don't go leave me, Brother," he cried, and he leaned toward the coffin. His hand, trembling, reached out, and

when he touched the casket he screamed. A screech owl flapped out of the box into our faces, scaring us and covering us with Paris green. Doodle was paralyzed, so I put him on my shoulder and carried him down the ladder, and even when we were outside in the bright sunshine, he clung to me, crying, "Don't leave me. Don't leave me."

When Doodle was five years old, I was embarrassed at having a brother of that age who couldn't walk, so I set out to teach him. We were down in Old Woman Swamp and it was spring and the sick-sweet smell of bay flowers hung everywhere like a mournful song. "I'm going to teach you to walk, Doodle," I said.

He was sitting comfortably on the soft grass, leaning back against the pine. "Why?" he asked.

I hadn't expected such an answer. "So I won't have to haul you around all the time."

"I can't walk, Brother," he said.

"Who says so?" I demanded.

"Mama, the doctor—everybody."

"Oh, you can walk," I said, and I took him by the arms and stood him up. He collapsed onto the grass like a half-empty flour sack. It was as if he had no bones in his little legs.

"Don't hurt me, Brother," he warned.

"Shut up. I'm not going to hurt you. I'm going to teach you

to walk." I heaved him up again, and again he collapsed.

This time he did not lift his face up out of the rubber grass. "I just can't do it. Let's make honeysuckle wreaths."

"Oh yes you can, Doodle," I said. "All you got to do is try. Now come on," and I hauled him up once more.

It seemed so hopeless from the beginning that it's a miracle I didn't give up. But all of us must have something or someone to be proud of, and Doodle had become mine. I did not know then that pride is a wonderful, terrible thing, a seed that bears two vines, life and death. Every day that summer we went to the pine beside the stream of Old Woman Swamp, and I put him on his feet at least a hundred times each afternoon. Occasionally I too became discouraged because it didn't seem as if he was trying, and I would say, "Doodle, don't you *want* to learn to walk?"

He'd nod his head, and I'd say, "Well, if you don't keep trying, you'll never learn." Then I'd paint for him a picture of us as old men, white-haired, him with a long white beard and me still pulling him around in the go-cart. This never failed to make him try again.

Finally one day, after many weeks of practicing, he stood alone for a few seconds. When he fell, I grabbed him in my arms and hugged him, our laughter pealing through the swamp like a ringing bell. Now we knew it

could be done. Hope no longer hid in the dark palmetto thicket but perched like a cardinal in the lacy toothbrush tree, brilliantly visible. "Yes, yes," I cried, and he cried it too, and the grass beneath us was soft and the smell of the swamp was sweet.

With success so imminent, we decided not to tell anyone until he could actually walk. Each day, barring rain, we sneaked into Old Woman Swamp, and by cotton-picking time Doodle was ready to show what he could do. He still wasn't able to walk far, but we could wait no longer. Keeping a nice secret is very hard to do, like holding your breath. We chose to reveal all on October eighth, Doodle's sixth birthday, and for weeks ahead we mooned around the house, promising everybody a most spectacular surprise. Aunt Nicey said that, after so much talk, if we produced anything less tremendous than the Resurrection, she was going to be disappointed.

At breakfast on our chosen day, when Mama, Daddy, and Aunt Nicey were in the dining room, I brought Doodle to the door in the go-cart just as usual and had them turn their backs, making them cross their hearts and hope to die if they peeked. I helped Doodle up, and when he was standing alone I let them look. There wasn't a sound as Doodle walked slowly across the room and sat down at his place at the table. Then Mama began to cry and ran over to him, hugging him and kissing him. Daddy hugged him too, so I went to Aunt Nicey, who was thanks praying in the doorway, and began to waltz her around. We danced together quite well until she came down on my big toe with her brogans, hurting me so badly I thought I was crippled for life.

Doodle told them it was I who had taught him to walk, so everyone wanted to hug me, and I began to cry.

"What are you crying for?" asked Daddy, but I couldn't answer. They did not know that I did it for myself; that pride, whose slave I was, spoke to me louder than all their voices, and that Doodle walked only because I was ashamed of having a crippled brother.

Within a few months Doodle had learned to walk well and his go-cart was put up in the barn loft (it's still there) beside his little mahogany coffin. Now, when we roamed off together, resting often, we never turned back until our destination had been reached, and to help pass the time, we took up lying. From the beginning Doodle was a terrible liar and he got me in the habit. Had anyone stopped to listen to us, we would have been sent off to Dix Hill.

My lies were scary, involved, and usually pointless, but Doodle's were twice as crazy. People in his stories all had wings and flew wherever they wanted to go.

His favorite lie was about a boy named Peter who had a pet peacock with a ten-foot tail. Peter wore a golden robe that glittered so brightly that when he walked through the sunflowers they turned away from the sun to face him. When Peter was ready to go to sleep, the peacock spread his magnificent tail, enfolding the boy gently like a closing go-to-sleep flower, burying him in the gloriously iridescent, rustling vortex. Yes, I must admit it. Doodle could beat me lying.

Doodle and I spent lots of time thinking about our future. We decided that when we were grown we'd live in Old Woman Swamp and pick dog-tongue for a living. Beside the stream, he planned, we'd build us a house of whispering leaves and the swamp birds would be our chickens. All day long (when we weren't gathering dog-tongue), we'd swing through the cypresses on the rope vines, and if it rained we'd huddle beneath an umbrella tree and play stickfrog. Mama and Daddy could come and live with us if they wanted to. He even came up with the idea that he could marry Mama and I could marry Daddy. Of course, I was old enough to know this wouldn't work out, but the picture he painted was so beautiful and serene that all I could do was whisper Yes, yes.

Once I had succeeded in teaching Doodle to walk, I began

to believe in my own infallibility and I prepared a terrific development program for him, unknown to Mama and Daddy, of course. I would teach him to run, to swim, to climb trees, and to fight. He, too, now believed in my infallibility, so we set the deadline for these accomplishments less than a year away, when, it had been decided, Doodle could start to school.

That winter we didn't make much progress, for I was in school and Doodle suffered from one bad cold after another. But when spring came, rich and warm, we raised our sights again. Success lay at the end of summer like a pot of gold, and our campaign got off to a good start. On hot days, Doodle and I went down to Horsehead Landing and I gave him swimming lessons or showed him how to row a boat. Sometimes we descended into the cool greenness of Old Woman Swamp and climbed the rope vines or boxed scientifically beneath the pine where he had learned to walk. Promise hung about us like the leaves, and wherever we looked, ferns unfurled and birds broke into song.

That summer, the summer of 1918, was blighted. In May and June there was no rain and the crops withered, curled up, then died under the thirsty sun. One morning in July a hurricane came out of the east, tipping over the oaks in the yard and splitting the limbs of the elm trees. That after-noon it roared back out of the west, blew the fallen oaks around, snapping their roots and tearing them out of the earth like a hawk at the entrails of a chicken. Cotton bolls were wrenched from the stalks and lay like green walnuts in the valleys between the rows, while the cornfield leaned over uniformly so that the tassels touched the ground. Doodle and I followed Daddy out into the cotton field, where he stood, shoulders sagging, surveying the ruin. When his chin sank down onto his chest, we were frightened, and Doodle slipped his hand into mine. Suddenly Daddy straightened his shoulders, raised a giant knuckly fist, and with a voice that seemed to rumble out of the earth itself began cursing heaven, hell, the weather, and the Republican Party. Doodle and I, prodding each other and giggling, went back to the house, knowing that everything would be all right.

And during that summer, strange names were heard through the house: Château Thierry, Amiens, Soissons, and in her blessing at the supper table, Mama once said, "And bless the Pearsons, whose boy Joe was lost at Belleau Wood."

So we came to that clove of seasons. School was only a few weeks away, and Doodle was far behind schedule. He could barely clear the ground when climbing up the rope vines and his swimming was certainly not passable.

We decided to double our efforts, to make that last drive and reach our pot of gold. I made him swim until he turned blue and row until he couldn't lift an oar. Wherever we went, I purposely walked fast, and although he kept up, his face turned red and his eyes became glazed. Once, he could go no further, so he collapsed on the ground and began to cry.

"Aw, come on, Doodle," I urged. "You can do it. Do you want to be different from everybody else when you start school?"

"Does it make any difference?"

"It certainly does," I said. "Now, come on," and I helped him up.

As we slipped through dog days, Doddle began to look feverish, and Mama felt his forehead, asking him if he felt ill. At night he didn't sleep well, and sometimes he had nightmares, crying out until I touched him and said, "Wake up, Doodle. Wake up."

It was Saturday noon, just a few days before school was to start. I should have already admitted defeat, but my pride wouldn't let me. The excitement of our program had now been gone for weeks, but still we kept on with a tired doggedness. It was too late to turn back, for we had both wandered too far into a net of expectations and had left no crumbs behind.

Daddy, Mama, Doodle, and I were seated at the dining-room table having lunch. It was a hot day, with all the windows and doors open in case a breeze should come. In the kitchen Aunt Nicey was humming softly. After a long silence, Daddy spoke. "It's so calm, I wouldn't be surprised if we had a storm this afternoon."

"I haven't heard a rain frog," said Mama, who believed in signs, as she served the bread around the table.

"I did," declared Doodle. "Down in the swamp."

"He didn't," I said contrarily.

"You did, eh?" said Daddy, ignoring my denial.

"I certainly did," Doodle reiterated, scowling at me over the top of his iced-tea glass, and we were quiet again.

Suddenly, from out in the yard, came a strange croaking noise. Doodle stopped eating, with a piece of bread poised ready for his mouth, his eyes popped round like two blue buttons. "What's that?" he whispered.

I jumped up, knocking over my chair, and had reached the door when Mama called, "Pick up the chair, sit down again, and say excuse me."

By the time I had done this, Doodle had excused himself and had slipped out into the yard. He was looking up into the bleeding tree. "It's a great big red bird!" he called.

The bird croaked loudly

again, and Mama and Daddy came out into the yard. We shaded our eyes with our hands against the hazy glare of the sun and peered up through the still leaves. On the topmost branch a bird the size of a chicken, with scarlet feathers and long legs, was perched precariously. Its wings hung down loosely, and as we watched, a feather dropped away and floated slowly down through the green leaves.

"It's not even frightened of us," Mama said.

"It looks tired," Daddy added. "Or maybe sick."

Doodle's hands were clasped at his throat, and I had never seen him stand still so long. "What is it?" he asked.

Daddy shook his head. "I don't know, maybe it's ———"

At that moment the bird began to flutter, but the wings were uncoordinated, and amid much flapping and a spray of flying feathers, it tumbled down, bumping through the limbs of the bleeding tree and landing at our feet with a thud. Its long, graceful neck jerked twice into an S, then straightened out, and the bird was still. A white veil came over the eyes and the long white beak unhinged. Its legs were crossed and its clawlike feet were delicately curbed at rest. Even death did not mar its grace, for it lay on the earth like a broken vase of red flowers, and we stood around it, awed by its exotic beauty.

"It's dead," Mama said.

"What is it?" Doodle repeated.

"Go bring me the bird book," said Daddy.

I ran into the house and brought back the bird book. As we watched, Daddy thumbed through its pages. "It's a scarlet ibis," he said, pointing to a picture. "It lives in the tropics— South America to Florida. A storm must have brought it here."

Sadly, we all looked back at the bird. A scarlet ibis! How many miles it had traveled to die like this, in our yard, beneath the bleeding tree.

"Let's finish lunch," Mama said, nudging us back toward the dining room.

"I'm not hungry," said Doodle, and he knelt down beside the ibis.

"We've got peach cobbler for dessert," Mama tempted from the doorway.

Doodle remained kneeling. "I'm going to bury him."

"Don't you dare touch him," Mama warned. "There's no telling what disease he might have had."

"All right," said Doodle. "I won't."

Daddy, Mama, and I went back to the dining-room table, but we watched Doodle through the open door. He took out a piece of string from his pocket and, without touching the ibis, looped one end around its neck. Slowly, while singing softly *Shall We Gather at the River*, he carried the bird around to the front yard and dug a hole in the flower garden, next to the petunia bed. Now we were watching him through the front window, but he didn't know it. His awkwardness at digging the hole with a shovel whose handle was twice as long as he was made us laugh, and we covered our mouths with our hands so he wouldn't hear.

When Doodle came into the dining room, he found us seriously eating our cobbler. He was pale and lingered just inside the screen door. "Did you get the scarlet ibis buried?" asked Daddy.

Doodle didn't speak but nodded his head.

"Go wash your hands, and then you can have some peach cobbler," said Mama.

"I'm not hungry," he said.

"Dead birds is bad luck," said Aunt Nicey, poking her head from the kitchen door. "Specially red dead birds!"

As soon as I had finished eating, Doodle and I hurried off to Horsehead Landing. Time was short, and Doodle still had a long way to go if he was going to keep up with the other boys when he started school. The sun, gilded with the yellow cast of autumn, still burned fiercely, but the dark green woods through which we passed were shady and cool. When we reached the landing, Doodle said he was too tired to swim, so we got into a skiff and floated down the creek with the

tide. Far off in the marsh a rail was scolding, and over on the beach locusts were singing in the myrtle trees. Doodle did not speak and kept his head turned away, letting one hand trail limply in the water.

After we had drifted a long way, I put the oars in place and made Doodle row back against the tide. Black clouds began to gather in the southwest, and he kept watching them, trying to pull the oars a little faster. When he reached Horsehead Landing, lightning was playing across half the sky and thunder roared out, hiding even the sound of the sea. The sun disappeared and darkness descended, almost like night. Flocks of marsh crows flew by, heading inland to their roosting trees, and two egrets, squawking, arose from the oyster-rock shallows and careened away.

Doodle was both tired and frightened, and when he stepped from the skiff he collapsed onto the mud, sending an armada of fiddler crabs rustling off into the marsh grass. I helped him up, and as he wiped the mud off his trousers, he smiled at me ashamedly. He had failed and we both knew it, so we started back home, racing the storm. We never spoke (What are the words that can solder cracked pride?), but I knew he was watching me, watching for a sign of mercy. The lightning was near now, and from fear he walked so close behind me he kept stepping on my heels. The faster I walked, the faster he walked, so I began to run. The rain was coming, roaring through the pines, and then, like a bursting Roman candle, a gum tree ahead of us was shattered by a bolt of lightning. When the deafening peal of thunder had died, and in the moment before the rain arrived, I heard Doodle, who had fallen behind, cry out, "Brother, Brother, don't leave me! Don't leave me!"

The knowledge that Doodle's and my plans had come to naught was bitter, and that streak of cruelty within me awakened. I ran as fast as I could, leaving him far behind with a wall of rain dividing us. The drops stung my face like nettles, and the wind flared the wet glistening leaves of the bordering trees. Soon I could hear his voice no more.

I hadn't run too far before I became tired, and the flood of childish spite evanesced as well. I stopped and waited for Doodle. The sound of rain was everywhere, but the wind had died and it fell straight down in parallel paths like ropes hanging from the sky. As I waited, I peered through the downpour, but no one came. Finally I went back and found him huddled beneath a red nightshade bush beside the road. He was sitting on the ground, his face buried in his arms, which were resting on his drawn-up knees. "Let's go, Doodle," I said.

He didn't answer, so I placed my hand on his forehead and lifted his head. Limply, he fell backwards onto the earth. He had been bleeding from the mouth, and his neck and the front of his shirt were stained a brilliant red.

"Doodle! Doodle!" I cried, shaking him, but there was no answer but the ropy rain. He lay very awkwardly, with his head thrown far back, making his vermilion neck appear unusually long and slim. His little legs, bent sharply at the knees, had never before seemed so fragile, so thin.

I began to weep, and the tear-blurred vision in red before me looked very familiar. "Doodle!" I screamed above the pounding storm and threw my body to the earth above his. For a long long time, it seemed forever, I lay there crying, sheltering my fallen scarlet ibis from the heresy of rain.

DISCUSSION

Every member of the family is usually asked to give more when one member has a significant handicap. In "The Scarlet Ibis," the older brother carries an inordinate share of the burden of caring for his younger brother. It is doubtful that the mother realizes the extent of the strain she imposes on him by asking him to "take along your little brother." When the older sibling complains of "dragging along" his little brother, there are overtones of embarrassment and fear mingled with his annoyance. The embarrassment stems from the ridicule he receives from peers when they see him with the misshapen Doodle, and the fear is for a sibling who is in physical jeopardy.

The brother goes about teaching Doodle to walk with the tenacity only a child can muster when he wants something badly enough. He uses cajoling, humor, and every other device at his disposal to get Doodle to work hard enough to achieve the almost miraculous accomplishment of standing and walking unaided. The older brother recognizes his ambivalent motivations. Therefore, he is proud because he has worked hard toward the achieved goal, but he also feels guilty because he is aware of his shame when pulling his disabled brother around in a go-cart. Parents and siblings of a handicapped child frequently have feelings of guilt and shame. These feelings are not transient because the adjustments necessary to accommodate the handicapped member of the family are ongoing. When these feelings are subconscious, they may surface as jealousy, anger, cruelty, or overindulgence. The older brother in this story finds that he is sometimes deliberately cruel to Doodle, although most often he is loving and appreciative of Doodle's good qualities. The duality of emotion felt by the older brother is not unlike the love-hate relationship all siblings experience in their growing up years. In "The Scarlet Ibis," the emotions are more intense. In complex family relationships, the addition of any burden magnifies the strains of everyday existence.

The family's excitement when they see Doodle walking unaided is touching. The small steps taken by the handicapped child often bring far more joy to families than the developmental milestones achieved by their normal children. Spurred on by their success, the brothers undertake the next challenge of making Doodle "like everybody else" by the start of school. In between an arduous program of swimming and climbing, the boys share many idyllic moments in Old Woman Swamp, away from the expectations that are imposed by other people. Families often find they can comfortably accommodate their retarded or physically disabled child in the circle of their home, but when adulthood is reached the goals for independent living and successful career choice may bring frustration and often failure.

This story is named for a rare bird that the author uses symbolically to foreshadow Doodle's death. The author compares Doodle's body to that of the ibis, with legs "so fragile and thin." The bird, which is obviously out of place away from the tropics, is the symbol for Doodle, who is sickly and crippled and out of place in the world of healthy children.

SPRINGBOARDS FOR INQUIRY

1. Go through the story and comment on the older brother's attitudes and feelings toward Doodle.

2. What are some of the constructive things the parents could do for the older brother and for Doodle?

3. Where would a family with a handicapped child go for emotional support, for information, and for diagnosis?

4. Describe some of the emotions felt by each member of this family when the scarlet ibis died.

5. If there were a family with a handicapped child on your street, in your churchgroup, or in your acquaintance, what are some of the things your family might do to be helpful?

CHAPTER TWELVE

The Exceptional Child in the Community

There are three types of communities, each of which can (with vary-ing degrees of effectiveness) provide support to families of the handi-capped.[1] These three communities are (1) the political community, (2) the professional community, and (3) the immediate community. Jerry W. Willis, Jeane Crowder, and Joan Willis suggest that the political and professional communities have the best potential for funded action in behalf of the community's handicapped population. These two com-munities exhort citizens to run for office, join political parties, and be-come part of the machinery that can legislate changes. A political battle in recent times in behalf of the handicapped children of a community has been described by Milton Budoff.[2] In 1968 the residents of the south end of Boston protested the inadequate special education program for their children and succeeded in legislation changes that eventually af-fected the entire state. Milton Budoff states, "The single most important principle established by the law is that the school district is responsible for all handicapped children of community residents, regardless of the degree of handicap."[3] In 1972, the Massachusetts legislature, after mas-

---

[1]Jerry W. Willis, Jeane Crowder, and Joan Willis, *Guiding the Psychological and Educa-tional Growth of Children* (Springfield, Ill.: Charles C. Thomas, Publisher, 1976).
[2]Milton Budoff, "Engendering Change in Special Education Practices," *Harvard Educa-tional Review*, vol. 45, no. 4 (November 1975), 507–26.
[3]Ibid., p. 517.

sive political support, was moved to pass Chapter 766, which was designed "to remedy past inadequacies and inequities by defining the needs of children requiring special education in a broad and flexible manner and by providing the opportunity for a full range of special education programs for children requiring special education; by requiring that a program which holds out the promise of being special actually benefits children assigned thereto."[4]

Perhaps the strongest, most pervasive influence on community attitudes will be the Education for All Handicapped Children Act of 1975 (P.L. 94–142). The following amendment to the act is of interest:

> 1. There are more than eight million handicapped children in the United States today;
> 2. the special educational needs of such children ar not being fully met;
> 3. more than half of the handicapped children in the United States do not receive appropriate educational services which would enable them to have full equality of opportunity;
> 4. one million of the handicapped children in the United States are excluded entirely from the public school system and will not go through the educational process with their peers;
> 5. there are many handicapped children throughout the United States participating in regular school programs whose handicaps prevent them from having a successful educational experience because their handicaps are undetected;
> 6. because of the lack of adequate services within the public school system, families are often forced to find services outside the public school system, often at great distance from their residence and at their own expense;
> 7. developments in the training of teachers and in diagnostic and instructional procedures and methods have advanced to the point that, given appropriate funding, state and local educational agencies can and will provide effective special education and related services to meet the needs of handicapped children.

Rather than the community educating the handicapped out of charity, education for the handicapped is now a right in law and as national policy.[5]

Robert Bogdan and Douglas Biklen use the term "handicapism" to describe the "set of assumptions and practices that promote the differential and unequal treatment of people because of apparent or assumed physical, mental, or behavioral differences."[6] Indeed, they claim that

---

[4]Massachusetts General Laws (Commonwealth of Massachusetts, 1972), chapter 766.

[5]National Advisory Committee on the Handicapped, *The Unfinished Revolution: Education for the Handicapped* (United States Government Printing Office, 1976, 017–080–01532–3), p. 1.

[6]Robert Bogden and Douglas Biklen, "Handicapism," 1977. Unpublished manuscript sent to the editors of this volume with permission to quote.

handicapism has many parallels to "racism" and "sexism." Essentially, the stereotyped view of the handicapped person actually teaches many such people to not expect education and opportunity but rather to put up with segregation (special classes and schools) and the cultural designation of "non-persons." The media perpetuate stereotypes of the handicapped as bizarre, dangerous, and physically different people; even the language ("moron," "stupid," "idiot," "crazy") of television cartoons encourages this generalization. The architecture of cities makes it virtually impossible for the handicapped to have equal access to public transit, toilets, and buildings.[7] Literacy barriers keep some handicapped from voting, getting credit, registering in schools, and even paying income taxes. Fund raising agencies often distort the image of handicapped persons by emphasizing the disabled as being incapable of self-help.

One example of the professional community's activities for the handicapped is described by Theodore Wasserman and Nancy Adamany.[8] These mental health professionals designed a program for children with severe behavioral, emotional, and learning disturbances. They realized that children with severe psychosocial problems were usually removed from the schoolroom to sheltered remedial settings and often did not find their way back to the schools. They decided to mainstream children part of the school day while providing treatment for specific disabilities during the other part. Utilizing a developmental model of diagnosis enabled the group to capitalize on a child's assets while developing areas of deficiency. An evaluation of the child tells the home school where to focus its attention while the remediation center located in the community (in this case, the Astor Day Treatment Center of the Bronx, New York) undertakes psychosocial and educational rehabilitation. Of particular importance is the contact made with parents, whose support is enlisted so that the behavior modification of the community agency and the school may be continued at home. The eventual aim of such a community-based program is to return children full time to the public school. Wasserman reports that

> of the twenty-five who began in September, 1974, seven (28%) have been returned to public school full time, six (24%) attend school for one or more full days in addition to the regular half day schedule. Three children (12%) are now considered ready to begin at least one full day, and two (8%)

---

[7] In April 1977 the HEW headquarters in San Francisco were occupied by handicapped persons for three weeks. Their demands for the removal of barriers that promote handicapism finally attracted the attention of the president of the United States.

[8] Theodore Wasserman and Nancy Adamany, "Day Treatment and Public Schools: An Approach to Mainstreaming," *Child Welfare*, vol. 55, no. 2 (February 1976), 117–24.

children who were in home instruction now attend school on half-day program. . . . thus 73% of the children have shown significant improvement.
. . . Although . . . the long-term effect . . . cannot be gauged . . . not
one of the seven children placed full time in school has needed further
intervention.[9]

For a variety of reasons the community prefers exceptional children and adults to be out of sight and consequently out of mind. Mental
health workers, on the other hand, have been stressing community-
based halfway houses, residences, and out-patient services. Small,
community centers do away with the need for large institutions and their
attendant problems. They keep the person in need of help closer to home
so that the transition from one type of care to another is not too much of a
strain. Patricia Stickney and Anthony Capaiuolo explain, "In the fields
of child welfare, juvenile and adult justice, and mental health and retardation, the emphasis has been on "normalization," returning already
institutionalized individuals to community life and directing others to
community services in lieu of institutionalization."[10] Their strategies,
like those of Robert Coates and Alden Miller, are to prepare the community to accept an alien philosophy of care for the exceptional person.[11]
Carol Sigelman has concluded that "many administrators have decided
to move in without informing neighbors or probing community attitudes
in advance. This strategy of *fait accompli* . . . has the advantage of pre-
venting moves to block the home's opening. And, if the present assessment of community attitudes is correct, it may be no less effective in the
long run than more elaborate strategies involving advance attitude sampling."[12]

In 1970, Wolf Wolfensberger, commenting on the concept of
"normalization" stated, "We should ask ourselves at all times whether
any service provided in conjunction with a residential service could not
be provided . . . by drawing upon . . . community resources."[13] Building upon this concept, Joel Ray developed a training center for families
of retarded children to teach them some behavior management skills and

[9]Ibid., p. 123.

[10]Patricia Stickney and Anthony Capaiuolo, "From CRISP: Strategies for Community Residences," *Child Welfare*, vol. 55, no. 1 (January 1976), 54.

[11]Robert Coates and Alden Miller, "Neutralization of Community Resistance to Group
Homes," in *Closing Correctional Institutions*, ed. Yitzhak Bakal (New York: D.C.
Heath & Company, 1973).

[12]Carol Sigelman, "A Machiavelli for Planners: Community Attitudes and Selection of
a Group Home Site," *Mental Retardation*, vol. 14, no. 1 (February 1976), 28.

[13]Wolf Wolfensberger, "The Principle of Normalization and Its Implication to Psychiatric
Services," *American Journal of Psychiatry*, 127:3, (September 1970), 294.

to "alert them to potential educational programs in their communities. Family training became an experiment in normalizing the relationships between delayed children and other members; its purpose was to help prevent institutionalization and to give families leverage in coping with their child at home and with his relationship to the community."[14]

One relatively new service to relieve stress upon the family from daily care for the disabled child is "respite care." This is reliable short-term home care for a day, a weekend, or a week so that parents can experience some worry-free time away from their child. There are training programs in various parts of the county for "providers" who receive a reasonable hourly wage for their sitter-companion service. The provider attends approximately thirty hours of training, which includes a Red Cross First Aid course, twelve hours of lecture by professionals in the field of developmental disabilities, and ten hours of field experience.

The ideal situation for exceptional persons in the community is the most normal and compassionate environment in which they may live with the least restrictions commensurate with their particular disability. In general, the closer the handicapped are to their home, the more the community senses its responsibility to envelop those who need its support. Once the community knows its responsibilities, it can provide for both the exceptional persons and the rest of the community.

[14]Joel S. Ray, "The Family Training Center: An Experiment in Normalization," *Mental Retardation*, vol. 12, no. 1 (February 1974), 13.

Clothe the Naked

by Dorothy Parker

Big Lannie went out by the day to the houses of secure and leisured ladies, to wash their silks and their linens. She did her work perfectly; some of the ladies even told her so. She was a great, slow mass of a woman, colored a sound brown-black save for her palms and the flat of her fingers that were like gutta-percha from steam and hot suds. She was slow because of her size, and because the big veins in her legs hurt her, and her back ached much of the time. She neither cursed her ills nor sought remedies for them. They had happened to her; there they were.

Many things had happened to her. She had had children, and the children had died. So had her husband, who was a kind man, cheerful with the little luck he found. None of their children had died at birth. They had lived to be four or seven or ten, so that they had had their ways and their traits and their means of causing love; and Big Lannie's heart was always wide for love. One child had been killed in a street accident and two others had died of illnesses that might have been no more than tedious, had there been fresh food and clear spaces and clean air behind them. Only Arlene, the youngest, lived to grow up.

Arlene was a tall girl, not so dark as her mother but with the same firm flatness of color. She was so thin that her bones seemed to march in advance of her body. Her little pipes of legs and her broad feet with jutting heels were like things a child draws with crayons. She carried her head low, her shoulders scooped around her chest, and her stomach slanted forward.

Big Lannie did not know it, when Arlene was going to have a baby. Arlene had not been home in nearly half a year; Big Lannie told the time in days. There was no news at all of the girl until the people at the hospital sent for Big Lannie to come to her daughter and grandson. She was there to hear Arlene say the baby must be named Raymond, and to see the girl die.

He was a long, light-colored baby, with big, milky eyes that looked right back at his grandmother. It was several days before the people at the hospital told her he was blind.

Big Lannie went to each of the ladies who employed her and explained that she could not work for some while; she must take care of her grandson. The ladies were sharply discommoded, after her steady years, but they dressed their outrage in shrugs and cool tones. Each arrived, separately, at the conclusion that she had been too good to Big Lannie, and had been imposed upon, therefore. "Honestly, those people!" each said to her friends. "They're all alike."

Big Lannie sold most of the things she lived with, and took one room with a stove in it. There, as soon as the people at the hospital would let her, she brought

Raymond and tended him. He was all her children to her.

She had always been a saving woman, with few needs and no cravings, and she had been long alone. Even after Arlene's burial, there was enough left for Raymond and Big Lannie to go on for a time. Big Lannie was slow to be afraid of what must come; fear did not visit her at all, at first, and then it slid in only when she waked, when night hung motionless before another day.

Raymond was a good baby, a quiet, patient baby, lying in his wooden box and stretching out his delicate hands to the sounds that were light and color to him. It seemed but a little while, so short to Big Lannie, before he was walking about the room, his hands held out, his feet quick and sure. Those of Big Lannie's friends who saw him for the first time had to be told that he could not see.

Then, and it seemed again such a little while, he could dress himself, and open the door for his granny, and unlace the shoes from her tired feet, and talk to her in his soft voice. She had occasional employment—now and then a neighbor would hear of a day's scrubbing she could do, or sometimes she might work in the stead of a friend who was sick—infrequent, and not to be planned on. She went to the ladies for whom she had worked, to ask if they might not want her back again; but there was little hope in her, after she had visited the first one. Well, now, really, said the ladies; well really, now.

The neighbors across the hall watched over Raymond while Big Lannie looked for work. He was no trouble to them, nor to himself. He sat and crooned at his chosen task. He had been given a wooden spool around the top of which were driven little brads, and over these with a straightened hairpin he looped bright worsted, working faster than sight until a long tube of woven wool fell through the hole in the spool. The neighbors threaded big, blunt needles for him, and he coiled the woolen tubes and sewed them into mats. Big Lannie called them beautiful, and it made Raymond proud to have her tell him how readily she sold them. It was hard for her, when he was asleep at night, to unravel the mats and wash the worsted and stretch it so straight that even Raymond's shrewed fingers could not tell, when he worked with it next day, that it was not new.

Fear stormed in Big Lannie and took her days and nights. She might not go to any organization dispensing relief for fear that Raymond would be taken from her and put in—she would not say the word to herself, and she and her neighbors lowered their voices when they said it to one another—an institution. The neighbors wove lingering tales of what happened inside certain neat, square buildings on the cindery skirts of the town, and, if they must go near them, hurried as if passing graveyards, and came home heroes. When they got you in one of those places, whispered the neighbors, they laid your spine open with whips, and then when you dropped, they kicked your head in. Had anyone come into Big Lannie's room to take Raymond away to an asylum for the blind, the neighbors would have fought for him with stones and rails and boiling water.

Raymond did not know about anything but good. When he grew big enough to go alone down the stairs and into the street, he was certain of delight each day. He held his head high, as he came out into the little yard in front of the flimsy wooden house, and slowly turned his face from side to side, as if the air were soft liquid in which he bathed it. Trucks and wagons did not visit the street, which ended in a dump for rusted bedsprings and broken boilers and staved-in kettles; children played over its cobbles, and men and women sat talking in open windows and called across to one another in gay, rich voices. There was always laughter for Raymond to hear, and he would laugh back, and hold out his hands to it.

At first, the children stopped

their play when he came out, and gathered quietly about him, and watched him, fascinated. They had been told of his affliction, and they had a sort of sickened pity for him. Some of them spoke to him, in soft, careful tones. Raymond would laugh with pleasure, and stretch his hands, the curious smooth, flat hands of the blind, to their voices. They would draw sharply back, afraid that his strange hands might touch them. Then somehow ashamed because they had shrunk from him and he could not see that they had done so, they said gentle good-bys to him, and backed away into the street again, watching him steadily.

When they were gone, Raymond would start on his walk to the end of the street. He guided himself lightly touching the broken fences along the dirt sidewalk, and as he walked he crooned little songs with no words to them. Some of the men and women at the windows would call hello to him, and he would call back and wave and smile. When the children, forgetting him, laughed again at their games, he stopped and turned to the sound as if it were the sun.

In the evening, he would tell Big Lannie about his walk, slapping his knee and chuckling at the memory of the laughter he had heard. When the weather was too hard for him to go out in the street, he would sit at his worsted work, and talk all day of going out the next day.

The neighbors did what they could for Raymond and Big Lannie. They gave Raymond clothes their own children had not yet worn out, and they brought food, when they had enough to spare and other times. Big Lannie would get through a week, and would pray to get through the next one; and so the months went. Then the days on which she could find work fell farther and farther apart, and she could not pray about the time to come because she did not dare to think of it.

It was Mrs. Ewing who saved Raymond's and Big Lannie's lives, and let them continue together. Big Lannie said that then and ever after; daily she blessed Mrs. Ewing, and nightly she would have prayed for her, had she not known, in some dimmed way, that any intercession for Mrs. Delabarre Ewing must be impudence.

Mrs. Ewing was a personage in the town. When she went to Richmond for a visit, or when she returned from viewing the azalea gardens in Charleston, the newspaper always printed the fact. She was a woman rigorously conscious of her noble obligation; she was prominent on the Community Chest committee, and it was she who planned and engineered the annual Bridge Drive to raise funds for planting salvia around the cannon in front of the D.A.R. headquarters. These and many others were for public activities, and she was no less exacting of herself in her private life. She kept a model, though childless, house for her husband and herself, relegating the supervision of details to no domestic lieutenant, no matter how seemingly trustworthy.

Back before Raymond was born, Big Lannie had worked as laundress for Mrs. Ewing. Since those days, the Ewing wash tubs had witnessed many changes, none for the better. Mrs. Ewing took Big Lannie back into her employment. She apologized for this step to her friends by the always winning method of self-deprecation. She knew she was a fool, she said, after all that time, and after the way that Big Lannie had treated her. But still, she said, and she laughed a little at her own ways. Anyone she felt kind of sorry for could always get around her, she said. She knew it was awful foolish, but that, she said, was the way she was. Mr. Ewing, she said outside her husband's hearing, always called her just a regular little old easy mark.

Two days' work in the week meant money for rent and stove-wood and almost enough food for Raymond and Big Lannie. She must depend, for anything further, on whatever odd jobs she could find, and she must not stop seeking them. Pressed on by fear and gratitude, she worked so well for Mrs. Ewing that there was sometimes expressed satisfaction at the condition of the lady's household linen and her own and her husband's clothing.

Big Lannie had a glimpse of Mr. Ewing occasionally, leaving the house as she came, or entering it as she was leaving. He was a bit of a man, not much bigger than Raymond.

Raymond grew so fast that he seemed to be taller each morning. Every day he had his walk in the street to look forward to and experience and tell Big Lannie about at night. He had ceased to be a sight of the street; the children were so used to him that they did not even look at him, and the men and women at the windows no longer noticed him enough to hail him. He did not know. He would wave to any gay cry he heard, and go on his way, singing his little songs and turning toward the sound of laughter.

Then his lovely list of days ended as sharply as if ripped from some bright calendar. A winter came, so sudden and savage as to find no comparison in the town's memories, and Raymond had no clothes to wear out in the street. Big Lannie mended his outgrown garments as long as she could, but the stuff had so rotted with wear that it split in new places when she tried to sew together the ragged edges of rents.

The neighbors could give no longer; all they had they must keep for their own. A demented colored man in a nearby town had killed the woman who employed him, and terror had spread like brush fire. There was a sort of panic in reprisal; colored employees were dismissed from their positions, and there was no new work for them. But Mrs. Ewing, admittedly soft-hearted certainly to a fault and possibly to a peril, kept her black laundress on. More than ever Big Lannie had reason to call her blessed.

All winter, Raymond stayed indoors. He sat at his spool and worsted, with Big Lannie's old sweater about his shoulders and, when his tattered knickerbockers would no longer hold together, a calico skirt of hers lapped around his waist. He lived, at his age, in the past; in the days when he had walked, proud and glad, in the street, with laughter in his ears. Always, when he talked of it, he must laugh back at that laughter.

Since he could remember, he had not been allowed to go out when Big Lannie thought the weather unfit. This he had accepted without question, and so he accepted his incarceration through the mean weeks of the winter. But then one day it was spring, so surely that he could tell it even in the smoky, stinking rooms of the house, and he cried out with joy because now he might walk in the street again. Big Lannie had to explain to him that his rags were too thin to shield him, and that there were no odd jobs for her, and so no clothes and shoes for him.

Raymond did not talk about the street any more, and his fingers were slow at his spool.

Big Lannie did something she had never done before; she begged of her employer. She asked Mrs. Ewing to give her some of Mr. Ewing's old clothes for Raymond. She looked at the floor and mumbled so that Mrs. Ewing requested her to talk up. When Mrs. Ewing understood, she was, she said, surprised. She had, she said, a great, great many demands on her charity, and she would have supposed that Big Lannie, of all people might have known that she did everything she could, in fact, a good deal more. She spoke of inches and ells. She said that if she found she could spare anything, Big Lannie was kindly to remember it was to be just for this once.

When Big Lannie was leaving at the end of her day's work, Mrs. Ewing brought her a package with her own hands. There, she said, was a suit and a pair of shoes; beautiful, grand things that people would think she was just crazy to be giving away like that. She simply didn't know, she said, what Mr. Ewing would say to her for being such a crazy. She explained that that was the way she was when anyone got around her, all the while Big Lannie was trying to thank her.

Big Lannie had never before seen Raymond behave as he did when she brought him home the package. He jumped and danced and clapped his hands, he tried to squeak and squealed instead, he tore off the paper himself, and ran his fingers over the close-woven cloth and held it to his face and kissed it. He put on the shoes and clattered about in them, digging with his toes and heels to keep them on; he made Big Lannie pin the trousers around his waist and roll them up over his shins. He babbled of the morrow when he would walk in the street, and could not say his words for laughing.

Big Lannie must work for Mrs. Ewing the next day, and she had thought to bid Raymond wait until she could stay at home and dress him herself in his new garments. But she heard him laugh again; she could not tell him he must wait. He might go out at noon next day, she said, when the sun was so warm that he would not take cold at his first outing; one of the neighbors across the hall would help him with the clothes. Raymond chuckled and sang his little songs until he went to sleep.

After Big Lannie left in the morning, the neighbor came in to Raymond, bringing a pan of cold pork and corn bread for his lunch. She had a call for a half-day's work, and she could not stay to see him start out for his walk. She helped him put on the trousers and pinned and rolled them for him, and she laced the shoes as snug as they would go on his feet. Then she told him not to go out till the noon whistles blew, and kissed him, and left.

Raymond was too happy to be impatient. He sat and thought of the street and smiled and sang.

Not until he heard the whistles did he go to the drawer where Big Lannie had laid the coat, and take it out and put it on. He felt it soft on his bare back, he twisted his shoulders to let it fall warm and loose from them. As he folded the sleeves back over his thin arms, his heart beat so that the cloth above it fluttered.

The stairs were difficult for him to manage, in the big shoes, but the very slowness of the descent was delicious to him. His anticipation was like honey in his mouth.

Then he came out into the yard, and turned his face in the gentle air. It was all good again; it was all given back again. As quickly as he could, he gained the walk and set forth, guiding himself by the fence. He could not wait; he called out, so that he would hear gay calls in return, he laughed so that laughter would answer him.

He heard it. He was so glad that he took his hand from the fence and turned and stretched out his arms and held up his smiling face to welcome it. He stood there, and his smile died on his face, and his welcoming arms stiffened and shook.

It was not the laughter he had known; it was not the laughter he had lived on. It was like great flails beating him flat, great prongs tearing his flesh from his bones. It was coming at him, to kill him. It drew slyly back, and then it smashed against him. It swirled around and over him, and he could not breathe. He screamed and tried to run through it, and fell, and it licked over him, howling higher. His clothes unrolled, and his shoes flapped on his feet. Each time he could rise, he fell again. it was as if the street were perpendicular before him, and the laughter leaping at his back. He could not find the fence, he did not know which way he was turned. He lay screaming, in blood and dust and darkness.

When Big Lannie came home, she found him on the floor in a corner of the room, moaning and whimpering. He still wore his new clothes, cut and torn and dusty, and there was dried blood on his mouth and his palms. Her heart had leapt in alarm when he had not opened the door at her footstep, and she cried out so frantically to ask what had happened that she frightened him into wild weeping. She could not understand what he said; it was something about the street, and laughing at him, and make them go away, and don't let him go in the street no more, never in the street no more. She did not try to make him explain. She took him in her arms and rocked him, and told him, over and over, never mind, don't care, everything's all right. Neither he nor she believed her words.

But her voice was soft and her arms warm. Raymond's sobs softened, and trembled away. She held him, rocking silently and rhythmically, a long time. Then gently she set him on his feet, and took from his shoulders Mr. Ewing's old full-dress coat.

DISCUSSION

Dorothy Parker is well known for her accurate observations of human characteristics. This story describes Big Lannie's efforts to keep her grandson in her home despite his handicap. Raymond is the only child Lannie has left, and her emotional ties to him are all-consuming. She has learned from bitter experience that she can expect nothing from the outside community. In addition, she and her friends have conjured lurid pictures of beatings and death inside the walls of the large institution on the outskirts of town that houses the misfits of society.

Because Lannie fears that Raymond may be taken away from her, she cannot go to any community agency for the help she desperately needs. Raymond seems like a delightful child who is probably of normal or above normal intelligence. Without education and with nothing but the essentials of life Lannie can scrape together, Raymond's future seems bleak. The neighbors try to be helpful, but they must go to work and cannot provide dependable care for Raymond. In terms of human warmth and sharing, Lannie's immediate community is supportive but that is not enough to satisfy Raymond's special needs.

Dorothy Parker is particularly accurate in her description of the do-gooders and "the pillars of the community." She captures their language and self-righteousness with perfection. Sometimes people who are active in raising funds in the community for worthy causes never get close to the people for whom the money is raised.

The smaller community in which Lannie lives is not prepared for the intermittent appearance of Raymond. The children on the street are apprehensive of a child who is blind. When they get used to him, they ignore him. If the children had been properly supervised, Raymond might have been included in some of their play activities. The children are not to blame for their reaction to Raymond when he appears in full dress suit after a long absence from the street. He is bizarre looking and inappropriate, and there is no one available to help them to understand his disability.

This is a sad story and not entirely fictional. There are many handicapped children who are kept at home and whose parents do not avail themselves of existing services. In many instances, misinformation about available services or prejudice about the service offered to the disabled keep people from contacting public agencies for assistance. Publicity about deaths and mistreatment in institutions for the retarded do not help to improve the image of community resources. In many instances, regional centers for a variety of handicaps are staffed by highly qualified personnel, and they have much to offer the family and the handicapped member.

SPRINGBOARDS FOR INQUIRY

1. What do you think will happen to Big Lannie and Raymond?

2. Discuss whether you think being physically handicapped creates more problems for members of minority groups than for Caucasians.

3. With community support, would there be an alternative to residential placement for Raymond?

4. Consult your county government and list the services they offer in the area of mental health, aid to dependent children, provision for medical examinations, social welfare, and options for education of the physically handicapped.

5. Comment on "handicapism" and discuss how the ordinary citizen can help to combat stereotyping the disabled.

Suggested Readings

ADULT FICTION, BIOGRAPHY AND AUTOBIOGRAPHY

The Mentally Retarded

ABRAHAM, WILLARD, *Barbara: A Prologue*. New York: Rinehart & Co., 1958.

BUCK, PEARL S., *The Child Who Never Grew*. New York: The John Day Company, Inc., 1950.

GANT, SOPHIA, *One of Those, The Progress of a Mongoloid Child*. New York: Pageant Press, 1957.

HUTCHINSON, R. C., *A Child Possessed*. New York: Harper & Row, Publishers, Inc., 1964.

KEYES, DANIEL, *Flowers for Algernon*. New York: Harcourt, Brace and World, Inc., 1966.

MOTTE, NEW, *The Hand of the Potter*. London: Cassell & Co., 1956

MURRAY, DOROTHY, *This Is Stevie's Story*. Elgin, Ill.: Brethren Publishing House, 1956.

SPENCER, ELIZABETH, *The Light in the Piazza*. New York: McGraw-Hill Book Company, Inc., 1960.

STEINBECK, JOHN, *Of Mice and Men*. New York: The Viking Press, Inc., 1963.

STOUT, LUCILLE, *I Reclaimed My Child*. Philadelphia, Pa.: Chilton Book Company, 1959.

WOLFF, RUTH, *A Crack in the Sidewalk*. New York: The John Day Company, Inc., 1965.

The Speech and Language Impaired

BUTLER, SAMUEL, *The Way of All Flesh*. New York: The Limited Editions Club, 1936.

CALDWELL, ERSKIN, *Tobacco Road*. New York: Grosset & Dunlap, Inc., 1948.

HUXLEY, ALDOUS LEONARD, *Eyeless in Gaza*. New York: Harper and Bros., 1936.

JOHNSON, WENDELL, *Because I Stutter*. New York: Appleton, 1930.

The Orthopedically Handicapped

BATTYE, LOUIS, *I Had A Little Nut Tree*. London: Martin Secker and Warburg, 1959.

BERG, MARGARET, *Wednesday's Child*. Philadelphia, Pa.: Muhlenberg Press, 1960.

BROWN, CHRISTY, *My Left Foot*. New York: Simon & Schuster, Inc., 1955.

CARLSON, EARL REINHOLD, *Born That Way*. New York: The John Day Company, Inc., 1941.

KILLILEA, MARIE, *Karen*. New York: Prentice-Hall., Inc., 1952.

MAUGHAM, WILLIAM SOMERSET, *Of Human Bondage*. New York: G. H. Doran Co., 1915.

STEELE, MAX, *Debby*. New York: Harper and Brothers, 1950.

WHITE, NELIA GARDNER, *Woman at The Window*. New York: The Viking Press, Inc., 1951.

The Multiply Handicapped

MONSARRAT, NICHOLAS, *The Story of Ester Costello*. New York: Alfred A. Knopf, Inc., 1953.

SMITHDAS, ROBERT J., *Life at My Fingertips*. Garden City, N.Y.: Doubleday & Company, Inc., 1958.

The Hearing Impaired

BOATNER, MAXINE TULL, *Voice of the Deaf: A Biography of Edward Miner Gallaudet*. Washington, D.C.: Public Affairs Press, 1959.

DES CARS, GUY, *The Brute*, trans. Michael Luke. New York: Greenberg, 1952.

FIELDS, RACHEL, *And Now Tomorrow*. New York: The Macmillan Company, 1942.

MCCULLERS, CARSON, *The Heart Is a Lonely Hunter*. Boston, Mass.: Houghton Mifflin Company, 1940.

PACE, MILDRED MASTIN, *Julliette Low*. New York: Charles Scribner's Sons, 1947.

WARFIELD, FRANCES, *Keep Listening*. New York: The Viking Press, Inc., 1957.

The Blind and the Partially Sighted

BJARNOP, KARL, *The Good Light*. New York: Alfred A. Knopf, Inc., 1960.

BJARNOP, KARL, *The Stars Grow Pale*. New York: Alfred A. Knopf, Inc., 1958.

CHEVIGNY, HECTOR, *My Eyes Have a Cold Nose*. New Haven, Conn.: Yale University Press, n.d.

HUSING, TED, *My Eyes Are in My Heart*. New York: Random House, Inc., 1959.

KENDRICK, BAYNARD, *Lights Out*. New York: William Morrow & Co., Inc., 1946.

MEHTA, VED P., *Face to Face*. Philadelphia, Pa.: Little Brown and Company, 1957.

MOORE, VIRGINIA BLANCK, *Seeing Eye Wife*. Philadelphia, Pa.: Chilton Book Company, 1960.

PUTNAM, PETER, *Keep Your Head Up*. New York: Harper & Bros., 1952.

TWERSKY, JACOB, *The Face of the Deep*. Cleveland, Ohio: World Publishing Company, 1953.

The Emotionally Disturbed

AIKEN, CONRAD, "Silent Snow, Secret Snow" in *Collected Stories of Conrad Aiken*. New York: The World Publishing Company, 1932.

BRAITHWAITE, E. R., *To Sir With Love*. Englewood Cliffs, N.J.: Prentice-Hall, Inc., 1959.

CATHER, WILLA, "Paul's Case" in *Youth and the Bright Medusa*. New York: Alfred A. Knopf, Inc., 1932.

GREENBERG, JOANNE, *I Never Promised You a Rose Garden*. New York: Holt, Rinehart and Winston, 1964.

RUBIN, THEODORE ISAAC, *David and Lisa*. London: McMillan, 1961.

SILLITOE, ALAN, *The Long Distance Runner*. New York: Alfred A. Knopf, Inc., 1959.

CHILDREN'S LITERATURE ABOUT THE DISABLED

The Mentally Retarded

BAASTAD, BABBIS FRIIS, *Don't Take Teddy*. New York: Charles Schribner's Sons, 1967.

CHRISTOPHER, MATT, *Long Shot for Paul*. Boston, Mass.: Little, Brown and Company, 1966.

CLEAVER, VERA and BILL CLEAVER, *Me Too*. New York: J. B. Lippincott Co., 1973.

FASSLER, JOAN, *One Little Girl*. New York: Behavioral Publications, 1969.

LITTLE, JEAN, *Take Wing*. Boston, Mass.: Little, Brown and Company, 1968.

REYNOLDS, PAMELA, *A Different Kind of Sister*. New York: Lothrop, Lee & Shepard Co., Inc., 1969.

WRIGHTSON, P. A., *A Racecourse for Andy*. New York: Harcourt, Brace and World, Inc., 1968.

The Learning Disabled

CORCORAN, BARBARA, *Axetime, Swordtime*. New York: Atheneum Publishers, 1976.

LASKEF, JOE, *He's My Brother*. Chicago, Ill.: Albert Whitman & Co., 1974.

SMITH, DORIS B., *Kelley's Creek*. New York: Thomas Y. Crowell Company, 1975.

The Speech and Language Impaired

BAASTAD, BABBIS FRIIS, *Kristy's Courage*. New York: Harcourt, Brace and World, Inc., 1965.

LEE, MILDRED, *The Skating Rink*. New York: Dell Publishing Co., Inc., 1970.

The Orthopedically Handicapped

ARMER, ALBERTA, *Screwball*. New York: Collins-World, 1963.

CHISTOPHER, MATHEW F., *Sink It, Rusty*. Boston, Mass.: Little, Brown and Company, 1963.

DE ANGELI; MARGUERITE, *The Door in the Wall*. Garden City, N.Y.: Junior Literary Guild, 1949.

FORBES, ESTHER, *Johnny Tremain*. Boston, Mass.: Houghton Mifflin Company, 1943.

LATHROP, WEST, *Monkey Ahoy!* New York: Random House, Inc., 1943.

MENOTTI, GIAN CARLO, *Amahl and the Night Visitors*. New York: McGraw-Hill Book Company, 1952.

SEREDY, KATE, *A Tree for Peter*. New York: The Viking Press, Inc., 1941.

SOUTHALL, IVAN, *Let the Balloon Go*. New York: St. Martin's Press, Inc., 1968

WAGONER, JEAN B. AND JANE ADDAMS, *Little Lame Girl*. Indianapolis, Ind.: Bobbs-Merrill Co., Inc., 1960.

The Multiply Handicapped

HUNTER, EDITH, F., *Child of the Silent Night*. New York: Dell Publishing Company, Inc., 1971.

PEARE, CATHERINE OWENS, *The Helen Keller Story*. New York: Thomas Y. Crowell Company, 1959.

The Hearing Impaired

BROWN, MARGARET WISE, *Dead Bird*. Reading, Mass.: Addison-Wesley Publishing Co., Inc., 1958.

BUCK, PEARL S., *Big Wave*. New York: The John Day Company, Inc., 1965.

COLE, SHEILA R., *Meaning Well*. New York: Franklin Watts, Inc., 1974.

CORCORAN, BARBARA, *A Dance to Still Music*. New York: Atheneum Publishers, 1974.

CUNNINGHAM, JULIA, *Wings of the Morning*. San Carlos, Calif.: Golden Gate Books, 1971.

LITCHFIELD, ADA B., *A Button in Her Ear*. Chicago, Ill.: Albert Whitman & Co., 1975.

PEARE, CATHERINE OWENS, *The Helen Keller Story*. New York: Thomas Y. Crowell Company, 1959.

ROBINSON, V., *David in Silence*. New York: J. B. Lippincott Co., 1965.

SMITH, VIAN, *Martin Rides the Moor*. Garden City, N.Y.: Doubleday & Company, Inc., 1965.

SPENCE, ELEANOR, *The Nothing Place*. New York: Harper & Row, Publishers, Inc., 1973.

The Blind and the Partially Sighted

ANDERSON, CLARENCE W., *Blind Connemara*. New York: The Macmillan Company, 1971.

BAWDEN, NINA, *The Witch's Daughter*. New York: J. B. Lippincott Co., 1966.

CANTY, MARY, *Green Gate*. New York: Thomas Y. Crowell Company, 1967.

CLEWES, DOROTHY, *Guide Dog*. New York: Coward, McCann & Geoghegan, Inc., 1965.

ERICSSON, MARY KENTRA, *About Glasses for Gladys*. Chicago, Ill.: Melmont Publishers, Inc., 1962.

GARFIELD, JAMES B., *Follow My Leader*. New York: The Viking Press, Inc., 1957.

JEWETT, ELEANORE M., *Mystery at Boulder Point*. New York: The Viking Press, Inc., 1949.

LITTLE, JEAN, *From Ann*. New York: Harper & Row, Publishers, Inc., 1972.

McDONNELL, LOIS EDDY, *Stevie's Other Eyes*. New York: Friendship Press, 1962.

MONTGOMERY, ELIZABETH R., *Tide Treasure Camper*. New York: Ives Washburn, Inc., 1963.

RYDBERG, ERVIE, *The Dark of the Cave*. New York: David McKay Co., Inc., 1965.

SOMMERFELT, AIMEE, *The Road to Agra*. New York: Criterion Books, 1962.

VANCE, MARGUERITE, *Windows for Rosemary*. New York: E. P. Dutton & Co., Inc., 1956.

The Emotionally Disturbed

ARTIUZ, RUTH M., *Portrait of Margarite*. New York: Atheneum Publishers, 1968.

PLATT, KIN, *The Boy Who Could Make Himself Disappear*. New York: Dell Publishing Co., Inc., 1971.

SPERRY, ARMSTRONG, *Call It Courage*. New York: The Macmillan Company, 1971.

Index

A

Abstract concepts
   autistic children and, 216
   blind children and, 160
Abstract language skills
   development of, in deaf children, 133
Abstract reasoning
   testing, 64
Achievement tests. See also Testing
   for orthopedically handicapped, 101
   scores of hearing impaired on, 137
Adamany, Nancy
   on professional community and the
      handicapped, 254
Adaptive behavior
   in classification of mentally retarded,
      17
   definition of, 16
   for levels of retardation, 19
Adaptive mechanisms
   in parents of hearing impaired, 140
Adventitiously deaf, 131
Aggression
   in behaviorally disordered children,
      178
   in parents of exceptional children, 235
American Association on Mental
      Deficiency, 15
"And Sarah Laughed," 142–55
Anxiety
   in parents of hearing impaired, 141

Aphasia
   and auditory-perceptual abilities, 85
Aphasic children
   with multiple handicaps, 105
Apraxia
   oral, 85
Articulation
   disorders, 83
   Goldman-Fristoe Test, 86
Asp, Carl W.
   on teaching deaf children, 135
Athas, Daphne
   The Fourth World, 166–75
Auditory association, 87
Auditory closure, 88
Auditory impairment. See Hearing
      impairment
Auditory perceptual ability
   Wepman Test of Auditory
      Discrimination, 86
Auditory reception. See Hearing
Auditory sequential memory, 88
Auditory stimulation
   in education of autistic children, 215
   in education of hearing impaired, 134
Aural training
   in education of hearing impaired, 134
Authority figure
   in educating the learning disabled, 66
Autism, 209–32. See also Autistic
   infantile, 209–10, 212–13

Autism (cont.)
    Kanner's theory of, 231
    schizophrenia and, 209–10
Autistic children, 209–32. See also
        Autism
    behaviors typical of, 210–11
    educational treatment for, 213–17
    emotional unresponsiveness of, 231
    with multiple handicaps, 105
    nonlearning behavioral characteristics
        of, 214–15
    parents of, 231
    personal relationships, 212
    vs. retarded, 212
    special education classes for, 232

B
Barg, C. Fisher
    on concept development in blind
        children, 160
Bartok, Lawrence
    on autism, 209
Becker, Howard S.
    on deviance and social rules, 4
Becker, L.
    on educating the learning disabled, 66
Behavior
    of autistic children, 210–11, 231
    management skills for families of
        retarded, 255
    nonlearning, of autistic, 214–17
Behavioral characteristics
    in defining special education
        categories, 106
Behaviorally disordered, 176–208. See
        also Emotionally disturbed
    education of, 178
    learning behaviors of, 178
Behavior disorders
    types of, 177–78
Behavior models
    for emotionally disturbed, 194
Behavior modification
    in autistic and schizophrenic, 213
    goals and technology, 23
    of mentally retarded, 21–22
    strategy for emotionally disturbed, 182
Bellugi, Ursula
    on language development in deaf
        children, 134
Bender Gestalt Test of Visual Motor
        Perception, 64
Berg, Frederick S.
    on classification of hearing
        impairment, 131

Bettelheim, Bruno
    on cause and treatment of autism and
        schizophrenia, 213
    denies special needs of gifted, 43
Biklen, Douglas
    on unequal treatment of handicapped,
        253–54
Bitter, Grant B.
    on mainstreaming the hearing
        impaired, 138
Blatt, Burton
    Christmas in Purgatory, 1
    on effects of labeling, 5
    on institutionalization of mentally
        retarded, 18
    on institutionalization of multiply
        handicapped, 104
Blind, 156–75. See also Blindness
    educational patterns for, 161–62
    education of, 159–65
    mannerisms of, 158
    multisensory approach to education of,
        160
    psychology of, 157
    society's attitudes toward, 157
Blindness, 3, 156–75
    compensation not automatic, 156–57
    definitions of, 159
    folklore of, 157
    social and psychological components
        of, 159
Body image concept
    of orthopedically handicapped, 98, 102
Bogdan, Robert
    on effects of labeling, 5
    on unequal treatment of handicapped,
        253–54
Boston, Bruce
    on the gifted as human resources, 44
Bower, Eli M.
    on emotionally disturbed children,
        176–77
    on learning levels of behaviorally
        disordered, 178
"The Boy Who Laughed," 26–36
Braginsky, Dorthea D. and Benjamin M.
    on effects of labeling, 5
    on institutionalization of mentally
        retarded, 18
Braille, 156
Brain damage
    as label for emotionally disturbed, 182
    in learning disabled, 65
    in multiply handicapped, 105
Budoff, Milton
    on legislation for special education, 252

Bulloch, Lyndal M.
  on education of emotionally disturbed,
    179
Burch, Catherine B.
  on identification of the gifted, 42
Bureau of Education for the
    Handicapped, 3
Buscaglia, Leo
  on counseling parents of disabled
    children, 235–36

C

Cameron, Norman
  on psychodynamics, 181
Cannery Row, 125–29
Capiuolo, Anthony
  on community services vs.
    institutionalization, 255
Caplan, Gerald
  on emotional complications of
    orthopedically handicapped, 103
Cecutients, 159. *See also* Partially sighted
Central dysacusis, 132
Cerebral palsy, 98, 105
Chinn, Phillip C.
  on mental retardation, 16
Christmas in Purgatory, 1
Clancy, Helen
  on treatment of autistic, 213
"Clancy Wants an Orangoutang," 47–60
Clarry, June
  on disorders in learning behaviors, 178
Cleft palate-associated defects, 84
"Clothe the Naked," 257–65
Coates, Robert
  on community services for the
    exceptional, 255
Cohen, Shirley
  on parental involvement in education
    of handicapped, 237
Communication disorders, 82–84. *See
  also* Speech defects
Communication skill development
  in curriculum for mentally retarded, 20
  in early childhood education, 107
Community
  as best environment for exceptional
    persons, 256
  and exceptional children, 252–65
  prefers exceptional persons out of
    sight, 255
  response to handicapped, 264–65
  services for exceptional persons,
    254–55, 265

Compensation
  adjustment to orthopedic handicap,
    100
Concept development
  in blind children, 160
Concrete concepts
  blind children and, 160, 163–64
Conductive hearing loss, 131
Conferences of Executives of American
    Schools for the Deaf, 131
Congenitally deaf, 131
Conner, Frances P.
  on education of orthopedically
    handicapped, 101
  on types of hearing impairment, 131
Conner, Leo
  on mainstreaming special schools for
    the deaf, 138–39
Constitutional origin
  in definition of mental retardation,
    16–17
Contingent stimulation
  in educating the learning disabled, 66
Creativity
  in emotionally disturbed children, 179
  in gifted students, 39–40
Cripple. *See* Orthopedically handicapped
Cross-mainstreaming
  of hearing impaired children, 138
Crowder, Jeane
  on exceptional child in the community,
    252
Cued speech
  in teaching deaf children, 136
Curriculum. *See also* Education
  for behaviorally disordered, 178
  for gifted children, 44–46
  for hearing impaired, 135
  for mentally retarded, 20–21
Curry, John
  on deprivation of the gifted, 44
Cutler, Richard L.
  on types of behavior disorders, 177–78
Cutsforth, Thomas
  on psychology of the blind, 157
  on verbalism by blind persons, 160–61

D

Day camp
  for emotionally disturbed children, 194
Deaf, 130–55. *See also* Hearing impaired
Deafness
  definition of, 130–31
Defense mechanisms
  of orthopedically handicapped
    persons, 98–100

Defiance
  in behaviorally disordered children,
    177–78
De Myer, Marian K.
  on autistic and schizophrenic, 212
Denial
  by orthopedically handicapped, 99
  by parents of exceptional children,
    234–35
Denny, M. R.
  on elicitation theory and incidental
    learning, 24
Detachment
  by parents of exceptional children, 234
Developmental period
  definition of, 16
Developmental strategy
  for teaching exceptional children,
    182–83
Deviants
  labeling creates, 5
Dokecki, Paul R.
  on verbalism by blind persons, 161
Douglas, Virginia I.
  on lack of imitation in autistic children,
    210
Downey, John A.
  on categories of orthopedic handicaps,
    101
Down's syndrome, 16
Dunn, Lloyd M.
  on exceptionality, 3
Dyslexia
  as label for emotionally disturbed, 182
  in learning disabled, 65

E

Education. See also Schools, Special
    education, and Teaching
  for autistic, 232
  of the blind, 159–65
  contributions in field of learning
    disabilities, 65
  educability of autistic, 216
  educability of mentally retarded, 17
  for handicapped a right in law, 253
  of hearing impaired, 134–40
  opportunities for exceptional child,
    236
  for orthopedically handicapped, 101–7
  parents and decisions involving, 233
  strategies for autistic, 214–17
  strategies for emotionally disturbed,
    180–82
  structured programs for autistic,
    216–17

Educational therapist
  as resource for learning disabled, 80
Education for All Handicapped Children
    Act
  amendment to, 253
  individualized educational programs,
    17
  provisions of, 3
  and role of learning disabilities teacher,
    66–67
Eisenson, Jon
  on childhood aphasia, 85
Ellis, N. R.
  on memory processes, 23–24
Emotional behavior
  deviations in, 2
Emotional disturbances
  in blind persons, 158
  diagnosis of, 62
  overlap with learning disabilities, 179
Emotionally disturbed, 176–208
  behavioral characteristics of, 177–78
  competency ratings for teachers of, 180
  day camp for, 194
  education for, 179–84
  learning characteristics of, 179
  with multiple handicaps, 105, 128
  severely, 209–32
Emotional needs
  of gifted children, 59
Emotional problems
  of orthopedically handicapped, 103
  statistics, 3
Engineered classroom, 21
Ennis, Bruce
  on mental retardation, 14
Environmental factors
  in mental retardation, 16
Epilepsy
  an invisible handicap, 12
  in multiply handicapped, 105
Epilepsy Foundation of America, 12
Ewing, Alexander and Ethel
  on educating deaf children, 134
Exceptional adults
  independent living and career choice,
    250
  practical aspects of life for, 236
Exceptional children. See also
    Exceptionality
  classification of, 2–5
  in the community, 252–65
  developing maximum capacity of, 2
  education for, 253
  and the family, 233–51
  legal right to education for, 253
  parents of, 233

Exceptionality, 1–13. *See also*
    Exceptional children
    definitions of, 1–5
    psychology of, 179
The Exceptional Parent (journal), 237

F
Failure
    of emotionally disturbed children in
        school, 183
    of hearing impaired children in school,
        139
Families of exceptional children, 233–51.
    See also Parents of exceptional
    children
    emotional and physical strain on, 234,
        256
    rights of, 236
    sibling relationships in, 236, 250
    training center for, 255
    training to prevent institutionalization,
        256
Family relationships
    of deaf children, 154–55
    integration of deaf into family, 140
    rejection and behavioral disorders in,
        177
    socialization of autistic with family,
        214
    of suicide victims, 206–7
Fantasy
    by orthopedically handicapped, 100
Fear
    of parents for handicapped children,
        12
Fernald, Grace
    on multisensory approach to learning,
        64
Fingerspelling, 136
Fisher, Mary Ann
    on attention-retention theory, 23–24
Fiske, Edward B.
    on special education in America, 1
Fletcher, Samuel D.
    on classification of hearing
        impairment, 131
Forness, Steven R.
    on behavior modification of mentally
        retarded, 22–23
The Fourth World, 166–75
Frostig Test of Visual Perception, 64
Frustration
    in learning disabled, 64
    low threshold in learning disabled,
        62–63
Functional analysis, 21–22

Funding
    community, for helping handicapped,
        252
    state, for special education programs,
        237
Fund raising agencies
    distort image of handicapped, 254

G
Gallagher, James
    on nonlearning behavior of autistic,
        214–17
Gearhart, Bill R.
    on special education, 2–3
Gewirtz, J. L.
    on observational learning theory,
        24–25
Gideon: A Boy Who Hates Learning,
    69–81
Gifted, 37–60
    characteristics of, 45, 58–59
    curriculum for, 44–46
    definition of, 38–39
    deprivation of, in average school, 44
    education of, 38–46
    emotional needs of, 59
    identification of, 37–43
    need for recognition, 58
Goals
    development sequence of educational,
        182–83
    in educating the learning disabled, 66
    in educating the orthopedically
        handicapped, 101
Goffman, Erving
    on effects of labeling, 5
Gofman, Helen
    on hyperkinetic syndrome, 63
Goldman-Fristoe Test of Articulation, 86
Gordon, Sol
    on guidance for handicapped and their
        families, 236
Gorham, Kathryn A.
    on labeling the multiply handicapped,
        104
Gowan, John C.
    on identification of the gifted, 42
Grades
    tyranny of letter grades, 79
Grammatical closure, 88
Graubard, Paul S.
    on education of behaviorally
        disordered, 178
Greenberg, Joanne
    "And Sarah Laughed," 142–55
    "Hunting Season," 6–13

Guilford, Joy P.
 on high IQ and high grades, 40
 on structure of intellect, 42
Guilt feelings
 in orthopedically handicapped, 99, 103
 in parents of exceptional children, 12,
  235
 in parents of hearing impaired, 141
 in parents of learning disabled, 80
 in parents of orthopedically
  handicapped, 122
 in siblings of exceptional children, 250

H

Handicapped. See Exceptional children
Handicaps. See also specific handicap
 invisible, 12
Hard of hearing. See also Hearing
  impaired
 defined, 131
Harris, Grace M.
 on educating the hearing impaired, 134
Hearing
 auditory reception, 87
 the blind and sense of, 160
 testing, of orthopedically handicapped,
  101
Hearing impaired, 130–55. See also
  Hearing impairment
 achievement test scores of, 137
 definition of, 130–31
 education of, 134–40, 154–55
 integration of, into family, 140
 language development in, 132–36
 with multiple handicaps, 105
 parental relationships, 140–41
Hearing impairment
 speech-hearing disability, 82
 statistics, 3
 types of, 131–32
Hewett, Frank
 on emotionally disturbed children,
  177, 180–83
Hewett, Lester E.
 types of behavior disorders, 177
Hexter, George
 on coping reactions of parents with
  exceptional children, 234–35
Hobbs, Nicholas
 on classification of the visually
  handicapped, 159
 on mental retardation, 16
Home. See Family and Parents
Hostility
 in behaviorally disordered child, 177
 in orthopedically handicapped, 123
 in parents of exceptional children, 235

House, B. J.
 on attention theory, 23–24
"Hunting Season," 6–13
Hurst, James
 "The Scarlet Ibis," 239–51
Hydrocephaly, 16
Hyperactivity
 in behaviorally disordered, 177
 in learning disabled, 62–63
 in multiply handicapped, 105
Hyperkinetic syndrome
 in learning disabled, 63
Hypersensitivity
 in emotionally disturbed, 178

I

Identification
 adjustment to orthopedic handicap,
  100
Illinois Test of Psycholinguistic Abilities,
  87
Imitation
 lack of, among autistic children, 210
Immaturity
 in emotionally disturbed children, 178
Incarceration. See Institutionalization
Incurability
 in definition of mental retardation,
  16–17
Individualized instruction
 for blind children, 163
 vs. personalized, 102
Institute for Educational Leadership, 43
Institutionalization
 of autistic and psychotic, 209
 of the blind, 174
 vs. community services, 255
 family training to prevent, 256
 vs. mainstreaming, 254
 of mentally retarded, 1–2, 14, 18, 34–35
 of misfits of society, 264
 of multiply handicapped, 104
 of severely and profoundly
  handicapped, 106
Intellectual abilities
 structure-of-intellect model of, 40–41
Intellectual functioning
 definition of, 16
Intelligence quotient. See IQ
Intelligence tests
 bias in standardized tests, 20
 group vs. individual, 42
 Otis Group Test, 42
 performance IQ, 19–20
 Stanford-Binet, 42
 Stanford-Binet and Wechsler Scales
  scores compared, 19

testing of orthopedically handicapped, 101
IQ
and adaptive behavior, 19
of behaviorally disordered, 176
in classification of mentally retarded, 17–20
in defining special education categories, 106
full scale, 20
high scores and identification of gifted, 39–40, 42
low scores in autistic children, 216
performance, 19–20
test scores and levels of retardation, 19
verbal, 20
IQ tests. See Intelligence tests
Isolation
of hearing impaired children, 141

J
Jenkins, Richard L.
on types of behavior disorders, 177
Jipson, Frederick J.
on performance IQ, 19–20
Johnson, Doris
on teaching aphasic preschool children, 85

K
Kanner, Leo
on infantile autism, 210
theory of autism, 231
Kaplan, Fred
Christmas in Purgatory, 1
Kaplan, Sandra
on curriculum for the gifted, 44
Kazin, Alfred
A Walker in the City, 90–97
Kelley, William Melvin
"The Life You Save," 185–95
Keogh, Barbara
on educating the learning disabled, 66
Kirk, Samuel A.
classification of hearing impairment, 131
definition of exceptionality, 2
Illinois Test of Psycholinguistic Abilities, 88–89
on voice disorders, 83
Klima, Edward
on language development in deaf children, 134
Knoblock, Peter
on education of emotionally disturbed children, 179

Kozloff, Martin A.
on teaching the mentally retarded, 21
Kvareceus, William
on education of emotionally disturbed, 179

L
Labeling
effects of, 4–5
as instruments of social control, 182
the mentally retarded, 17
mislabeling of learning disabled, 61–62
of multiply handicapped, 103–5
Lambert, Nadine M.
assessment of mental retardation, 20
Language development
in autistic and schizophrenic, 209, 213–14, 216
in deaf children, 132–36
reception, processing and expression, 84–85
Language disorders. See Speech defects
Language impaired, 82–97. See also Speech defects
classification of, 83–88
and learning problems, 65, 85–86
teaching practices, 88–89
Language Sampling Analysis and Training, 86–87
Learning. See also Education, Memory, and Teaching
attention-retention theory, 23–24
behavioral disorders interfere with, 177
behaviors that interfere with, 182
developmental sequence for successful, 182–83
elicitation theory and incidental learning, 24
multisensory approach, 64
nonlearning behavior of autistic, 214–15
observational learning theory, 24–25
preferred learning style, 102
social learning theory, 23–24
Learning diagnostician
role in education of learning disabled, 67
Learning disabilities. See also Learning disabled
definition of, 65
diagnosis of, 62–65
and emotional disturbances, 179
multidisciplinary approach to, 67
specific learning disorders, 66
statistics, 3

Learning disabled, 61–81. *See also*
    Learning disabilities
    with multiple handicaps, 105
    organic impairment in, 65
Learning triangle
    for teaching emotionally disturbed,
        183–84
Levitt, Edith
    on parental involvement in education
        of handicapped, 237
L'Heureux, John
    "Something Missing," 196–208
    "The Life You Save," 185–95
Limits
    imposing, for behaviorally disordered,
        194
Lipreading, 136
Listening skills
    teaching the mentally retarded, 21
"Little Baseball World," 108–24
Litvinov, Ivy
    "The Boy Who Laughed," 26–36
Lovaas, O. Ivar
    on education of autistic and
        schizophrenic, 213
Lowenfeld, Berthold
    principles for teaching blind children,
        162–64
    on sensory deprivation of the blind,
        159–60
Low, Niels L.
    categories of orthopedic handicaps,
        101
Lowry, Robert
    "Little Baseball World," 108–24

M
McBride, Glen
    on treatment of autistic, 213
McConnell, Freeman
    on language learning in deaf children,
        132–33
McDowell, Floyd
    on special education categories, 106
MacGintie, Walter H.
    on language development in deaf
        children, 132
McKee, Beverly E.
    on educating the learning disabled, 66
Mackie, Romaine P.
    on education of emotionally disturbed,
        179
MacKinnon, Donald W.
    on unfulfilled potential, 37
Macmillan, Donald L.
    on behavior modification of mentally
        retarded, 22–23

Mainstreaming
    cross and reverse, 138
    educable mentally retarded, 17
    in education of learning disabled,
        67–68
    of hearing-impaired children, 138–40
    vs. institutionalization, 254
    of severely and profoundly
        handicapped 106–7
    of special schools for the deaf, 139–40
Mannerisms
    of the blind, 157
Manual alphabet, 136
    negative attitudes toward, 155
Manual expression, 87
Manualism
    in teaching deaf children, 135
Marland, Sidney P.
    on education of the gifted, 37–38
    on procedures to identify the gifted,
        42–43
Martinson, Ruth A.
    definition of gifted, 38
    on identification of the gifted, 42
Meadow, Kathryn P.
    on language development in deaf
        children, 134
Medical care
    parents and decisions involving, 233
Medical history
    in school records, 12
Medication
    in treating learning disabilities, 63
    school children on, 12
Medicine
    contributions in field of learning
        disabilities, 65
Meeker, Mary
    on Stanford-Binet test, 42
Memory
    auditory, of orthopedically
        handicapped, 101
    input organization theory, 23–24
    multiprocess memory model, 23–24
    sequential, 88
    short-term memory defect in autistic,
        214
    short-term memory defect in learning
        disabled, 62
Mental deficiency. *See* Mental retardation
Mentally ill. *See* Emotionally disturbed
Mentally retarded, 14–36. *See also*
    Mental retardation
    educational curriculum, 20–21
    incarceration of, 14
    institutionalization vs. normalization,
        18

intellectual and social potential of, 34
training center for families of, 255
Mental retardation, 14–36. *See also*
    Mentally retarded
    assessment of, 20
    classification of, 16–20
    definition of, 15–16
    diagnosis of, 62
    environmental factors, 16
    levels of, 19
    literature on, 18
    in multiply handicapped, 104–5, 128
    President's Committee on, 14–15
    in psychotic and autistic, 209
    statistics, 3, 15
Mental Retardation (journal), 18
Mercer, Cecil D.
    on teaching retarded children, 22
Mercer, Jane
    on labeling the mentally retarded, 17
    on retardation and socioeconomic
        status, 19
    System of Multi-Cultural Pluralistic
        Assessment, 20
Michaux, Louis
    on physical handicaps, 98
Microcephaly, 16
Miller, Alden
    on community services for the
        exceptional, 255
Minimal brain dysfunction
    in learning disabled, 65
    in multiply handicapped, 105
Minimal neurological impairment, 176
Minority group children
    mental retardation among, 19
Mongolism, 16
Moores, Donald F.
    on language development in deaf
        children, 134
Morehead, Donald M.
    on language development in deaf
        children, 133–34
Morse, William C.
    on types of behavior disorders, 177–78
Motility
    in autistic children, 211, 215
Motor coordination
    deficient fine and gross, in multiply
        handicapped, 128
    development in early childhood
        education, 107
    gross, of orthopedically handicapped,
        101
    in learning disabled, 62
Multidisciplinary team
    diagnosis of learning disabilities, 62

Multiply handicapped, 2, 98–129
    classification of, 103–5
    diagnosing, 128
    education for, 128
    institutionalization of, 104
    recognition and diagnosis of, 103–4
    services limited for, 104
    severely and profoundly handicapped,
        106
Multisensory approach
    in education of the blind, 160
Myklebust, Helmer R.
    on hearing impairment, 130–31
    on teaching aphasic preschool
        children, 85

N

Natchez, Gladys
    Gideon: A Boy Who Hates Learning,
        69–81
National Association for Retarded
    Children, 237
National Information Center for the
    Handicapped, 237
Neisworth, John T.
    on exceptionality, 2
Neurological dysfunction, 61–81
Neurological impairment
    in multiply handicapped, 105, 128
Neuromuscular characteristics
    deviations in, 2
Nix, Gary
    on teaching deaf children, 136
Normalization. *See* Mainstreaming

O

Oates, Joyce Carol
    "Wednesday's Child," 218–32
Occupational therapists
    in special education, 107
Occupational training. *See* Vocational
    training
Ogden, Charles K.
    on language complexity, 133
Oralism
    in teaching deaf children, 135
Organic impairment
    in learning disabled, 65
Orthopedically handicapped, 98–129
    definition and categories of, 101
    education for, 101–7
    emotional complications of, 103
Orton, Samuel
    on reading disability, 65–66
Otis Group Test, 42. *See also* Intelligence
    tests
Overinhibited child, 177

P

Paraplegics, 99–100. *See also*
    Orthopedically handicapped
Paraprofessionals, 107
Parents of exceptional children, 233–51.
    See also Families of exceptional
    children
    autistic children, 213–14, 231
    coordination with, in teaching learning
        disabled, 67
    counseling for, 234
    The Exceptional Parent (journal), 237
    gifted children, 58–59
    guilt and fear of, 12
    hearing impaired. 140–41
    involvement in organizations, 237
    learning disabled, 80
    mentally retarded, 34–35
    multiply handicapped, 104
    problems in child-parent relationships,
        34–35, 234
    role in education of handicapped, 17
    schizophrenic, 213–14
    support in rehabilitation, 254
Parker, Dorothy
    "Clothe the Naked," 257–65
Partially sighted, 156–75
Pathological behaviors
    in autistic children, 211
Peabody Picture Vocabulary Test, 86
Peer relationships
    of emotionally disturbed, 207
Pegnato, Carl W.
    on identification of the gifted, 42
Perceptual skill development
    in early childhood education, 107
Permissiveness
    in treatment of autistic and
        schizophrenic, 213–14
Personality problems
    of emotionally disturbed children, 178
Personalized instruction
    vs. individualized, 102
Personal relationships
    among autistic and schizophrenic, 212
Physical characteristics,
    deviations in, 2
Physically handicapped, 98. *See also*
    Orthopedically handicapped
Physical therapists
    in learning disabilities, 65
    in special education, 107
Piaget, Jean
    on language development in deaf
        children, 134
Pinckney, Edward and Cathey
    on psychoanalysis, 181

Pity
    for exceptional children, 236
P. L. 94–142. *See* Education for All
    Handicapped Children Act
Plowman, Paul
    on special education for the gifted, 46
Potential
    vs. performance in emotionally
        disturbed child, 179
Prejudice
    about available services, 265
President's Committee on Mental
    Retardation, 14–15
Pringle, Mia K.
    on prevalence of multiple handicaps,
        103
Problem-solving abilities
    testing, 64
Profoundly handicapped, 106
Projection
    by orthopedically handicapped, 100
Psychodynamic-interpersonal strategy
    for teaching emotionally disturbed, 180
Psychodynamics
    in treatment of autistic and
        schizophrenic, 213
Psycholinguistic abilities
    Illinois Test of Psycholinguistic
        Abilities, 88
Psycholinguistic theory
    and verbalism, 161
Psychological adjustment
    to physical disability, 98
Psychological development
    deficiencies in hearing impaired,
        140–41
Psychology
    of the blind, 157
    contributions in field of learning
        disabilities, 65
    of exceptionality, 179
Psychosocial problems
    institutionalization of children with,
        254
Psychotherapy
    in treatment of autistic and
        schizophrenic, 213
Psychotic children, 209
Public school system. *See also* Schools
    education for severely and profoundly
        handicapped, 106
    returning handicapped to, 254
    services for handicapped in, 253

Q

Quay, Herbert C.
    types of behavior disorders, 177–78

R

Rains, Prudence M.
  on exceptionality, 3–5
Rationalization
  by orthopedically handicapped, 100
Reaction formation
  by orthopedically handicapped, 99
Reading
  difficulties and visual motor
    perception, 64
  disabilities, 79–80
  disorders and learning disabilities, 65
  teaching the learning disabled, 66
Recognition
  gifted child's need for, 58
  orthopedically handicapped child's
    need for, 103
Recreation
  parents and decisions involving, 233
Regression
  by orthopedically handicapped, 99
Rehabilitation
  psychosocial and educational, 254
Reinforcement
  in educating the learning disabled, 66
Rejection
  of emotionally disturbed by peer group,
    207
Repression
  by orthopedically handicapped, 99
Reschly, Daniel
  performance IQ, 19–20
Resentment
  in siblings of exceptional children, 236
Residential care. See
    Institutionalization
Residential services. See
    Institutionalization
Resource personnel
  in special education, 107
Resource room
  in education of the blind, 161
  for learning disabled, 64
Respite care, 256
Retention
  of learning disabled, 80
Reverse mainstreaming
  of hearing impaired children, 138
Richards, Ivor A.
  on language complexity, 133
Rimland, Bernard
  on lack of imitation in autistic children,
    210
Robinson, Nancy M. and Halbert B.
  on mental retardation, 16
Rochester method
  for teaching deaf children, 136

Rosenhan, David L.
  on effects of labeling, 5
Rosenstein, Joseph
  on language development in deaf
    children, 132
Rubin, Eli Z.
  on learning levels of behaviorally
    disordered, 178
Rutter, Michael
  on autism, 209, 212–13

S

Sailor, Wayne
  plan for special education, 106–7
Sanders, Frances A.
  on lack of imitation in autistic children,
    210
Sara
  "Clancy Wants an Orangoutang,"
    47–60
"And Sarah Laughed," 142–55
Sarason, Seymour
  on institutions for the retarded, 1–2
Sarbin, Theodore R.
  on mental retardation, 18
"The Scarlet Ibis," 239–51
Schizophrenia
  and autism, 209–10
  childhood, 209–10
  educational treatment for, 213–17
  in multiply handicapped, 104
  and personal relationships, 212
  vs. mental retardation, 212
Schlesinger, Hilde
  on language development in deaf
    children, 134
School administrator
  role in education of learning disabled,
    67
School nurse
  role in education of learning disabled,
    67
School psychologist
  as resource for learning disabled, 80
  role in education of learning disabled,
    67
School records
  medical history in, 12
Schools. See also Public school system
  classroom management in teaching
    learning disabled, 67
  exclusion of multiply handicapped
    from public, 104
  legal responsibility for handicapped,
    252–53
  physical organization of, for learning
    disabled, 67

Schools *(cont.)*
  practices modified for exceptional
    children, 2
  services for diagnosing and
    remediating learning disabilities, 81
  special schools for the deaf, 130–39
Security
  needs of orthopedically handicapped,
    103
Self-activity
  in teaching blind children, 164
Self-esteem
  needs of orthopedically handicapped,
    103
Self-fulfilling prophecy
  labeling becomes, 5
  and the mentally defective, 2
Self-help
  in curriculum for mentally retarded, 20
  in early childhood education, 107
  in emotionally disturbed, 182
  teaching the mentally retarded, 21
Self-image
  of blind persons, 157
  labeling affects, 5
  of orthopedically handicapped, 123
Self-motivation
  in emotionally disturbed, 182–83
Sensory abilities
  deviations in, 2
Sensory-neural hearing loss, 132
Sensory-neurological strategy
  for teaching emotionally disturbed, 181
Severely handicapped, 106–7
Shame
  in parents of exceptional children, 235
  in siblings of exceptional children, 250
Sheltered workshops, 237
Sholl, Geraldine
  on sensory deprivation of the blind,
    159–60
Siblings. *See also* Families of exceptional
    children
  love-hate relationships in, 250
Sigelman, Carol
  on community services for the
    handicapped, 255
Sign language. *See* Manual alphabet
Singh, Sadanand
  on language development in deaf
    children, 133–34
Skinner, B. F.
  behavior modification techniques, 22
Slow learner
  with multiple handicaps, 105
Smith, Judy
  plan for special education, 106–7

Smith, Robert M.
  on exceptionality, 2
Snell, Martha E.
  teaching retarded children, 22
Social behavior
  deviations in, 2
Social development
  in autistic and schizophrenic, 213
  deficiencies in hearing impaired,
    140–41
Socialization
  in curriculum for mentally retarded, 21
  primary, of autistic, 214
Socialized delinquent, 177
Social judgment
  testing, 64
Social Learning Theory, 23–24
Social rules
  deviance defined by, 4
Social skill development
  in early childhood education, 107
Social workers
  and families of exceptional children,
    237
  role in education of learning disabled,
    67
Society
  attitudes of, toward the blind, 157
  negative self-regard induced in blind
    by, 158
  rejection of physically handicapped by,
    98
Society for the Prevention of Blindness,
    159
Socioeconomic background
  and mental retardation, 19
Somatopsychology. *See* Body image
    concept
"Something Missing," 196–208
Sontag, Ed
  on special education, 106–7
Sorosky, Arthur D.
  on behaviors of autistic children,
    210–11
Sound blending, 88
Spatial organization
  improvement in orthopedically
    handicapped, 102
Special education. *See also* Education
  children requiring, 2
  classes for the blind, 161
  definition of, 2
  general, 106–7
  legislation for, 252
  parents and, 233
  plan for, 106–7
  state funding for, 237

Speech defects. *See also* Language
    impaired
    categories of, 83–84
    definition of, 82
    delayed speech development, 84
    oral apraxia, 85
    statistics, 3
Speech impaired, 82–97. *See also*
    Language impaired
Speech production
    testing of orthopedically handicapped,
    101
Speech skills
    teaching the mentally retarded, 21
Speech therapists
    in special education, 107
Spitz, H. H.
    input organization theory, 23–24
Stanford-Binet test, 19. *See also*
    Intelligence tests
Steinbeck, John
    Cannery Row, 125–29
Stereotyping
    effect of, 4–5
    and unequal treatment of handicapped,
    254
Stickney, Patricia
    on community services vs.
    institutionalization, 255
Stigma
    of epilepsy, 12
Stimuli
    autistic prefer visual over auditory, 215
Stocker, Claudell S.
    on listening classes for the blind,
    156–57
Stokoe, William
    on language development in deaf
    children, 133–34
Stress
    in emotionally disturbed, 206
Stuttering, 83
    psychological factors, 96
Suicide
    in emotionally disturbed children, 206
System of Multi-Cultural Pluralistic
    Assessment, 20

T

Tactual perceptions
    the blind and, 160
Talented. *See* Gifted
Tannenbaum, Abraham J.
    on personalized instruction of
    orthopedically handicapped, 102
Taylor, Steven
    on effects of labeling, 5

Teachers
    competency ratings for teaching
    emotionally disturbed, 180
    failure causes child failure, 183
    itinerant, 162
    role in education of the blind, 165
    training in special education, 253
Teaching. *See also* Education
    autistic children 213–17
    blind children, 162–64
    the gifted, 46
    individualized vs. personalized
    instruction, 102
    language-impaired children, 85–86,
    88–89
    the learning disabled, 66–68
    the mentally retarded, 21–23
    methods for hearing impaired, 135–36
    the orthopedically handicapped,
    102–3
    precision teaching, 21
    of reading to learning disabled, 66
Temper
    in learning disabled, 64
Testing. *See also* Intelligence tests
    Bender Gestalt Test of Visual Motor
    Perception, 64
    Frostig Test of Visual Perception, 64
    language disabilities, 86–88
    of learning disabled, 62, 80
    orthopedically handicapped, 101–2
    Wide Range Achievement Test, 64
Throne, J. M.
    on educating the learning disabled, 66
Titicut Follies, 1
Total communication
    in teaching deaf children, 135–36
Touch. *See* Tactual perceptions
Twain, Mark
    on unfulfilled potential, 37

U

Unified instruction
    in teaching blind children, 164
United Cerebral Palsy Association for
    Neurologically Handicapped
    Children, 237
Unresponsiveness
    emotional, of autistic children, 231
Unsocialized aggressive child, 177

V

Van Uden, Anthony
    on mainstreaming the prelingually
    deaf, 139
Van Riper, Charles
    definition of speech defect, 82
    stuttering, 83

Verbal expression, 87
Verbalism
   by blind persons, 161
Verbal unreality. See Verbalism
Visual association, 87
Visual closure, 88
Visual functioning
   testing of orthopedically handicapped,
      101
Visual information processing
   deficiency in autistic, 215
Visually handicapped. See Blind and
      Partially sighted
Visual motor perception
   and reading difficulties, 64
Visual perceptual disturbance
   in learning disabled, 62
Visual reception, 87
Visual sequential memory, 88
Visual stimuli
   autistic children prefer, 215
Vocabulary
   of deaf students, 136
   Peabody Picture Vocabulary Test, 86
   testing of orthopedically handicapped,
      101
Vocational training
   for mentally retarded, 21
   for orthopedically handicapped, 123
   parents and decisions involving, 233
Voice disorders, 83. See also Speech
      defects

W

A Walker in the City, 90–97
Wasserman, Theodore
   on professional community and the
      handicapped, 254–55
Wechsler Intelligence Scale for Children,
      19–20. See also Intelligence tests
   in diagnosing learning disabilities, 64

   identifying depressed language
      functioning, 86
Wedell, Klaus
   behavior modification of retarded
      children, 21
"Wednesday's Child," 218–32
Wepman Test of Auditory
      Discrimination, 86
Whelan, Richard J.
   on education of emotionally disturbed,
      179
White, Mary A.
   on disorders in learning behaviors, 178
Wide Range Achievement Test, 64
Wiegerink, Ronald
   nonlearning behavior of autistic,
      214–17
William, Harold
   on education of emotionally disturbed,
      179
Willis, Jerry W.
   on exceptional child in the community,
      252
Willis, Joan
   on exceptional child in the community,
      252
Withdrawal
   by orthopedically handicapped, 99
Wolfensberger, Wolf
   on community services vs.
      institutionalization, 255

Z

Zeaman, D.
   on attention-retention theory, 23–24
Zigler, E.
   on social learning theory, 24
Zweibelson, Irving
   on concept development in blind
      children, 160